Shall We Sin?

american
university
studies

Series VII
Theology and Religion

Vol. 226

PETER LANG
New York • Washington, D.C./Baltimore • Bern
Frankfurt am Main • Berlin • Brussels • Vienna • Oxford

Jeffrey K. Mann

Shall We Sin?

Responding to
the Antinomian Question
in Lutheran Theology

To Pastor Sweet,
   With appreciation for your hospitality and
best wishes for a lifetime of learning.

[signature]

PETER LANG
New York • Washington, D.C./Baltimore • Bern
Frankfurt am Main • Berlin • Brussels • Vienna • Oxford

Library of Congress Cataloging-in-Publication Data

Mann, Jeffrey K.
Shall we sin?: responding to the antinomian question
in Lutheran theology / Jeffrey K. Mann.
p. cm. — (American university studies. Series VII,
Theology and religion; v. 226)
Includes bibliographical references.
1. Antinomianism—History of doctrines. 2. Luther, Martin, 1483–1546.
3. Melanchthon, Philipp, 1497–1560. 4. Spener, Philipp Jakob,
1635–1705. 5. Kierkegaard, Søren, 1813–1855. 6. Bonhoeffer, Dietrich,
1906–1945. 7. Lutheran Church—Doctrines—History.
I. Title. II. Series.
BT1330.M36   230'.41—dc21   2002154658
ISBN 0-8204-6372-8
ISSN 0740-0446

Die Deutsche Bibliothek-CIP-Einheitsaufnahme

Bibliographic information published by **Die Deutsche Bibliothek**.
Die Deutsche Bibliothek lists this publication in the "Deutsche
Nationalbibliografie"; detailed bibliographic data is available
on the Internet at http://dnb.ddb.de/.

© 2003 Peter Lang Publishing, Inc., New York
275 Seventh Avenue, 28th Floor, New York, NY 10001
www.peterlangusa.com

To my parents,
Karl-Otto and Anita Jane Mann

ଠ TABLE OF CONTENTS

       Imitation and Despair 111
       The Leap 118
       The Requirement 128
       Conclusion 136

V.   **Dietrich Bonhoeffer** **139**
       Obedience 142
       The Example 152
       Christology 161
       Conclusion 168

       Epilogue **171**
       Orthodoxy and Orthopraxy 175
       A Final Analysis 177

       Bibliography **183**

ℭ ACKNOWLEDGMENTS

I would like to express my thanks to several people who have helped me in a variety of capacities over the years that I have worked on this project. To Gene TeSelle and Paul DeHart, who helped guide and direct the entire project, I am grateful.

To Erik Trovall, who first made me understand Luther's theology, despite my objections, my sincerest thanks.

A word of thanks is also due to Jen Bowden, whose assistance in the preparation of this manuscript was a real blessing.

And finally, to my wife, Neneth, whose constant support helped make this labor of love a reality, I am deeply appreciative.

ABBREVIATIONS

CD	Dietrich Bonhoeffer. *The Cost of Discipleship*. New York: Macmillan Publishing Company, 1959.
CR	*Corpus Reformatorum. Philippi Melanchthonis opera quae supersunt omnia*. eds. Karl Bretschneider and Heinrich Bindseil. Halle and Braunschweig: Schwetschke, 1834–1860.
DB	Eberhard Bethge. *Dietrich Bonhoeffer*. ed. Victoria J. Barnett. Minneapolis: Fortress Press, 2000.
DBW	*Dietrich Bonhoeffer Werke*. ed. Eberhard Bethge. Gütersloh: Chr. Kaiser, 1986–1999.
DBWE	*Dietrich Bonhoeffer Works*, English edition. ed. Wayne Whitson Floyd, Jr. Minneapolis: Fortress Press, 1996–.
LW	*Luther's Works*. ed. Jaroslav Pelikan and Helmut T. Lehmann. Philadelphia and St. Louis, 1958–1986.
MBW	*Melanchthons Briefwechsel: Kritische und kommentierte Gesamtausgabe*. ed. Heinz Scheible. Stuttgart–Bad Cannstatt: Frommann–Holzboog, 1977–.
Pap	*Søren Kierkegaards Papirer*, ed. Niels Thulstrup. Copenhagen, 1968–78.
PD	Philip Jacob Spener. *Pia Desideria*. Fortress Press, 1964.
PJSS	*Philipp Jakob Spener Schriften*. ed. Erich Beyreuther. Hildesheim: Georg Olms Verlag, 1979–.
SKJP	*Søren Kierkegaard's Journals and Papers*. eds. Howard V. Hong and Edna H. Hong. Bloomington: Indiana University Press, 1967–978.
WA	*D. Martin Luthers Werke*. Kritische Gesamtausgabe. Weimar: H. Böhlau, 1883–1993.
WA Br	*D. Martin Luthers Werke*. Briefwechsel. Weimar: H. Böhlau, 1930–1985.
WA TR	*D. Martin Luthers Werke*. Tischreden. Weimar: H. Böhlau, 1912–1921.

⊄ℜ INTRODUCTION

Even before St. Paul had committed his theology to writing, a question was raised which has dogged Christian theologians for the past two millennia. Anticipating this theological objection in his epistle to the church in Rome, he posed the problem: *"And so what shall we say? Shall we sin because we are not under the law but under grace? By no means!"* [Rom. 6:15] This question, which appears in various forms throughout the New Testament, can be termed the *"antinomian question."* It is, of course, not only a matter for biblical scholars or historical theologians; it continues to be asked in various forms still today. Not long ago, on a late night talk show, the host was reminiscing about life in Catholic school and posed the rhetorical question: *"So you sin all week, go to confession on Friday, and everything is cool, right?"*

While this TV personality appeared more interested in justifying inappropriate behavior than raising a theological point for discussion, the apostle's concern in raising this question was quite the opposite; Paul wanted to point out that there is no inconsistency between being freed from the law and the obligation to abide by the law. What is noticeably lacking, however, in Paul's answers to various forms of this question is a precise explication of the implications that follow from choosing to sin. His brief response to the antinomian question is far from exhaustive. As a result, attempts at a more complete response have appeared from time to time, most markedly whenever Pauline theology, with all of its difficult implications, is being defended most vigorously.

This supposed moral loophole in Paul's radical emphasis on God's grace has frequently been given the name antinomianism. The difficulty with this label is that it has been used to refer to a variety of religious movements or theological positions that vary significantly from one another. The *Oxford Dictionary of the Christian Church* includes a short entry for *"Antinomianism"* that includes very brief references to the Gnostics, Anabaptists, Johann Agricola, and certain English sects. It begins with the following statement: *"A general name for the view that Christians are by grace set free*

from the need of observing any moral law."[1] This definition is obviously
inadequate. On this basis one could conclude that Augustine, Martin Luther,
John Calvin, and a whole host of other "orthodox" theologians were
antinomians. It is not the belief that Christians are set free from the law
which makes one an antinomian, but the judgment of another that one is
neglecting the law in one's own life or teaching.

Among certain Gnostics in the second century, the belief that there were
"pneumatic" or spiritual people whose knowledge of divine matters elevated
them to a level above "psychic" and "hylic" humans who do not enjoy this
saving knowledge led to a disturbing level of trust in knowledge over
behavior, spiritual information over moral conduct. As J.G. Davies explains,
"As, therefore, the material cannot affect the spiritual, the gnostic may do
what he likes, in the sure confidence of his ultimate ascension into eternity."[2]
Whereas the Catholic Church eventually condemned Gnosticism as a heresy,
partly because of this undue emphasis on knowledge above morality, history
remembers the Gnostics as being antinomian.

At the beginning of the fifth century, a theological debate, with certain
parallels to the second century, erupted between Augustine and the British
monk Pelagius. Pelagius was concerned that Augustine's magnification of
the importance of faith over good works left the Christian life of obedience
in the lurch. Augustine was ultimately vindicated in his position, while his
opponent has had his name attached to a heresy that still suggests legalism. If
the judgment of the Church at the time had been reversed—and I am among
those who are happy that it was not—it is likely that we would be reading
about St. Pelagius' defeat of the antinomian Augustine in our Church History
texts today. Antinomianism is not always a clear-cut position; it exists
wherever the commitment to the Christian life, theologically or actually,
does not measure up to another's expectations.

The other specific school of theological thought that comes to mind
when one hears the name antinomianism is the position of Johann Agricola
in the sixteenth century. As we shall see in more depth in the following
chapters, Agricola held a real distaste for the preaching of the law, believing
that the saving work of Christ alone should be taught and preached by the
Church. While Agricola never suggested that it is immaterial what kind of
behavior a Christian engages in, his opponents believed that position was the
inevitable consequence of his message. Agricola's theology was geared
toward a magnification of God's glory and grace, but it was judged to be

---

[1] *The Oxford Dictionary of the Christian* Church, ed. F. L. Cross and E. A. Livingstone
(Oxford: Oxford University Press, 1983), 65.
[2] J. G. Davies, *The Early Christian Church* (Grand Rapids: Baker Book House, 1965), 71.

dangerous in its implications for Christian morality and became branded as antinomian.

While I do not wish to argue through these examples that antinomianism exists only in the eye of the beholder, it can be the case that one person's antinomianism is another's evangelical liberty. For our purposes in this project, I make the above observations for the sake of pointing out that antinomianism is a difficult "ism" to point to or nail down. It exists where one Christian believes that others have abused the freedom they have in Christ. When exactly that point is breached cannot be objectively defined, as it is subject to individual understandings of the place of the law and the gospel.

The most common manifestation of antinomianism, and that which concerns us here, may be seen among a large number of Christian believers who might be tempted to take advantage of the freedom from the law which Paul described in his epistle to the Romans. Many times, these people are contemplating not a systematic approach to theology or ethics but the occasional indiscretion or vice. This project, therefore, in addressing the antinomian question, is concerned not so much with a life of libertine excess but with the more immediate query a Christian may ask, "What really is going to happen if I don't do my best to live according to God's law?" Even when the question is not specifically articulated, it is this excessive reliance upon grace to excuse moral inactivity or vice that has been bemoaned by theologians and pastors alike, especially since the Reformation. Thus, the antinomian question encompasses the positions of those who might suggest absolute lawlessness as well as the single individual who wants to know what will happen if she puts aside a commandment "just this once." For this reason, in the context of this paper, unless otherwise indicated, the term "antinomianism" will be used in its broader understanding to refer to the abuse of Christian freedom that may follow from the asking of the antinomian question.

It may also be worth pointing out from the start that there can be no "answer" to the antinomian question, if by that we mean a reply that will silence any further discussion every time the question is asked. To begin with, people ask different versions of this question for a variety of reasons: some out of theological curiosity, others in the attempt to find an excuse to indulge sinful desires. Different occasions call for different responses. Moreover, if the one inquiring is trying to discover if there are eternal consequences to the occasional abuse of Christian liberty, it is impossible for anyone to make that judgment. No person is in the place of being able to declare the eternal fate of another on the basis of particular behaviors. While it is possible to *respond* to the antinomian question with advice, insights, or warnings, there can be no *answer*, properly speaking.

Antinomianism in the Lutheran Church

The history of Lutheranism, more than that of any other denomination, has been filled with accusations of fostering this abuse of Christian freedom. Martin Luther's revival of Pauline theology, along with his continual insistence on Christian liberty, contributed substantially to the developing Lutheran theology's susceptibility to this critique; and, as we shall see, the Catholic party did not miss the chance to strike home with this point. From the earliest years of the Reformation, Luther and his disciples were subject to repeated accusations by Rome of either fomenting libertine lifestyles among their hearers, or themselves living in a manner that took little account of the will of God.[3] Whether or not Lutherans have indeed been less pious than their separated brethren in other denominations is a question we shall leave to others. Nevertheless, the accusation of antinomianism did not end with the passing of the period we call the Reformation. The subsequent four centuries have contained their fair share of critics with fingers pointing at Lutheranism for allowing or even creating this abuse of Christian freedom. Still today, Lutherans maintain a reputation as having something of an antinomian bent. At the very least, there are a great many who may ask with Carter Lindberg, "Do Lutherans shout justification but whisper sanctification?"[4]

At the same time that accusations of libertinism have come from outside of Lutheranism, a great number of Lutherans themselves have shared this same concern about their own tradition. Various individuals—from Johann Arndt[5] to Paul Tillich[6]—and movements—as in the case of contemporary

---

[3]See, for example Johann Eck, *Enchiridion of Commonplaces*, trans. Ford Lewis Battles (Grand Rapids: Baker Book House, 1979).

[4]Carter Lindberg, "Do Lutherans Shout Justification But Whisper Sanctification?" *Lutheran Quarterly* 13 (1999): 1-20.

[5]"Dear Christian reader, that the holy Gospel is subjected, in our time, to a great and shameful abuse is fully proved by the impenitent life of the ungodly who praise Christ and his word with their mouths and yet lead an unchristian life that is like that of persons who dwell in heathendom, not in the Christian world." Johann Arndt, *True Christianity*, trans. Peter Erb (New York: Paulist Press, 1979), 21.

[6]"The consequence of the absence in Lutheranism of the Calvinistic and Evangelistic valuation of discipline was that the ideal of progressive sanctification was taken less seriously and replaced by a great emphasis on the paradoxical character of the Christian life. In the period of orthodoxy, this led Lutheranism to that disintegration of morality and practical religion against which the Pietistic movement arose." Paul Tillich, *Systematic Theology* (Chicago: The University of Chicago Press, 1963), 3:230f.

political theology[7]—have expressed their dissatisfaction with moral apathy within the confessional Lutheran church that they believe has often led to inactivity or impiety. Still today, among those who call themselves Lutherans, there remains an abiding concern to address the antinomian question and explain *why* Lutherans need to be very concerned with the life of sanctification.

The difficulty faced by those who have sought to address this question from within a Lutheran framework has been how to insist on the importance, or even necessity of good deeds, without compromising Luther's doctrine of *sola fide*. How do you tell someone that they have to do good works at the same time that you tell them they do not have to do good works? That is, if one, with Luther, insists that works are not necessary for my salvation, what is the motivation for me to engage in good works that do not strike my fancy? Granted, there are times when I may *want* to do the right thing. The question here has to do with those times when I do *not* want to do the right thing. If good works do not obtain or maintain my salvation, as Luther has insisted, then what is the reason for me to do them? The dilemma in which this problem places my interlocutor should not be underestimated. As any continuing dialogue on this point usually demonstrates, it becomes very easy to compromise Luther's remarkable emphasis on the completely free gift of grace in the attempt to make sure that one does not abuse the moral freedom that follows.

In the work of those who have sought to address this issue, we may identify two approaches in responding to the antinomian question. The first is by identifying the error in reasoning that lies behind the antinomian objection in the first place. By making the antinomian question into a logical problem, one may seek to unravel the argument, expose its internal inconsistencies, and thereby close the moral loophole. After all, our intuition tells us there is something wrong with this line of reasoning; the trick is to identify the logical mistake and correct it. Thus, the first approach is to face the antinomian question as a question of logic, and then to articulate a response while being careful not to violate Luther's theology of radical grace in the process. One needs to acknowledge, however, that walking this tightrope is not an easy task, if it is possible at all. As we shall see, more than a few attempts to offer logical answers to the antinomian question while remaining loyal to Luther have ended disappointingly: either the question was not adequately answered, or Luther's abiding principle of *sola fide*, his

---

[7]E.g., Dorothee Soelle, *Against the Wind: Memoir of a Radical Christian*, trans. Barbara and Martin Rumscheidt (Minneapolis: Fortress Press, 1999).

unwavering belief that it is faith alone without any works through which one is saved, was sacrificed—often unwittingly—in the process.

The second approach is rather different from the first. The antinomian can also be addressed or responded to by presenting a counterclaim that trumps the initial position. That is, one may pose a rhetorical question or thought to the individual considering the libertine abuse of Christian freedom that leads that person to retract their previous statement, to withdraw the antinomian question altogether. For example, let us imagine a teenage boy who poses the antinomian question to his parish pastor, attempting to justify his ongoing sinful behavior. The pastor may not answer him a word, but lead him to a corner of the church where there is a striking portrayal of Christ's suffering on the cross and bid him to sit there a short time. We might easily imagine the young man rising from his seat after a few minutes being a bit embarrassed, never to pose the antinomian question again. At the same time, we might equally as well imagine him leaving after a few minutes only being perturbed that the pastor tried to use a guilt-trip to make him change his behavior. Whether or not it is effective, and whether or not it is motivated by guilt or gratitude, this type of response to our perennial problem represents the second possible approach that may be taken to the antinomian question, an appeal to one's sense of conscience or duty.

Making use of some combination of these two approaches, attempts have been made over the centuries to address the antinomian question. Within Lutheranism, there have been a significant number of theologians who were deeply concerned with this issue—theologians who wanted to minimize or avoid libertine abuses that might follow from Luther's gospel message of radical grace. By way of logical solutions or psychological/spiritual appeals to one's conscience, the past five centuries have witnessed men and women who attempted to do just that. It is the purpose of this project to consider the contributions of a small number of them—to look at the ideas, suggestions, and theologies of different Lutheran theologians writing at different times under different circumstances, but with one goal in mind: to respond to the antinomian question.

After a careful consideration of the theology of Luther as it pertains to this issue, each of the following chapters will offer a look at the theological contributions of a specific Lutheran theologian who was particularly in-terested in this problem of the abuse of Christian freedom. By considering the work of Philipp Melanchthon, Philipp Jakob Spener, Søren Kierkegaard, and Dietrich Bonhoeffer, I intend not only to examine their contributions in responding to the antinomian question, but the degree to which they were faithful to Luther's principle of *sola fide* in the process. Moreover, I will argue that it was Luther's unwillingness to clearly and forthrightly address the antinomian question that led later Lutheran theologians to attempt to make up for this deficiency. While many were able to make positive contributions through their recovery of various under-emphasized aspects of Luther's thought (under-emphasized by both Luther and his theological heirs), they also allowed themselves to be led outside the parameters of the Reformer's theology in their attempts to add to or move beyond his work. While all four theologians treated here were committed to the fundamentals of Luther's theology—most particularly the idea that salvation is attained by grace alone through faith alone—the degree to which they were able to hold together this commitment with the need they felt to respond to those who saw this as an excuse for libertinism needs to be closely considered.

The History of Scholarship

The majority of research in this area is limited to bits and pieces within larger works that seek to elucidate the connection between one of the four latter figures and Luther. To my knowledge, no monograph has been published which focuses primarily on the faithfulness of any of these theologians to Luther's doctrine of *sola fide*, with the possible exception of the incriminating exposition of Melanchthon in F. Bente's *Historical Introductions to the Book of Concord*.[8] Rather, one finds a few pages, an occasional chapter, or, from time to time, an article that addresses the theological relation between Luther and one of the four figures treated here. However, in the cases of Melanchthon, Spener, and Bonhoeffer, who claimed to teach a theology in keeping with the Reformer, most scholars are generally content to grant their solidarity with Luther's teachings. Very rarely does one find an author willing to scratch beneath the surface to see if the two theological perspectives are consistent.

The research on Luther's doctrine of *sola fide* has been enormous, and so it is not difficult to find first-rate scholarship on the subject. The work of Paul Althaus[9] continues to be an excellent resource for understanding the theology of Luther, although contemporary research coming out of Finland has raised the issue of serious shortcomings in his understanding of Luther's doctrine of sanctification.[10] This debate allows us to explore this relevant

---

[8] F. Bente, *Historical Introductions to the Book of Concord*, (St. Louis: Concordia Publishing House, 1965).
[9] First and foremost, Paul Althaus, *The Theology of Martin Luther*, trans. Robert C. Schultz (Philadelphia: Fortress Press, 1966).
[10] E.g. *Union with Christ: The New Finnish Interpretation of Luther*, ed. Carl E. Braaten and Robert W. Jenson (Grand Rapids: William B. Eerdmans, 1998.)

issue as we seek a firmer grasp of Luther's understanding of the Christian life.

Melanchthon scholarship, which traditionally has been oblivious to his concern with the antinomian question, has received a substantial boost in recent years from Timothy J. Wengert.[11] His concern for uncovering Melanchthon's battles against antinomianism has contributed significantly to the research in the area and has been an invaluable resource for understanding previous commentaries on Melanchthon's theological peculiarities. The scholarship in this area is finally moving beyond its understanding of Melanchthon as a closet-humanist and has allowed much more fruitful work to take place on the impulses behind his theological work, specifically those issues relevant to his concern with Christian immorality.

Research in the theology of Spener has been seriously lacking in recent years, especially in the United States. While there has been enough basic interest to keep *Pia Desideria* in print, precious little work has been added to the study of his theology. The contributions of James K. Stein in English,[12] and Paul Grünberg in German[13] continue to be the best resources for understanding his life and work. While these and other secondary sources allow productive research in Spener's theology to take place, there is presently very little scholarship being done that considers the continuities and discontinuities between the work of the Father of the Reformation and the Father of German Pietism.

Kierkegaard, on the other hand, continues to be the subject of extensive theological work. Additionally, there has been a significant amount of scholarship on the subject of the relationship between Luther and the melancholy Dane. Walter Lowrie's authoritative biography[14] continues to be an invaluable resource for understanding Kierkegaard's attitude toward Luther. Likewise, Regin Prenter's article "Luther and Lutheranism" in the *Bibliotheca Kierkegaardiana*[15] provides a helpful framework for any further comparative work between these two theological giants. While he may see more disparity between them than really exists, his contribution to the discussion is significant.

[11] E.g. Timothy J. Wengert, *Human Freedom, Christian Righteousness: Philip Melanchthon's Exegetical Dispute with Erasmus of Rotterdam*, (New York: Oxford University Press, 1998).
[12] James K. Stein, *Philipp Jakob Spener: Pietist Patriarch* (Chicago: Covenant Press, 1986).
[13] Paul Grünberg, *Philipp Jakob Spener*, 3 vols. (Göttingen: Vandenhoeck & Ruprecht, 1893-1906).
[14] Walter Lowrie, *Kierkegaard* (New York: Harper and Brothers, 1962).
[15] Regin Prenter, "Luther and Lutheranism." in *Bibliotheca Kierkegaardiana* (Copenhagen: C.A. Reitzels Boghandel, 1981), 6:121-172.

As in the case with Kierkegaard, there is a significant amount of new scholarship coming out on the work and legacy of Bonhoeffer as well. After bemoaning the lack of comparative work on Luther and Bonhoeffer, Christian Gremmels released the well-received series of article in *Bonhoeffer und Luther* (1983),[16] and continued his own work on the subject into the 1990s.[17] However, a considerable gap exists today between the academic research on Bonhoeffer and the popular interest in his fight against cheap grace, which is what interests us here. While Gremmels has made real contributions to this area, the majority of scholarship on the subject still exists as sweeping comments about the consistency of thought between the two men with little attention to the subtle differences in their approaches to the Christian life of discipleship.

The Four Chosen

Among the many who could have been selected to represent Lutheranism's response to the antinomian question, why these four? There are indeed, I admit, a great many figures from whom one could choose. Such a project could conceivably be extended to include individuals like Johann Gerhard, Johann Arndt, August Hermann Francke, Henry Melchoir Mühlenberg, Wilhelm Löhe, Paul Tillich, or Dorothee Sölle. Why these four? First, since this undertaking follows a diachronic approach to the problem, the selected figures should represent different time periods. Admittedly the first two chapters, dealing with Luther and Melanchthon, address figures who lived during the sixteenth century. However, this is, I believe, in the best interest of the overall project insofar as a contemporary response to Luther offers us an insight that later generations cannot afford.

Second, as suggested above, all four of these figures were particularly interested in responding to the antinomian question. While their historical contexts differ, as did the manifestations of perceived antinomianism, all four held an overarching concern to respond to moral laxity that was based on the abuse of Christian liberty. In the works of Spener and Bonhoeffer it is easy to see their preoccupation with this threat. I will argue, however, that Melanchthon and Kierkegaard were equally occupied with this social and theological conundrum. In the case of all four theologians, the antinomian question and their varied responses to it make up the core of their theological particularity. It is impossible to understand their theological contributions

---

[16] *Bonhoeffer und Luther*, ed. Christian Gremmels (München: Chr. Kaiser Verlag, 1983).
[17] Christian Gremmels, "Rechtfertigung und Nachfolge: Martin Luther in Dietrich Bonhoeffers Buch 'Nachfolge,'" in *Dietrich Bonhoeffer Heute*, ed. Rainer Mayer und Peter Zimmerling (Giessen: Brunnen Verlag, 1992).

apart from this very practical problem; it is impossible to understand them as individual people of faith apart from this concern as well.

Lastly, these four theologians were chosen because of their far-reaching influence, both within Lutheranism and wider historical Christianity. Students of Church history easily recognize all four names. Their books are still regularly assigned and read around the world. (The Book of Concord, the works of Kierkegaard, and Bonhoeffer are presently being released in new authoritative English editions, and those of Spener in German.[18]) There are few Lutheran theologians who could be placed alongside these four in terms of influence and authority in Lutheranism; in Protestantism; in Christianity. Those others who can, however, did not share the same degree of concern for responding to the antinomian question. While I respectfully acknowledge those who might suggest a fifth figure I did not include, or might prefer to see one of these four replaced by another, I remain convinced that these four theologians are the most representative and influential respondents to antinomianism in the history of the Lutheran church. The project may certainly be extended to include others, but it should begin with these four.

Goal and Purpose

In answer to the question of what I hope to accomplish by undertaking this project, I should be clear that I do not intend to offer my own answer or response to the antinomian question. As an historical theologian I prefer to point my reader to the contributions of others. This work functions merely to direct those interested in this question to individuals who sought to address this problem and to evaluate their responses according to the standard of Luther's conception of the gospel, specifically the principle of *sola fide*. Insofar as one may wish to discover the logical arguments posed by these figures, the reader will find them summarized herein. However, if one desires to be inspired and strengthened in one's faith in such a way as to render the antinomian question moot in one's own life, I must direct the reader to the original works of these various authors, including Luther. One will find in the pages of this book a few morsels that may whet one's appetite, but the real intellectual and spiritual meal awaits us in the pages scribed by these five men. Their complete responses to the antinomian question can only be found in their own words.

---

[18] The new Book of Concord was released by Fortress Press in 2000. The Hong and Hong series of Kierkegaard translations published by Princeton University Press is nearing completion, as are *Dietrich Bonhoeffer Works* (Fortress Press) and *Philipp Jakob Spener Schriften* (Georg Olms Verlag).

✆ CHAPTER ONE

Martin Luther

When students encounter Martin Luther and his theology in passing, if they happen to remember anything it may be his advice to Philipp Melanchthon, "Sin boldly!" Words like these tend to stick with us; they shock, surprise, and confuse us, and thereby have a way of embedding themselves in our memories. As Luther shared many students' appreciation for bold rhetoric designed to topple existing assumptions about morality, faith, and religion, this famous bit of advice, characteristic of his caustic personality, is hard to forget. As a radical theological innovator (despite his protests to the contrary), Luther offered in this statement a particularly insightful look into the changes in the theological landscape which he was effecting during his time. "Sin boldly!" Viewed cynically and apart from their original context, these words can easily be misunderstood and have been tossed around in support of a lifestyle that Luther would certainly not have countenanced. Considered sympathetically and appreciated in their relation to Melanchthon's tendency to engage life in cautious baby-steps, these words still confuse us.

While we know that Luther was not advocating crass libertinism, was this not just another example of the Reformer's reactionary tendency to overstate his claims without consideration for the moral and theological repercussions that might follow from such careless language? Didn't Luther once again sacrifice the importance of a life of piety in favor of his emphasis on the importance of grace? Perhaps so. However, as with most of his extreme statements, his theological genius cannot be seen by glancing at the letters his pen produced—however well appreciated within their context—but only by carefully pondering them in the spirit in which Luther wrote. Luther not only failed to write a systematic theology, but the words he left us do not lend themselves well to formulation into a systematic approach to understanding God's dealing with humanity, either. The poetic element and fiery rhetoric in his writings make an exposition of his thought tricky business, as innumerable authors have discovered since the sixteenth century. Nonetheless, if we are to understand and discuss the intention behind such antinomian advice as *"Sin boldly!,"* some presentation and analysis of his thought become necessary.

We may certainly leave aside many particulars of Luther's theology in this attempt to grasp his raising of and responses to the antinomian question. While they are certainly related, his understanding of christology, the sacraments, eschatology, ecclesiology, and government may be left aside in an effort to maintain our focus in this work. We shall limit ourselves to an all-too-quick exposition of Luther's anthropology, distinction between law and gospel, and the nature of faith before continuing on to discuss his role in the Antinomian Controversy with Johann Agricola. This chapter will conclude with an analysis of the importance of his theology in understanding the antinomian question, an issue and concern which was magnified as a result of his radical insistence on grace.

Luther and His Theology

After some deliberation, John Calvin decided that it would be more appropriate to begin his *Institutes* with the doctrine of God rather than of humanity. This should come as no surprise to those who are familiar with his constant emphasis on the glory of God. However, in our efforts to understand Luther's theology, it may be best for us to begin with what human beings do before discussing what God does. In the same way that Calvin's *Institutes* betray the legal training which helped shape him as a person, Luther's theological writings are unable to hide their author's personality as well. The latter's theological passion and conviction arose as a result of the experience of his own impotence before God and manifest themselves on almost every page he wrote. However, without his existential acknowledgment of his inability to fulfill the law of a perfect God, and without his liberating "tower experience" that convinced him of the freedom and joy found through the gospel, he would likely have remained an obscure monk and priest in the relatively unknown university at Wittenberg. For Luther the law must come before the gospel (despite Karl Barth's objections to the contrary[1]); he insisted that we must understand our own works before we understand the works of God. Therefore we begin with Luther's anthropology before proceeding to his doctrine of justification.

Human Nature

According to Luther, human nature has been completely corrupted since the fall of Adam and Eve in the garden. Augustine had fought tooth and nail in

---

[1]See Karl Barth, *Evangelium und Gesetz* (1935).

the early fifth century to establish his view of original sin, only to have it steadily disintegrate in the centuries that followed. As Adolf von Harnack has pointed out, "the history of Church doctrine in the West was a much disguised history of struggle against Augustine."[2] Roughly a millennium later, Luther and the reformers were adamant not only about reviving the beloved Bishop of Hippo's anthropology but taking it a step further as well. For Luther, who never enjoyed a love affair with philosophy as Augustine had, not only is the human will corrupt, but human reason as well. While our cognitive abilities are solely to be relied upon in secular matters, they constantly betray us in spiritual ones. Luther's reference to "Madam Reason"[3] was not intended to undermine trust in the power of the human mind to understand the cosmos or establish governments, but to insist that in areas of spiritual concern she would sell herself out, defending the corrupt human will that wants to justify itself rather than be justified by God. For Luther, then, original sin not only left the human will depraved but rendered human reason and judgment as corrupt and incapable of grasping God's righteousness as the decaying body in which they dwell.

With the human will and reason rendered impotent by sin, it comes as no surprise that the daily conduct of persons is often less than laudatory. The world in which we live, Luther noted, is nothing more than "a mad dog with bloody teeth"[4] in which we are governed by evil and greedy despots who shamelessly abuse those under them and where the only thing that is rarer than a wise prince is a morally upright one.[5] At the same time, he acknowledged that humanity is also capable of establishing good government, promoting peace, keeping order, and even practicing the noble virtues of which the Greeks had spoken so well. While one's outward works may be praiseworthy and beneficial for one's neighbor, their inner motivation, however, remains as selfish and corrupt as those of the murderer across the street. While this insistence did not sit well with many in the sixteenth century (as it surely does not with many still today), Luther is echoing the concern of Augustine in noting that without grace, human beings are capable only of serving themselves and their own interests. While experience may teach us that kindness and civility have their many rewards—offering a more prudent approach to the attaining of one's desires—human beings are incapable of transcending their own natures. It is part of who we are as fallen

---

[2]Adolph von Harnack, *History of Dogma*, trans. Neil Buchanan (New York: Russell and Russell, 1958), 6:167.
[3]*LW* 33, 122.
[4]*WA* 27, 264.
[5]*LW* 45, 113.

people that we seek nothing but our own happiness. The good deeds that we do for our neighbors are nothing other than works that function to serve our own desires. As Jesus had sought to convey in his teaching, broadening and deepening the intentions of the law, so Luther wanted to communicate that human life is characterized by nothing more than sin and rebellion. Luther believed that only after understanding this may one begin the journey of faith. First, however, one needs to hear God speaking through the law, communicating "how all your life and deeds are nothing before God, but that you, together with everything in you, must perish eternally. If you believe this aright—that you are guilty—you must despair of yourself."[6]

For Luther, the first thing that is necessary for one to begin to be reconciled to God is to acknowledge one's corruption, sinfulness, and impotence. The problem is that human nature being what it is, and human reason being the *"whore"* that cannot help but serve that nature, humans are incapable of realizing this. Between the tendencies either to justify one's actions or oneself, we find humanity attempting to take its salvation into its own hands. This, for Luther, is not only impossible but blasphemous, making God a liar; God has declared that He is the author of salvation. "The notion of being able to achieve one's own righteousness is the cesspool (*sentina*) of all evils and the very worst sin (*peccatum peccatorum*) of the world."[7] Rather, the entire act of justification is the work of God and begins with His use of the law to show us exactly how powerless we are.

The Law

Luther clearly spoke of two uses of the law. While the question as to whether he also allowed for a third use of the law is a subject of considerable debate, and one to which we will return, his understanding of the first two uses of the law is not generally disputed. The first use of which he spoke, the *usus politicus,* functions as a curb on the excesses of human behavior so that civil society can exist and the Word of God can be preached. For God "wants to preserve order among us and compel us to lead an externally honorable life, that we may live together without devouring one another, which would happen if there were no law."[8] Thus this function of the law has nothing to do directly with a sinner's reconciliation, but merely helps create the conditions under which God's salvific act may take place. In keeping with Luther's concern for maintaining the focus of theology on the justification of the individual sinner, one finds little discussion of this use of the law in his

---

[6]*WA* 7, 22.
[7]WA 40¹, 477.
[8]*WA* 10¹, 1, 454f.

writings; and from many of his remarks about the law, one might even forget that it exists.

The second use of the law, the *usus theologicus*, is the primary and central use for Luther. This second use "shows us our sins spiritually, terrifying and humbling us, so that when we have been frightened this way, we acknowledge our misery and our damnation. And this latter is the true and proper use of the Law."[9] The law, understood through its *usus theologicus*, tells us not what to do but what we have failed to do. In this way it prepares the sinner for the gospel, the "good news" of the forgiveness of sins. The law, functioning in this accusatory way, makes the sinner aware of her own sinfulness. Hence we find in the history of Lutheran theology numerous references to the metaphor of a mirror to elucidate this second use of the law.

To comprehend more properly what Luther intended when he spoke of the law in this way, it is necessary not only to stipulate that the law is found in the New Testament as well as the Old, but to insist that we overcome our tendency to think of the law as a set of moral rules or regulations. The law for Luther is not limited to a legal code that one may find in the Decalogue, the Sermon on the Mount, or Canon Law. We do not see it exhausted in the collective genius of moral and religious leaders from Confucius to Gandhi. The law, rather, consists of whatever makes us aware of our finitude, depravity, and impotence in the face of the eternal.[10] As Gerhard Ebeling explains in his *Wort und Glaube:* "Law for Luther is not a revealed statutory norm to which man then adopts this attitude or that, but law is for Luther an existentialist category which sums up the theological interpretations of man's being as it is in fact. Law is therefore not an idea or an aggregate of principles, but the reality of fallen humanity."[11] For Luther, the primary importance of the *demand* in the law is not to provide rules for social interaction, but to assist the individual in discovering what Schleiermacher would later call our "absolute dependence" on God. That is, God's demands in the law function, first and foremost, by revealing human impotence.

As a result, the law is not limited to the recitation of and commentary on ethical mandates from Scripture, as important as these may be. No, the law also may be encountered in such things as the religious teachings of Muhammad, the terror of a thunderstorm or earthquake, or the passing of a loved one. This awareness of the multifaceted nature of the law was

---

[9] *LW* 26, 337.

[10] *WA* 39[1], 354.

[11] Gerhard Ebeling, *Word and Faith*, trans. James W. Leitch (Philadelphia: Fortress Press, 1963), 75.

expressed particularly well by a professor of mine years ago who advised his
seminary students that they should avoid preaching the *"law"* at funerals for
it is already present staring everyone in the face. It follows, moreover, that
while Luther adamantly insisted that one needs to differentiate law from
gospel in reading Holy Writ, a particular passage need not be either one or
the other; in fact, much in Scripture is both at the same time. As Luther
articulated in his discussion with Agricola, and as we shall see below, the
Gospel writers' account of Christ on the cross, suffering because of and for
the sake of our sins, is both law and gospel simultaneously. Luther's most
direct articulation of this matter was included in the Formula of Concord,
Solid Declaration, Article V, "Everything that preaches about our sin and the
wrath of God, no matter how or when it happens, is the proclamation of the
law."[12]

The reception of the law, as Luther pointed out, is only the first step, the
prerequisite for hearing and truly understanding the gospel. The message of
the forgiveness of sins makes sense and can be personally appropriated *pro
me* only if the awareness of one's sinfulness has preceded it. For those who
have been brought to despair through the law, however, the gospel becomes
the power of God unto salvation. It requires nothing on the part of the sinner,
who has come to understand that he is powerless to offer his assistance in
any way; it consists of pure grace. Thus he states: "The gospel, however,
does not preach what we are to do or to avoid. It sets up no requirements but
reverses the approach of the law, does the very opposite, and says, 'This is
what God has done for you....' So, then, there are two kinds of doctrine and
two kinds of works, those of God and those of men."[13]

This free and unconditional gift of the Holy Spirit and the forgiveness of
sins, if it is received, have a profound effect on the law. With the complete
reconciliation of the individual believer to God and the removal of all guilt,
the accusing voice of the law is silenced. There is nothing left to condemn,
for the penalty has been paid by Christ on the cross. With the sinner's
acquittal, the power of the law is not merely vitiated, not only overcome and
transcended, it has become opposed to the message of grace. Paul Althaus
has correctly pointed out that while St. Paul taught that justification takes
place *"without the law"* (Rom. 3:21), Luther, while in fundamental agreement, puts an even sharper edge on Paul's words, preferring to describe
justification as taking place *"against the law."*[14] For Luther, the point could

---

[12] See further *WA* 15, 228.
[13] *LW* 35, 162.
[14] Paul Althaus, *The Theology of Martin Luther*, trans. Robert C. Schultz (Philadelphia:
Fortress Press, 1966), 257.

not be emphasized enough that the law focuses on what we do while the gospel brings to our attention what God does. The former demonstrates our inability to justify ourselves; the latter announces that God has justified sinners by Himself. Therefore, the works of the law are in complete opposition to the work of the gospel. Whoever attempts to bring the law into the discussion of reconciliation, beyond its limited role of demonstrating human weakness, not only usurps God's authority to be the author of salvation but makes a liar of the God who has declared all sins forgiven and all human works void of any merit. Thus Luther points out, "It is a marvelous thing and unknown to the world to teach Christians to ignore the law and to live before God as though there were no law whatever. For if you do not ignore the law and thus direct your thoughts to grace as though there were no law but as though there were nothing but grace you cannot be saved."[15] At the same time, he never insisted that Christians have no further use for the law. The second use of the law continues its function throughout the believers' life of faith, constantly reminding them of their dependence on God and ever-present need of forgiveness. While Luther relished the rhetorical shock value of statements like that just quoted, and could use phrases as unprecedented as *"lex est negatio Christi"* ("law is the negation of Christ"),[16] he would have been the last one to claim that the law's usefulness ends with the reconciliation of the sinner. As he admitted in 1539, during his battle with Agricola, "I myself, as old and as learned as I am, recite the commandments daily word for word like a child."[17]

Reconciliation

The implications of Luther's radical notion of grace, however, go beyond his surprising statements about the freedom from the law. If Luther was to argue that human works count for nothing in the attainment of salvation, he would have to follow that premise consistently, even when it led him to some rather unpopular conclusions. If he was to argue that our human works make no contribution whatsoever to our reconciliation, then, like Augustine, he would have to insist that Christians do nothing that makes them more or less ready than anyone else. Grace comes without any preparation on the part of the redeemed, Luther believed, and it takes place without any assistance or cooperation on their part as well. "Thus I am justified as though I were a piece of material and I suffer; I do not do anything."[18] While this notion that

---

[15] *LW* 26, 6.
[16] *WA* 40^2, 18; *LW* 27,16
[17] *LW* 47, 109.
[18] *WA* 39^1, 447.

reconciliation happens to an individual without any involvement, participation, or cooperation on her part struck many as absurd or even dangerous,
Luther was undaunted in his insistence that *"grace alone"* means *"grace
alone."* In his 1535 commentary on Galatians, he uses the language of passive righteousness: "But this most excellent righteousness, the righteousness
of faith, which God imputes to us through Christ without works, is neither
political nor ceremonial nor legal nor work-righteousness but is quite the
opposite; it is a merely passive righteousness, while all others, listed above,
are active. For here we work nothing, render nothing to God; we only receive
and permit someone else to work in us, namely, God."[19] We will see in the
next chapter that this would later become a point of contention within
Lutheranism during the Synergistic Controversy. From the very beginning,
however, words like these could easily give offense to moderate Catholics
trying to diffuse tensions between Rome and Wittenberg. The obvious
danger was that Luther's audiences would simply resort to religious apathy
or fatalism. If it is all in God's hands whether one is granted saving faith,
there is little point in trying to do the right thing to get to heaven. However,
despite such protests, Luther made no compromise of his position. "Then do
we do nothing and work nothing in order to obtain this righteousness? I
reply: Nothing at all."[20]

Faith

There is often some confusion on the part of Lutherans as to the role which
faith plays in salvation. The tendency to interpret Luther's insistence on *sola
fide* as suggesting that we are saved by faith is common but inaccurate. The
correct formula should read that we are saved by grace *through* faith. Alister
McGrath is correct in insisting that we need to understand that for Luther,
justification is *"propter Christum*, and not *propter fidem,"* that is, on account
of Christ, not on account of our faith.[21]

Properly speaking, then, faith does not justify us. What it does is receive
the justification which is offered by virtue of the work of Christ. Christ offers
the sinner forgiveness, and it is faith which is able to accept the gift. As
Luther explains, "Faith does not reconcile us of itself, but it grasps and
obtains the reconciliation which Christ has wrought for us."[22] Or again,
"[Faith] holds out the hand and opens the bag and is content to receive

---

[19] *LW* 26, 4f.
[20] *LW* 26, 8.
[21] Alister E. McGrath, *Iustitia Dei: A History of the Christian Doctrine of Justification*,
Second Edition (Cambridge: Cambridge University Press, 1998), 201.
[22] *WA* 8, 519.

nothing but benefactions."[23] At times, Luther's fluid use of language permits him to make statements that suggest that faith is what makes us righteous before God. The context, however, will always demand recognition of his position that our faith is not gaining reconciliation for us but merely receiving it, as when he writes, "Therefore faith justifies because it takes hold of and possesses this treasure, the present Christ."[24]

Furthermore, as we have seen above, this faith is not something that we decide to do or to have. Fallen humanity does not have the luxury to decide whether or not to have the faith in God which liberates one from sin. Luther explains that it is not an act (*actio*) which we do, but should be called an influence (*passio*) which powerfully changes our souls and allows us to receive reconciliation with our Maker.[25] Faith, like the accompanying justification, is a gift from God. Neither is received on the basis of any human merit, act, or decision. Rather, this passive influence, or faith, is freely received along with the passive righteousness that justifies the sinner in the eyes of God. That is, however, where the passive nature of faith ends, for faith does not remain passive in the soul of the believer. Faith is indeed the power of God that manifests itself in works of love. The necessary complement of faith being given freely apart from human works or merit is that God is giving His Spirit to the redeemed sinner. Therefore, by necessity, the man or woman who believes will begin to live a life of faith. This theme will be explored more fully below. Here it is enough to remark that for Luther, faith not only receives the forgiveness of sins, but compels works of love as well. It is because of this, then, that humanity observes the difference between what is true and illusory faith. Without the good works and battle against sin that follow upon the reception of faith and imputed righteousness, one can be sure that what is under consideration is not truly faith. Faith then performs two functions. First it justifies the sinner; second it empowers him to a life of new obedience. Neither the faith nor the new obedience justifies; rather, the former receives justification and the latter accompanies it.

Unfortunately, this faith, through which one is saved, is too often viewed as a simple task by which we assure ourselves entrance into heaven. Five centuries of Protestantism have struggled with this misconception, both from within its own ranks and in criticisms from without. Meaningless, almost Gnostic statements about "believing in Jesus" in order to be saved have lulled many into a false security regarding the strength or even existence of their faith and have rightly drawn indignation from Christianity's critics.

---

[23] *WA* 21, 488.
[24] *LW* 26, 130.
[25] *WA* 42, 452.

Likewise, Luther's critics, when the Reformation was dawning, could not understand how he could say that it is through faith alone that one is justified, without the *charitas*, the works of love, which appear to make our role in reconciliation meaningful. Otherwise, it begins to sound like Bonhoeffer's "cheap grace." For Luther, however, faith is far from a simple undertaking. "To be sure, faith does seem to be an easy matter; but it really is a difficult art. Temptation and experience certainly teach that, on the contrary, we must say that clinging to God's Word so that the heart is not afraid of sins and death but trusts and believes God, is a far more bitter and difficult task than observing all the rules of the Carthusian and monastic orders."[26]

To repeat, faith is not something one decides to do. One does not have the luxury to wait until an appropriate time and then believe. "This sort of [false] faith is, moreover, very harmful. It would be better not to have it at all. A philosopher who is moral is better than a hypocrite who has such a faith."[27] True faith does not appear out of our own willing or desire to be saved; it is, as we have seen above, entirely the work of God. While human beings generally perceive that they have the free will to choose to believe or not, for Luther this is an illusion. For Luther, our will can cooperate with God only after our justification. Faith comes to the believer from God alone, despite our perception that we make the decision; hence the Lutheran distaste for altar calls and "decision-theology." Unlike the false, convenient faith which masquerades as authentic belief, "the real faith, of which we are speaking, cannot be brought into being by our own thoughts. On the contrary, it is entirely God's work in us, without any cooperation on our part."[28]

Secondly, and perhaps more importantly, faith is not subscription to a particular theology or list of doctrines. Luther could not be more emphatic that true faith is the personal appropriation of the claims of Christianity *pro me*. "Accordingly, that 'for me' or 'for us,' if it is believed, creates that true faith and distinguishes it from all other faith, which merely hears the things done."[29] This is what the Spirit of God allows the believer to do. Overcoming doubts as to the claims of Christianity that cannot be verified through experience,[30] the Holy Spirit creates faith in the heart of the believer that Christ died *"for me."* True faith does not simply accept the Nicene Creed, but understands, grasps, accepts, and believes that the Christ spoken of

---

[26] *WA* 33, 284.
[27] *WA* 40¹, 421.
[28] *WA* 10³, 285.
[29] *LW* 34:111.
[30] *WA*, 52, 517.

therein died to save me personally from the sins that I know are weighing me down with guilt.

Grace and the Gift

As this discussion of faith shows, God does not come to the sinner presenting merely the faith that justifies, but provides two different things.[31] In the act of justification the sinner receives by virtue of Christ's work on the cross first *gratia*, or grace, and secondly *donum*, or the gift.[32] The grace of God is that forgiveness of sins which reconciles us with our Creator and assures us of salvation. The gift is the power of the Holy Spirit in our lives that provides the strength to stop sinning and to live a God-pleasing life of piety.[33] Heinrich Bornkamm offers particularly clear definitions of these two aspects of justification: " 'Grace' means a change in a person's situation toward God, so that grace really reaches the person from without, from God's point of view.... 'Gift' means the change in a person as accomplished by grace, the inward event in faith and in the attendant overcoming of sin which faith brings about."[34] These two aspects of the Christian life necessarily exist together and cannot be separated. However, the degree to which each one is emphasized has varied significantly, not only in subsequent Lutheran theology but in later commentaries on Luther as well. Which one of these, the grace or the gift, did Luther place more emphasis on? Which one should be emphasized in discussing Luther's theology? These questions continue to dog theologians as accusations fly about other groups or individuals who may have neglected one or the other.

Today it is being argued that the legacy of Immanuel Kant on subsequent Lutheran theology has led to an overemphasis on the imputed grace of God, to the neglect of consideration of the gift of the Spirit of God which enlivens the believer's soul. In his philosophical and theological writings, Kant insisted that we can speak only of *relations*, not of *being* itself. Thus, while Christianity can speak meaningfully of the restored relationship between God and humanity which is offered through the redeeming work of Christ, statements about God's actual *being* coming to dwell within the individual human are tenuous at best. Therefore, we can speak about God's action in justifying sinners, but to make metaphysical claims about human nature's

---

[31] It would be easier to call them both "gifts," for that is what they are, but Luther has given one of them the name *donum* ,or "gift," and so we must be careful in our language so that we do not confuse the two in speaking of the both as gifts.

[32] *WA* 49, 94f.

[33] *WA* 50, 599f.

[34] Heinrich Bornkamm, *Luther in Mid-Career*, trans. E. Theodore Bachmann (Philadelphia: Fortress Press, 1983), 186. See further *LW* 32, 226-29.

union with Christ through the presence of the Holy Spirit is beyond the limits of religious knowledge or speech. Moreover, as Sammeli Jununen and others have pointed out, we find that representatives of "neo-Protestant" Luther-scholarship such as Albrecht Ritschl and Wilhelm Herrmann as well as those of the Luther-renaissance movement such as Karl Holl, Erich Vogelsang, Reinhold Seeberg and Erich Seeberg, tend to concede to the Kantian resistance to metaphysical language, thereby reducing Luther's conception of faith to "ethical or relational concepts" rather than ontological *"Seins-Aussagen."*[35] The concern here is that the twofold nature of faith is being reduced to a single component; i.e. that the "grace" of God comes to encompass the entire essence of faith, while the "gift" of the Holy Spirit, indwelling the believer, is pushed into the background as a philosophical embarrassment.

Recently there has been an increased effort, particularly among the Finns, to restore Christianity's focus on the "union with Christ" in faith. Much of this effort is welcome for its ability to reclaim a neglected and undervalued component of Luther's conception of faith from various rationalizing tendencies. McGrath correctly points out that Luther used more "images and categories of personal relationship to describe the union of the believer and Christ (such as the *commercium admirable* of a human marriage paralleling that between the soul and Christ), [while] Melanchthon increasingly employed images and categories drawn from the sphere of Roman law."[36] Unfortunately, much of this language has become understated in Lutheranism since Luther's death.

In the latter half of the twentieth century, there has been a move to rectify this situation. Lutheran theologians in the United States have been making strides to correct this imbalance,[37] but most of the efforts have come from Finnish scholars. Luther's emphases on love and participation as essential aspects of Christian faith have come to the forefront in Finland. Tuomo Mannermaa insists:

---

[35] Sammeli Juntunen, "Luther and Metaphysics: What is the Structure of Being According to Luther," in *Union with Christ: The New Finnish Interpretation of Luther*, ed. Carl E. Braaten and Robert W. Jenson (Grand Rapids: William B. Eerdmans, 1998), 129-160. We see this tendency in Althaus as well who is willing to grant that "Christ is not only the 'object' of faith but is himself present in faith," (1966, 231) but generally limits his differentiation between genuine and false faith to the ability to appropriate the facts of salvation "for me" and "for my sake." (1966, 230).

[36] McGrath, *Iustitia Dei*, 211.

[37] E.g. Gerhard O. Forde, "Forensic Justification and the Law in Lutheran Theology," in *Justification by Faith* (Minneapolis: Augsburg Publishing House, 1985), and Bengt R. Hoffman, "On the Relationship Between Mystical Faith and Moral Life in Luther's Thought," in *Encounters with Luther*, vol. 1 (Gettysburg: Lutheran Theological Seminary, 1980).

> In contrast to Luther's theology, forgiveness [*gratiam*]...and the real presence of God (*donum*) in faith are in danger of being separated by the one-sidedly forensic justification adopted by the Formula of Concord and by subsequent Lutheranism. In Luther's theology, however, both of these motifs are closely united in his understanding of the person of Christ.[38]

Thus, the Finns urge us to remember that Luther's theology encompasses both aspects of faith. Both the grace of forensic justification, which grants the forgiveness of sins and the gift of the Holy Spirit need to be emphasized. Simon Peura reminds us, "The believer receives through faith a pure, unselfish love from God, who is himself this love and who gives it to the believer who desires to receive him."[39]

Unfortunately, in their passionate embrace of this neglected yet essential component of Luther's thought, coupled with their attempt to establish more common ground with the Eastern Orthodox churches, the Finns have a tendency to push their position too hard. In insisting on the "gift," they tend to neglect God's "grace" of justification. As a result, sanctification becomes based largely on the indwelling Spirit of God with little if any mention of the gratitude which the Christian has for the forgiveness of sins. This is certainly not an insignificant concern, as gratitude is central to Luther's understanding of sanctification and of utmost importance for our discussion of the antinomian question. The "gift" may be the power of God to enable the redeemed sinner to undertake her own battle against sin, but this battle against the sinful flesh is based on the gratitude that comes with knowing that her sins are forgiven. The Finns tend to neglect this essential relation of "grace" and "gift" in sanctification. One cannot help but notice the lack of discussion of gratitude in their discussion of the life of faith. While this does conveniently play into their agenda of ecumenism with the Eastern Orthodox, which likewise bases its discussions of *theosis*, or deification, not on gratitude toward but on union with Christ, it is not any truer to Luther than the theology of the heirs of Kant.[40] The Finns swing the pendulum back past a balance of "grace" and "gift" to an overemphasis on the latter.

---

[38] Tuomo Mannermaa, "Justification and *Theosis* in Lutheran-Orthodox Perspective, in *Union with Christ*, 28.

[39] Simon Peura, "What God gives Man Receives: Luther on Salvation," in *Union with Christ*, 78-79.

[40] Dennis Bielfeldt has expressed a similar concern, noting a tendency on the part of the Finns to rely in large part on passages from the early Luther. See "Response to Sammeli Juntunen, 'Luther and Metaphysics'," in *Union with Christ*, 163. Also, Klaus Schwarzwaller has raised some critical questions about the Finnish agenda in his "Verantwortung des Glaubens," in *Freiheit als Liebe bei Martin Luther* ed. Dennis Bielfeldt and Klaus Schwarzwaller (Frankfurt: Peter Lang, 1995), 146ff.

Sanctification

Sanctification, literally the process of becoming holy, is an area of theology that Luther has often been accused of neglecting. He certainly had less to say about this topic than about his primary concern, justification. Despite his unwillingness to say more about it, however, his contribution to Christian theology on this topic is far from insignificant. In the same way that he frustrates contemporary readers with his minimal concentration on this topic, his contemporaries throughout Germany were, at times, equally impatient with his resistance to saying more about it. In 1520, Georg Spalatin again encouraged him to write a sermon on good works, sharing his concern that Luther's writings were fodder for the accusations of his enemies that his theology would lead to lawlessness and a total lack of respect for righteous living. Still, Luther was not inclined to produce such a work. Finally he relented, remembering an earlier promise to do so and penning one of his most influential and praised theological productions, his *Treatise on Good Works.*

Luther began this work by insisting that, of course, he did not oppose good works but greatly encouraged them. His primary concern was that people realize what are and what are not truly good works. Emphasizing that the key is to look at the person doing the work, not simply the works themselves, he stated: "He who would have a person do good works must not begin with the works but with the person who is to do them."[41] Attempts to curry God's favor, get oneself into heaven, or even maintain one's status as a child of God cannot be described as good works. Truly good works spring not from self-interest but from love for God. Those with faith realize not only that they cannot obtain or maintain their own salvation through their own works, but that God has already undergone the requisite good works and paid the penalty for sin. Thus the believer, in gratitude toward God for doing what sinners are unable to do, responds with good deeds. Thus Luther pointed out that "God's children do what is good because they want to and not for selfish reasons. They seek no reward except to be praised by God and to do his will,"[42] and commented further, "This is the reason that when I exalt faith and reject such works done without faith they accuse me of forbidding good works. The fact of the matter is that I want very much to teach the real good works which spring from faith."[43] Luther's extreme position, that good works can spring only from genuine Christian faith, is based on his understanding of the role of gratitude. Only in Christianity,

---

[41] *WA*, 7, 33.
[42] *WA* 18, 694.
[43] *LW* 44, 24.

Luther argues, can one find the free forgiveness of sins. As a result, only in Christianity can one find the eradication of the attempt to gain God's favor with our alleged *"good works,"* and only in Christianity can there be gratitude toward God for the greatest work ever performed, the sacrifice of the Son of God on the cross. Consequently, it is only through true Christian faith that one abandons the self-interested motive of gaining one's salvation and expresses gratitude toward God which spontaneously manifests itself in good works. This deduction is not much in favor in today's global society, where any claim for the superior, unique, and essential nature of one religion will likely be confronted with manifold objections; as a result, it is too frequently glossed over. However, it is of central importance in understanding Luther's theology, despite its propensity to offend, for Luther is unintelligible without the recognition that specific knowledge of Christ's actions creates liberation, peace, and gratitude in the sinner.

Luther was obviously elucidating not only the source of good works in Christians, but their inevitability as well. "Where there is genuine faith, there good works will certainly follow, too."[44] If one truly believes the Christian message, two implications must follow. First, the person must have the power of the Holy Spirit dwelling within, which makes possible not only saving faith, but the life of faith as well. Second, the person must have personally appropriated the law and gospel message of Christ to herself, so that she will necessarily feel gratitude toward God. These two factors necessarily imply that the redeemed sinner will live a life of piety and struggle against the sin which remains in her temporal body. As Luther stated: "For as naturally as a tree bears fruit, good works follow upon faith."[45] And, "Just as there is not fire without heat and smoke, so there is no faith without love."[46]

The opposite obviously holds true as well. Where there are no good works, there can be no faith. "For although faith is enough for salvation and I obtain the kingdom of heaven through faith, good works must nonetheless follow, or my faith is not genuine. For faith is so serious a matter that it does not remain without good works."[47] Of course one needs to be careful when making judgments of this sort. Sin still abounds. The believer is both righteous and a sinner at the same time, *simul iustus et peccator*. It is not always apparent what are good works and what is hypocritical self-righteousness. Moreover, as Paul Tillich points out, we do not see in Luther's conception of

---

[44] *LW* 21, 150.
[45] *WA* 10³, 285.
[46] *WA* 17², 275.
[47] *WA* 47, 114.

sanctification the steadily improving life on its way to perfection, as he finds
in Calvin. "It was seen instead as an up-and-down of ecstasy and anxiety, of
being grasped by *agape* and being thrown back into estrangement and
ambiguity. This oscillation between up and down was experienced radically
by Luther himself, in the change between movements of courage and joy and
moments of demonic attacks, as he interpreted his states of doubt and
profound despair."[48] McGrath has observed the same tendency in Luther.
Contrasting him with the famous bishop of Hippo: "For Luther, man may
thus only progress in the spiritual life by continually returning to Christ
semper a novo incipere. Thus Luther interprets *semper iustificandus* as 'ever
to be justified anew,' while Augustine treats it as meaning 'ever to be made
more and more righteous.'"[49] That is, Luther sees the individual believer
drawing strength from continually returning to the font of God's grace rather
than slowly building up a greater and greater store of faith during one's
lifetime. While Luther would also at times speak about the progressive
development of sanctity in the life of the believer, Tillich's and McGrath's
point is well-taken. Identifying faith in another or in oneself is not so simple
as trying to observe a steady improvement in character. Indeed, Calvin
rejected this tactic as well. Religious conviction, gratitude, and passion wax
and wane during the believer's pilgrimage on this earth. What remains
constant is the faith that assures the redeemed sinner through the dark and
heavy times.

In any discussion of Luther's understanding of sanctification, the
question may arise whether good works are performed for the sake of God or
for the sake of the neighbor. The answer to this question is readily apparent
in Luther's writings, as long as we carefully define our terms. Luther made it
clear that the good works which Christians do are done for the benefit of the
neighbor; neither for God, as if God required our efforts, nor for ourselves.
"On the last day he will ask you whether you have done any deeds not for
the sake of yourself being justified by them but for the sake of your
neighbor's being served."[50] He advises that the Christian should "think of
nothing more than doing to your neighbor as Christ has done to you, and let
all your works with your entire life be directed to your neighbor."[51]

---

[48] Paul Tillich, *Systematic Theology*, vol. 3 (Chicago: University of Chicago Press, 1963), 230.
[49] McGrath, *Iustitia Dei*, 200.
[50] *WA* 11, 94. Note that he does not say that the works are done for the sake of the neighbor,
but for the sake of the neighbor being served. Here he is drawing a contrast between doing
good works for our own sake or for another's, not addressing here the motive of the behavior.
[51] *WA* 10¹, 2, 168.

At the same time, however, it is necessary also to remember that the motive for these good deeds is again gratitude toward God. They are based not on the love we may have for our neighbor but on the love which we have for God. Christians do these good deeds because God desires that they be done. "He does these things to his neighbor, and this is called doing them to God and serving God, because God has commanded and enjoined such conduct. "[52] Furthermore, as we have seen, this obedience to God is not based on fear or self-interested hope for salvation, but is done freely out of gratitude for all that God has done for the sinner. While there certainly may be an earnest desire to help one's neighbor, the Christian is not to wait for that feeling to come first. These acts of love, which we perform out of gracious obedience to God, are frequently less than pleasurable. "Our old Adam finds such washing of feet very sour work...And he is especially hurt when gratitude fails to follow.... Therefore we need not only diligent practice but also constant prayer that God would give us His grace to be patient and humble. "[53] In other words, Luther does not ask whether it is better to give to the neighbor joyfully or begrudgingly; that would be to miss the point since God commands that we engage in both pleasant and unpleasant works of love. Rather, it is a question of how much gratitude we feel toward God so that we will willingly undertake the tasks He gives His children. Good works are done for the benefit of the neighbor, but for the sake of God.

The Third Use of the Law

Whether or not Luther considered there to be a third use of the law in addition to the two he directly expressed has been a subject of considerable disagreement among historians and theologians. Unfortunately, for all the ink that has been spilled on the subject, little productive dialogue on the subject has taken place. The primary reason for this has been the failure to agree upon a common definition of this third use of the law when considering Luther's theology.

In the 1534 edition of his *Scholia*, Melanchthon introduced a third use of the law to the theology of the Reformation. He would later define this use of the law rather succinctly in the following words: "The law must be proclaimed in such a manner that it teaches certain works through which God wants us to exercise obedience. God does not want us to devise our own works or worship, because reason, unless it is guided by God's Word, can easily err and through wrong desires be misled into the creation of faulty

---

[52] *WA* 52, 462.
[53] *WA* 52, 225.

works, as becomes evident in the legislation of the heathen. "[54] This third use, then, was to be an application of the law for the Christian believer alone. It does not exist to rein in the excesses of evil people, as does the first use, nor does it condemn one's actions, pointing out to the sinner his sins, as we find in the second use, but offers to the believer direction on how to live a Christian life—what rules to follow and prohibitions to observe. Insofar as Calvin would later make this third use the primary function of the law, there can be no disagreement that Luther would have rejected such a claim. The primary function of the law for Luther was always its second use. The issue is not whether Luther allowed a third use of the law like Calvin, which supersedes the other uses, but whether he accepted this additional function of the law as Melanchthon had described it.

At first glance it could appear that Luther would not have permitted such a use and in fact went out of his way to avoid it. Time and again, Luther insisted that the redeemed would automatically discern proper conduct without having to be taught how; that a good tree produces good fruit without requiring instruction from a thick book of laws.[55] Likewise, we may recall that he could speak of the law coming to an end in Christ; *lex est negatio Christi*. Furthermore, in his exegesis of Scripture, in the very places where we would certainly expect to find some hint of a third use of the law, it is frequently lacking. Consider his First Lecture on the Psalms, where, in his exposition of Psalm 119, he appears to bend over backwards to avoid speaking of the law in this way. When he discusses the author's words, "And I will consider the wondrous things of Thy law," and "My soul has coveted to long for Thy ordinances at all times," it is remarkable that he has nothing to say about the law as a blessing which provides the child of God with ethical direction. Rather, he looks beyond the obvious literal meaning of the text, providing a spiritual interpretation that dovetails with his radical insistence on grace. The importance of this text for Luther is not that it reminds its readers of how wonderful God's laws are, but that it reminds them that they are never to think they have fulfilled God's law and need no longer pursue His commands. "Therefore those who are proud do not covet to desire the Lord's ordinances but think themselves richly justified and already in possession of all ordinances.... The proud and slothful, who seek to be holy or at ease, covet a quick end to work and an arrival at the top.... Let us therefore covet this, that we may always be able to progress and not pause at any time or have reached perfection."[56]

---

[54] *CR* 21, 719.
[55] *WA* 11, 250.
[56] *LW* 11, 428f.

While it is certainly not easy to find a third use of the law in Luther's writings, even where we would most expect it to be, it is still there if one is willing to look closely for it. We first need to understand that, despite some of Luther's extreme statements about the destructive nature of the law, he still believed it to be holy and good. It has been humanity's own depravity that has made the law destructive. "The whole law was holy, just and good, as Paul says in Rom. 7 [:12]; but because of our fault, that which is good cannot be good to us, nor does it make us alive, but kills."[57]

While the condemnation of the law disappears with the forgiveness that comes through faith, the positive moral foundation and direction in the law remains. "In the Ten Commandments," Luther stated, "we have a summary of divine teaching. They tell us what we must do to make our whole life pleasing to God.... No deed or conduct can be good or pleasing to God unless it is in accord with the Ten Commandments, however great and precious it may be in the eyes of the world."[58] That is to say, while Christian believers may spontaneously engage in acts of love, there are times when one may make mistakes, no matter how well intentioned one may be. God's law, then, offers assistance in directing the love-inspired conduct of His children in productive directions. Furthermore, as Althaus has pointed out, Luther did follow up his statements about how Christians are moved by the Holy Spirit, no longer being dependent on the Decalogue, by reminding his hearers that not everyone enjoys the same measure of the Spirit.[59] Those who are weaker in the faith require more direction.

Moreover, Luther could insist, "The commandments are necessary, not that we should be justified through their works but that we, as those already justified, may know in which way our spirit should crucify the flesh and direct us in the affairs of this life, so that the flesh may not turn wanton and, snapping the reins, throw the rider, the spirit of faith. The reins must be put not on the rider but on the horse."[60] Similarly, in his 1524 hymn based on the Ten Commandments, after one verse dedicated to each commandment, the eleventh verse reads:

> God these commandments gave therein
> To show, thee, child of man, thy sin
> And make thee also well perceive
> How man unto God should live.
>   Have mercy Lord![61]

---

[57] *LW* 32, 178.
[58] *WA* 30[1], 178.
[59] *The Theology of Martin Luther*, 270.
[60] *WA* 2, 498.
[61] WA, 35, 428.

Lastly, it must be pointed out that Melanchthon wrote in his *Instructions for the Visitors of Parish Pastors in Electoral Saxony* (1528): "Therefore again and again the Ten Commandments are to be assiduously taught, for all good works are therein comprehended."[62] This work of Luther's younger colleague not only received his mentor's stamp of approval, but has been included in the English edition of Luther's Works, as it has been judged to be consistent with his own views. Neither did Luther oppose the third use of the law when Melanchthon officially presented it six years later.

Still, one cannot help but notice the obvious scarcity with which this use of the law appears in Luther's writings. Even after Melanchthon began to write about a third use, one still finds very little from Luther's pen on the subject. The explanation can be found in Luther's understanding of the proper domain of theology. In his lectures on Psalm 51, he wrote, "The proper subject of theology is man guilty of sin and condemned, and God the Justifier and Savior of man the sinner. Whatever is asked or discussed in theology outside this subject is error and poison."[63] The third use of the law simply does not figure into this prescription very neatly. In the first part, the primary use of the law is to function like a mirror. In the second part, the principle point is that the believer is freed from the tyranny of the law. Yes, the law does function as a guide for believers, but that does not really fall within these relatively narrow parameters of what theology is. When coupled with Luther's concern that Rome had been using the law to weigh down the consciences of believers, it can hardly surprise us that he would have little to say about its third use, even if he did accept it in principle.

Others have objected to the claim that Luther allowed for a third use of the law. Werner Elert has argued vigorously against such a use being present in his hero.[64] He has discredited the chief proof text for a third use in Luther

---

[62] *LW* 40, 277.

[63] *LW* 12, 310.

[64] To be more precise, what Lutheran theologians like Elert and Gerhard Forde are objecting to is a "notion of a 'third use of the law'...understood in purely informatory terms." (Werner Elert, *Law and Gospel,* trans. Edward H. Schroeder [Philadelphia: Fortress Press, 1967], 43). They are willing to grant a third use "as it is in the *Formula of Concord* only for answering the question of the *realm* of the law's validity, but not for indicating a special function of the law" (Ibid.). That is to say, they are willing to grant a third use, if by that term one means the first and second use of the law as applied to the believer. Rather than some new function, "the believer would see that law is needed in exactly the same way as the rest of fallen humanity needs it; to restrain from presumptive and evil ways and to convict sin." (Forde, "Forensic Justification," 302) The primary reason for holding on to the name "third use of the law" is clear from Elert's quote above; Lutheran theologians tend to be wary of opposing the *Formula of Concord.* However, despite the claims of both Elert and Forde that this watered-down third use is consistent with their Confessions, the Solid Declaration, Article VI of the *Formula* is

(*WA* 39^1, 485) by arguing that its appearance in Luther's corpus is due to a forgery.[65] Even if we grant his claim, which certainly would remove the clearest case of Luther speaking directly to a third use, we are still left with a significant number of other references to this function of the law. Moreover, those who oppose finding a third use in Luther do not do so on the basis of an argument from silence, discarding the few supporting cases, but have a larger concern behind their objections.

The main thrust of the argument of theologians like Elert and Gerhard Forde is a concern that the third use will come to replace the first two uses in the lives of Christians. Forde expresses his concerns, writing, "But this rejection [of the third use] involves precisely a more serious consideration about the place of the law in the life of the one who believes, waits, and hopes for the end. It means that for the time being the law remains in force, there is no watering down, no shift to a third use. It is the sinner who must die and be made new, not the law that must be watered down or changed."[66] Unfortunately, Forde is fighting the wrong battle. No leading Lutheran theologian has argued that the law should be watered down to accommodate a third use. While it may be true that the Reformed tradition has adopted a third use of the law which minimizes the role of the former two in discussions of the life of the redeemed, that is certainly not what was being suggested by Melanchthon or the authors of the *Formula*. As we have seen, a third use of the law, alongside the other two, being of secondary importance in relation to the second use, was not only approved by Luther but even commended by him from time to time as well.

Ultimately, I find it hard to imagine how one can respond to an ethical command with recognition of one's own moral shortcoming without at the same time concluding that this same moral command is worth implementing in one's life.

---

pretty clear on this point: "Then [the Holy Spirit] employs the law to instruct the regenerate out of it and to show and indicate to them in the Ten Commandments what the acceptable will of God is (Rom. 12:2) and in what good works, which God has prepared beforehand, they should walk (Eph. 2:10)" (Tappert, 566). And again, "Believers, furthermore, require the teaching of the law so that they will not be thrown back on their own holiness and piety and under the pretext of the Holy Spirit's guidance set up a self-elected service of God without his Word and command" (Tappert, 567).

[65] See his article, "Eine theologische Fälschung zur Lehre vom Tertius usus legis," in *Zeitschrift für Religions- und Geistesgeschichte* 1, (1948), 168-70.

[66] "Forensic Justification", 302.

Luther and Agricola

Luther's involvement with what was called antinomianism during his time centered on the person of Johann Agricola. Born in 1494, in the town of Eisleben—the hometown of Luther as well—Agricola was raised within the same cultural and religious milieu as his future mentor and later nemesis. He began his studies at Wittenberg in 1515, falling under the spell of Luther's theology and personality. After spending some time studying medicine, he pursued a career in theology. He had hoped to fill a chair on the theological faculty at Wittenberg, but saw the position go to Melanchthon instead. With some bitterness toward his onetime friend, he subsequently accepted a position back in Eisleben, as the director of a Latin School, where he excelled as a preacher, although he had not been ordained to the clergy.

Agricola had been a close personal friend of both Luther and Melanchthon, but the tensions between them began to rise when Agricola's developing theology began to contradict first the work of Melanchthon and later of Luther himself.[67] The essence of his position was that the law should play no part in the conversion of the sinner. True repentance consists of a changed way of life and is based on love for God, not fear of punishment. As a result, there can be no second use of the law, neither before nor after conversion; and there is certainly no third use. The law may be useful for keeping public order, *via* the first use, but plays no role in salvation. Hence his statement, "The Decalogue belongs in the courthouse, not in the pulpit."[68]

His theological posture toward the law was called "antinomianism," although his concerns were quite different from those whose antinomian spirit may have come from a desire to live a more libertine lifestyle. Rather, he wanted to remove any suggestion that human beings play a role in their own salvation, and thereby to give God's grace and work all the more glory. That is to say, if the sinner first considers the law in a way that brings her to repentance, and then receives faith in forgiveness through Christ, she was the one who made the first move, so to speak, before receiving faith. Wengert

---

[67] For a detailed discussion of the history of Agricola's conflicts with Melanchthon and Luther, see Timothy Wengert, *Law and Gospel: Philip Melanchthon's Debate with John Agricola of Eisleben over* Poenitentia (Grand Rapids: Baker Books, 1997) and F. Bente, *Historical Introductions to the Book of Concord* (St. Louis: Concordia Publishing House, 1965), first published in *Concordia Triglotta*, 1921.
[68] From his *Annotations to the Gospel of St. Luke*, quoted in Bente, *Historical Introductions*, 163.

explains, "In order to keep the focus solely on Christ and his grace, Agricola was determined to eliminate all externals from faith."[69]

Agricola argued that faith does not presuppose contrition. One can come to faith without having to confront the accusing voice of the law first. In fact, the law only functions to drive the sinner further away from God, who is perceived as being a harsh judge. The true *poenitentia* which is required for faith involves a turning away from past sins and living a new life of piety, not just contrition for one's sins. Thus, the necessary *poenitentia* arises not from the law, which only creates fear, but from the message of the gospel, which brings the love of God to the sinner. Faith springs from love, not fear. It is this infused love, which comes through the message of God's grace, of Christ's salvific act on the cross, which allows the *poenitentia* of a new life to take place. As a result, the preacher's job is not to preach the law, but to announce the gospel. It is enough to preach Christ crucified for one to come to faith; no law is necessary.

Moreover, Agricola continued to create a theological system that avoided all use of the law. If the law is not preached prior to justification, it certainly should not be after the sinner has been redeemed. Christianity consists solely of the message of the gospel. The law could and should be completely avoided. God's commandments had no place in a Christian pulpit for Agricola, and he had little sympathy for those who were concerned that this would lead to license; to him the purity of the gospel was more important. As he explained, "When they see that the people live in such disorderly ways, along come the saintliest people and want to help the situation with commands, rules, statutes, and other ceremonies. And as soon as the gospel and Christian life are comprehended in rules, then it is no longer the gospel, and God is denied, who wants his word comprehended voluntarily."[70]

Through the latter half of the 1530s, Luther and Melanchthon squared off time and again with Agricola. A disputation would be held; Agricola would either recant or simply not show up. Later he would be restored to good standing in the Lutheran community only to revert to his previous positions. As a result, we have six lists of theses that Luther wrote against the Antinomians, providing ample material with which to gauge Luther's reaction to this movement. While this antinomianism did continue on after Agricola, furthered by Andreas Poach and Anton Otto, this Second Antinomian

---

[69] *Law and Gospel*, 87.
[70] From *Colosser*, J.vi.r, quoted in *Law and Gospel*, 86.

Controversy was not as extreme as the first, although the positions were essentially the same.[71]

Throughout the Antinomian Controversies, the adherents of this new school of thought did not fail to make use of Luther's own words in arguing their position. Statements that Luther had made, particularly the young Luther, were proving to be vital ammunition for Agricola as he began his early assault on Melanchthon. Pulled from their contexts, words like the following from Luther's *The Freedom of a Christian* could offer substantial support to Agricola's cause: "A Christian has no need of any work or law in order to be saved, since through faith he is free from every law and does everything out of pure liberty and freely."[72] Or again, "Moses is dead. His rule ended when Christ came. He is of no further service...even the Ten Commandments do not pertain to us."[73] Luther was aware of this. He acknowledged, "True it is that at the early stage of this movement we began strenuously to teach the gospel and made use of these words which the Antinomians now quote. But the circumstances of that time were very different from those of the present day."[74] There were certainly authentic aspects of Luther's thought that Agricola drew from the reformer's earlier writings; however, these were not being tempered with Luther's understanding of human sinfulness, both before and after conversion.

The Antinomian Controversy took its toll on Luther, who felt personally injured and betrayed by the events that took place. On Dec. 21, 1537, during the beginning of the controversies with Agricola, Luther was recorded as saying with a deep sob, "How painful it is to lose a good friend, one who is cherished with a great love! I've had him at my table, he has laughed with me, and yet he opposes me behind my back. I won't stand for it."[75]

Luther's response to these Antinomians essentially took the form of two arguments. First, the law remains in effect both to accuse and condemn. The second use of the law is not negotiable. Luther would later have to distinguish between general and justifying faith (general faith being sufficient for contrition, but not yet sufficient for justification), a move that undermined his earlier position on the simplicity of faith. He was thereby able to maintain his insistence that the terrors of the law must precede reconciliation with God. After all, as we have seen, without the law the

---

[71] On this last point, see Matthias Richter, *Gesetz und Heil* (Göttingen: Vandenhoeck & Ruprecht, 1996).
[72] *LW* 31:361.
[73] *LW* 35, 165.
[74] *LW* 47, 104.
[75] *LW* 54, 228; no. 3650a.

gospel fails to make sense. Furthermore, one must remember *lex semper accusat*, the law always accuses. The second use applies to the redeemed as much as to the unrepentant sinner. "The repentance of believers in Christ goes beyond the actual sins, and continues through our life until death."[76] Even the believer needs to hear the accusing voice of the law, constantly drawing him to repentance. For a Christian to forget that the law accuses him as well leads to a dangerous complacency. Luther saw this tendency during his own day, stating that, "they have grown so accustomed to nothing but sweet security that they sink helplessly into hell. For they have learned to perceive nothing in Christ but sweet security."[77]

Second, the law is necessarily present and will remain eternally. As Luther reminded Agricola, one cannot simply decide to remove the law. As discussed above, the law is present not just when the Decalog is read but may be encountered at any moment in any place. It is not merely something external that we encounter, but the internal reaction to our place in this temporal world. "The devil knows very well too that it is impossible to remove the law from the heart."[78] Thus it is actually impossible to be an antinomian, as one can never eradicate the law. Indeed, to remove the law would also require the removal of the Lord's Prayer, for this prayer, "taught by the Lord Himself to the saints and believers, is a part of repentance, containing much of the doctrine of the law."[79] Moreover, "whoever prays it aright confesses with his own mouth that he sins against the law and repents."[80] "Therefore also the Lord's Prayer itself teaches that the law is before, below, and after the gospel...and that from it repentance must begin."[81] Luther's point here is that one cannot escape the law, that it is present on every page of scripture, throughout the Lord's Prayer, and within our very souls. As Freud would deny that one can simply eradicate the superego, so Luther is saying that it is impossible to dispense with the law. Even Agricola's attempt to base *poenitentia* on the message of Christ on the cross turns out to be a use of the law. Luther's younger colleague failed to appreciate the intimate connection between law and gospel, as well as Luther's notion of *simul iustus et peccator*, and as a result created a theological system which was self-contradictory. However, while his theology proved to be nonviable, it did serve the purpose of forcing Luther to

---

[76] WA 39¹, 350.
[77] *LW* 47, 111.
[78] *LW* 47, 111.
[79] WA 39¹, 351.
[80] Ibid.
[81] Ibid.

clarify some of his earlier statements and set the record straight where he was being misunderstood. Lamenting, "I am afraid that if I had died at Smalcald, I would forever have been called the patron of such spirits, since they appeal to my books,"[82] Luther's brief encounter with antinomianism was really a blessing in disguise.

Luther's Response to the Antinomian Question

Returning to our concern regarding the possible moral license which Luther's theology allows, we see at this point that the Reformer's radical insistence on grace placed so much emphasis on what God does in the act of salvation, and so little on what humanity contributes, that he set the stage for centuries of fierce debate on the topic. On the one hand, he had erected a theological edifice that practically insisted that sinners do not have to worry about what they do and the decisions they make. All of the work and decision is left to God; humanity is passive in its justification. On the other, he also outlined a model in which good works and proper moral decision-making will necessarily happen and cannot, by definition, be absent. Our next consideration, then, is twofold. First, how well did Luther balance his preaching of justification and sanctification? Second, we consider what specific responses he offered to the rather practical and pointed antinomian question, which is concerned with what repercussions there are if I occasionally forgo my moral responsibilities and do not act as a Christian should. This section begins with a look at Luther's preaching and will conclude by considering what is at the heart of the problem, his conception of *simul iustus et peccator*.

Luther in the Pulpit

Luther was a voracious preacher. We have the benefit of more than 2300 extant sermons to draw from, which is both fortuitous and daunting at the same time. As a result, few discussions of Luther's sermons can ever be exhaustive. Nonetheless, key traits and themes are observable and can be used to serve our investigation of the effects of his theology. Luther's sermons, mostly preached in the parish church in Wittenberg, were the medium for most of his contact with the laity of his time. For those who did not have the benefit of access to his vast literary production (recall that literacy rates were in the single digits!), Luther's sermons provided the time and place where the rubber hit the road.

---

[82] *LW* 47, 107f.

The great Reformer's primary intention in his preaching was to help his listeners appreciate and understand the gospel message of Jesus as he had found it, primarily in Paul's epistles. His overarching concern was that Roman Catholic theology, which neglected God's grace and placed the onus of reconciliation with God on the individual instead, was leaving sinners in despair or permitting them to trust in their own pharisaic self-righteousness. This led him to emphasize the wholly sufficient work of Christ that stands in contrast to the impotent, passive nature of humanity that only receives what is offered freely. While Luther always insisted that people need to hear both law and gospel, one does not always find the neat balance in his own writings that one might expect. He would insist that preaching too much law would lead one's congregants to trust in themselves, while focusing too intently on the gospel leads people to neglect good works. "For this reason it is difficult to preach to people: it is never right, no matter how you preach to them; they always lean to one side."[83] And so while Luther knew that it is a difficult juggling act to properly balance law and gospel in preaching, his preference is obvious. Luther was almost always reacting to what Rome was teaching. Thus, his insistence on emphasizing the gospel was designed, as we have seen, to make up for Catholicism's neglect of this essential teaching. In his own mind, Luther reasoned that the previous centuries' accentuation of the law had already been internalized by society, and that what was now needed was a strong dose of the gospel to create some balance in the Church. While it is not difficult to sympathize with Luther in his context, wanting to counterbalance the Roman emphasis on law, he struggled to remember that law and gospel need to be balanced not only in the Church at large but also in the lives of individuals daily. Trying to make up for the imbalance in the Church can have uncomfortable implications for individual believers.

By the same token, when Luther wanted to lay down the law, he could do it with a passion and conviction that could rival more than a few Lutheran Pietists of later years. Consider "The Eight Wittenberg Sermons" given upon his return from the Wartburg.[84] Likewise, his "Sermon on Soberness and Moderation" (1539) pulled no punches in spelling out exactly what kind of behavior was unacceptable for Christians. Luther may not have spent much of his time outlining codes of moral conduct, but the fact that he felt strongly about them is hard to deny, as this sermon illustrates. "If you do not wish to conduct yourself this way, if you are going to go beyond this and be a born pig and guzzle beer and wine, then, if this cannot be stopped by the rulers, you must know that you cannot be saved. For God will not admit such

---

[83] *WA* 45, 688.
[84] *LW* 51, 67ff.

piggish drinkers into the kingdom of heaven.*"*[85] This occasional passion for preaching piety is not limited to his later years, when his primary focus on grace began to bear a fruit he did not intend. As Elmer Carl Kiessling has pointed out, among Luther's earliest sermons, a "striking characteristic is their tone of high ethical seriousness. The preacher is full of impatience with things as they are."[86] Luther knew how to powerfully preach the law, but for various reasons chose not to engage in such tactics very often.

Luther was more concerned with a higher spiritual goal than with improving the conduct of a Christian society. Of course, he could have focused more on the law and motivated his parishioners to a more active life of piety. However, for Luther the highest good is genuine, liberating Christian faith, not simply moral virtue; and he would not sacrifice the former in an attempt to achieve the latter. "I would much rather hear people say of me that I preach too sweetly and that my sermon hinders people in doing good works (although it does *not* do so) than not preach faith in Christ at all."[87]

Of course there is not an either/or between preaching the gospel and encouraging good works. What Luther was insisting on was that the law should not be preached with the primary intent of improving civil behavior, but that it be preached to draw sinners to Christ, who will empower them to carry out genuine good works of gratitude. In this way, Luther was insisting that the cart should not be put before the horse, even if this carried with it the charge that he was neglecting civil righteousness. Luther believed himself to be under a higher calling than merely to improve public morals. We may see this in his First Advent Sermon of 1532, in which he stated that he was preaching "a different sermon from the one that is preached with good works as the basis. True, Hans, Paul, and Peter should and must do good works. But this sermon reaches higher."[88] He went on to explain:

> That is why I am not as much disturbed by people's greed, harlotry, fornication, so prevalent now everywhere, as I am by the despising of the gospel. Avarice, harlotry, and unchastity are indeed great and terrible sins, sins which the Lord God punishes severely with plague and famine, though land and people still survive. But this sin is not adultery or harlotry; it is not even of human origin but of the devil, causing God's fatherly visitation of grace to be so terribly despised, laughed to scorn, and

---

[85] *LW* 51, 293.
[86] Elmer Carl Kiessling, *The Early Sermons of Luther and Their Relation to the Pre-Reformation Sermon* (Grand Rapids: Zondervan Publishing House, 1935).
[87] *WA* 37, 394.
[88] *Sermons of Martin Luther: The House Postils,* trans. Eugene F. A. Klug (Grand Rapids: Baker Books, 1996),1:18.

mocked. Such sin, you may be sure, prompts God's severest judgment to WIPE IT CLEAN![89]

As a consequence, Luther chose to use the law relatively sparingly in his preaching. The focus on grace always answered and outweighed the accusing voice of the law. Luther failed, however, to recognize two things in his preaching which exacerbated the problem of his emphasis on the gospel. The first, as discussed above, was that he was reacting to the legacy of centuries of semi-Pelagian Catholicism. He himself had internalized all of the accusations, guilt, shame, struggle, and *Anfechtung* that come with the law through his intensive religious studies and lifestyle as an Augustinian monk and priest. He was, after all, a remarkably spiritual man with a gift for critical self-analysis. What he forgot was that others did not necessarily share the same struggles. For Luther, the spiritual battle was to overcome his self-loathing and intention to establish his own righteousness. The temptation of worldly vices was never a major factor in his life. For others, however, the problem is just the opposite. As we shall see in the following chapters, much of humanity struggles to overcome the tendency to let God do all the work. They rest idly in the belief that their efforts do not obtain salvation or that their sins may be forgiven by purchasing an indulgence or going to confession. Luther's contention was that the law had reigned supreme throughout the Middle Ages. As a result, the people, so weighed down by its condemnation, would leap with joy, gratefully dedicating their lives to God for the forgiveness they were hearing about in the gospel. However, in the same way that this optimism did not work as planned with the Jews, the legacy of moral license in Wittenberg after Luther's death is further evidence that not everyone struggled with the same temptations as Luther.

Luther's other error involved his application of the law. When he did preach the law, he frequently had the unfortunate habit of applying it to those who were not present. For instance, in his sermon for Invocavit Sunday, 1534, on the temptation of Jesus in the wilderness, Luther discussed how the temptations that the Lord faced from the devil are shared by all of humanity. However, he devoted the majority of his preaching on this subject to pointing out how the Papists had succumbed to these temptations, rather than how his own parishioners did.[90] Similarly, two weeks later, on Oculi Sunday, he spent a great deal of time railing against the Papists and the "village bigwigs" who were curtailing the free preaching of the gospel.[91] The majority of those present, being neither Papists nor bigwigs, were thereby not

[89] Ibid., 1:21f.
[90] Ibid., 1:312-320.
[91] Ibid., 1:329-343.

hearing the law preached to them. At other times, however, the balance was laudable. His 1532 Laetare Sunday sermon contained relatively little about the heretics in Rome. Here he encouraged his hearers to be satisfied with what God had given them, not coveting what others might have been given, and to be careful that they not take the gospel for granted. He reminded them that their behavior does have implications, and that if they ignored the preaching of law and gospel these would be taken away from them.[92] Still, Luther's tendency to engage in polemics toward his Catholic opponents from the pulpit robbed his audience of hearing the law preached to them. As he himself rightly taught, "A law that does not condemn is a fictitious and painted law like a chimera or tragelaphus."[93] When Luther condemned the behavior of those who were not present instead of the people sitting right in front of him, he not only robbed them of hearing the law, but potentially contributed to a pharisaic attitude among those in the congregation who could feel smug that they were not sinners like those papists.

As a result of these two aspects of his preaching, Luther's sermons did not contain the balance of law and gospel which is necessary, according to his own theology, to effectively bring people to understand, appreciate, and believe the gospel. The problem was not, as some would contend, a lack of the third use of the law, but of the second. Luther struggled at times to understand how to let the law accuse those in his congregation. Either he used the law to attack the sins with which he struggled personally, but which did not necessarily trouble others, or he aimed his arrows at those who were not even present. Either way, it is clear that Luther's greatest gift lay in his theological genius. He did not enjoy the psychological insight that would have enabled him to hold the law as a mirror directly in front of his parishioners in such a way as to make them look at their own sins rather than the sins of others. Luther knew quite well that "God saves real, not imaginary, sinners, and he teaches us to mortify real rather than imaginary sin."[94] The difficulty was to use the law in a way that reflected his hearers' real sin back to them.

Simul iustus et peccator

The key to understanding Luther's contribution to the antinomian question lies in his view of the anthropology of the Christian believer who is at the same time both sinner and saint, *simul iustus et peccator*. Despite what may sound like a neo-Platonic notion of a duality of the human being which

---

[92] Ibid., 1:344-350.
[93] *WA* 39[1], 358.
[94] *LW* 32, 229.

combines different moral components into one whole, Luther did not want to glue two parts together into one. The redeemed sinner is completely righteous in her status before God while remaining an absolute sinner through her will and actions in this world. Wilfred Joest expresses this remarkable notion of anthropological union as follows:

> The *simul* is not the equilibrium of two mutually limiting partial aspects but the battleground of two mutually exclusive totalities. It is not the case that a no-longer-entirely sinner and a not-yet-completely-righteous one can be pasted together in a psychologically conceivable mixture; it is rather that real and complete righteousness stands over against real and total sin.... The Christian is not half free and half bound, but slave and free at once, not half saint, but sinner and saint at once, not half alive, but dead and alive at once, not a mixture but a gaping opposition of antitheses.[95]

Thus, to understand Luther one must overcome the tendency to think of the *simul* as two coexisting parts, and instead think of two separate and complete entities present within an individual at the same time. As McGrath correctly points out, for Luther the believer is *"extrinsically righteous* and *intrinsically sinful,"* in contradistinction from Augustine and Karlstadt who taught that the justified Christian is *"partly* righteous and *partly* sinful (*ex quadum parte iustus, ex quadam parte peccator*)."[96] Contrary to Andreas Osiander, the imputation of righteousness does not change our status as sinful human beings. The focus is on God's declaration that the believer is a saint, not the believer becoming something new which warrants that title.

In addition to being a rather penetrating interpretation of the new life in Christ, Luther's notion of the *simul* also functions as a great source of comfort for the individual believer. The pressure to examine oneself to make sure the sin is gone before feeling confident of one's righteousness is done away with. The remaining presence of sin does not frighten the believer into becoming enslaved to the law in the pursuit of holiness. Instead, he understands that the sin will remain, and can thereby be liberated to pursue a life of faith and piety without having to consider the remaining sin with despair or anxiety. Christians need to know that even their good deeds will constantly be marred by sin. This creates not sadness but relief. For God "has made us certain that [our good works] are not sinless and faultless (so that our trust is not in them), with the result that we can acknowledge in a confession without doubt or falsity that we are sinners in all our works and

---

[95] Wilfred Joest, *Gesetz und Freiheit* 2nd ed. (Göttingen: Vandenhoeck & Ruprecht, 1956), 58f. As quoted in Forde, 282.
[96] McGrath, *Iustitia Dei*, 209.

are men whom mercy has found."⁹⁷ Thus, the presence of sin in our lives functions as a reminder that it is not we who earn salvation, but that Christ earned it for us and has given it to us freely.

However, it is the flip side of this liberating message of the *simul* that interests us here in our discussion of the antinomian question. If the "new man" reacts to this news with thanksgiving and grace, the "old man" tends to see in this doctrine a loophole allowing moral laxity. I recall that as a teenager I tended to drive my youth counselors at church close to the point of desperation and infuriation. I remember one particular incident in which one counselor, having had his patience tested enough, announced to me that the sinner in him was going to slap me in the head, while the saint in him was going to be forgiven for doing so. Moreover, it is not even necessary to be pushed to the edge by a frustrating teenager before one realizes that Luther's *simul* can be used as a means to permit impiety. As discussed in the introduction, we are talking not about a lifestyle of moral license but about the daily encounters with ethical choices where obvious sin is the more attractive option.

Now it is true that Luther reminds us that "we do not tell people to believe that all is done when we believe, and that we need not do good works. No, we must not divorce the two. You must perform good works and do good to your neighbor at all times, so that the inner faith of your heart may glow outwardly and be reflected in your life."⁹⁸ However, this does not get us very far in solving the problem. First, as noted above, Luther did not spend a great deal of time on this topic. Second, it tells us what we already know: Christians should and must perform good works. The person asking the antinomian question, however, wants to know what harm will be done if she doesn't do the right thing *this afternoon*. After all, one cannot ever avoid sinning; one's good works are even tainted with it, as Luther insisted to Latomus (a theme we will return to in the third chapter). So what really is the harm of just one more sin today, as long as I do not become addicted or enslaved to it?

Luther did give some advice to preachers, pastors, and theologians who might have to deal with this question. He tells them, "In order to understand this use [of the law for Christians], you must divide man into two parts and distinguish well between them, namely, into the old and the new man, as St. Paul has divided him. Leave the new man entirely undisturbed by laws; drive the old one unceasingly by laws, and be sure not to grant him any rest from

---

⁹⁷ LW 32, 193.
⁹⁸ *LW* 23, 110.

them."[99] Thus, those with a pastoral role need to confront the sinful side of believers with the harshness of the law, to rein in the excesses of their behavior, and force them to remember their need for forgiveness, while at the same time comforting their righteous side with the gospel. He goes on to say, "So, then, God comes and frightens [the old man] with the law; He commands us to preach it forcibly to the people, so that they must fear death, shame, and hell. Not that he intends to make them better by it, but He intends to repress the wickedness, of which they are full, so that they dare not break through the restraint and carry on as they please."[100]

We find Werner Elert echoing the same approach to the potential problem of Christians abusing their freedom from the law:

> It is not the new pardoned man who is endangered by libertinism because he is guided by the Spirit of God and cannot go wrong. The danger exists for the 'old' man, the flesh which desires participation in the new liberty. It is a very real danger because the old and the new man are biographically the same individual. It can only be averted when man learns from God what he is and spends his life under God's judgment.... The old man is continually brought in contact with the law and chastised by it. That is the proper use, the theological or pedagogical use of the law. Only in this manner can libertinism be avoided.[101]

The potential problem here involves the dividing of the believer into two people, or at least two personalities. One cannot selectively preach the law to the old man alone while reserving the gospel for the new. The Christian is *simultaneously* saint and sinner; what the former hears, the latter hears as well. It is impossible to announce grace and the forgiveness of sins to the new man and keep the old man from hearing. Likewise, when Elert tells us that "the old man is continually brought in contact with the law and chastised by it," we have to recognize that the new man is receiving the same chastise-ment. There cannot be two messages given. The problem remains. The justified sinner may hear the condemnations of the law and be brought to repentance, but when the good news of freedom from the law is announced, there is no way of keeping this from the old man. Consequently, the theological or pedagogical use of the law may continue to hammer at the old man until death, but he can always respond with, "Yes, but I do not need to worry so much, for I know I am justified freely without works. God knows I am both sinner and saint, and so there is no reason to get too upset about a few more sins."

---

[99] *WA* 17¹, 122f.
[100] WA 17¹, 123. See further on this issue Gottfried G. Krodel, "Luther—an Antinomian?," in *Lutherjahrbuch* (Göttingen: Vandenhoeck & Ruprecht, 1996), 85.
[101] Werner Elert, *The Christian Ethos*, trans. Carl J. Schindler (Philadelphia: Muhlenberg Press, 1957), 297.

Fortunately Luther has left us with some additional ways of responding to the antinomian question. Perhaps the most important was his insistence that the Scriptures do not teach any perseverance of the saints. Once saved does not mean always saved. The Christian believer can indeed lose her salvation. This results not from sinning *per se*, but from the greatest sin, the rejection of faith. A person who once enjoyed genuine faith can later reject that faith, thereby forfeiting her salvation.

We see this perhaps most clearly in Luther's discussion of baptism. While Paul used the perfect form of the verb to describe the dying that takes place in baptism, so that the sinner *has died* to sin through baptism, Luther used the present progressive tense, describing how Christians are *dying* to sin because of their baptism. Althaus commented on this difference, writing, "The symbolic act of baptism, according to Luther, does not signify something which has taken place once in the past but something which must continually take place. The old man 'should' be drowned, etc. Luther thus applies Paul's statement about the meaning of baptism not to the initial act of baptism but to the lifelong realization of the meaning of baptism."[102] By means of this interpretation of baptism, then, Luther can insist that one's baptism is valid insofar as it is an ongoing event in one's life. However, when one rejects one's baptism, ceasing to put the old man to death, faith has been rejected as well. Therefore faith exists *as long as* one is actively involved in putting the old man to death. While Althaus may have overstated his claim that Luther "*repeatedly* emphasizes that forgiveness of sin and justification for the sake of Christ are valid for those who fight against sin"[103] (emphasis mine), he was correct in pointing out that the requirement for the continuation of these blessings is the battle against the flesh.[104] Likewise, Christians who betray an absence of love in their behavior are demonstrating that they may have lost their faith as well. "Whoever has had faith at some time but now has no love, no longer has that faith."[105] However, to reiterate once more the objection of our interlocutor, for many Christians the temptation is not to give up completely the effort to put the old man to death or stifle all opportunities to engage in acts of love, but to see what the harm would be if it were done *just today*. Whether the fear of losing one's salvation is sufficient to keep our friend on the right path is not clear.

---

[102] Althaus, *The Theology of Martin Luther*, 357.
[103] Ibid., 244n.
[104] See further *LW* 32, 239: "For God has made a covenant with those who are in Christ, so that there is no condemnation if they fight against themselves and their sin."
[105] *WA* 34[1], 168.

Finally, Luther wanted his readers to know that good works carry with them the promise of temporal rewards while vice can lead to all sorts of punishment short of the loss of salvation. In his Small Catechism he concluded his discussion of the commandments by reminding us, "God threatens to punish all who transgress these commandments. We should therefore fear his wrath and not disobey these commandments. On the other hand, he promises grace and every blessing to all who keep them. We should therefore love him, trust in him, and cheerfully do what he has commanded."[106] While this is not a particularly strong theme in Luther, it is nonetheless present, giving further encouragement to stay on the right path. Once again, regrettably, we must point out that this statement does not answer the antinomian question. While it does provide a good reason—even a self-interested reason—to avoid sin, the temptation to leave the straight and narrow comes from, among other things, the perception that the benefits of the illicit behavior will outweigh the costs. Despite the fact that one may know that punishment may come from the hand of God, experience tells us that guilty pleasures all too often go unpunished. For many of us, engaging in that guilty pleasure may be worth the risk.

Conclusion

The intention of this chapter has been to outline where and whence in Luther's theology the antinomian question arises as well as Luther's various approaches to dealing with the issue. We have seen that this was never a primary concern for the Reformer, who was much more interested in correcting the legalistic errors of Rome than the libertine excess that might follow from what we have called his radical insistence on grace. Luther's strongest weapons against antinomian tendencies, therefore, were not fully utilized in his part-time effort to curb these excesses. In his preaching, he demonstrated that he was quite capable of utilizing the full force of the second use of the law when he wanted, but much too often was distracted by his concerns over the Roman denigration of faith. Admittedly, Luther was a man of his times, responding to the needs of his times. However, when attacking the errors of Rome got in the way of rooting out the sin in the lives of his congregants, we need to acknowledge that his reactionary tendencies kept him from doing his job as a preacher.

Likewise, the brilliance of his teaching about the *simul iustus et peccator* was a much needed remedy to the overly optimistic anthropology of his opponents. His discussions of the liberation that comes with the knowledge

---

[106] Tappert, 344. See also LW 54, 240, *Tischreden* No. 3600.

that sinners receive the grace of God with no preconditions are unsurpassed. His concern for the other side of this coin, however, that not having to do anything means *not having to do anything*, can be disheartening. The proposed solution of preaching the condemnation of the law to the old man alone demonstrates a lack of thought and consideration which otherwise characterize his theology. In other words, the lack of priority which sanctification receives in Luther has contributed to a less than satisfactory response to our problem.

Luther has left us a theological legacy that many have attempted to complement, but none have succeeded in superseding. As with any theological system, model, or foundation, there is additional work to be done. Alterations, corrections, and additions can be brought to bear on the original contribution of an individual like Luther to make up for any oversights and even errors. However, such constructive work is a tricky business. The bold individual who seeks to contribute to the Lutheran legacy needs to be clear about understanding what Luther has done and why before making any changes. While certain externals and accents can be modified in an attempt to improve the entire edifice, the foundation must be left alone if one is to remain faithful to Luther and maintain theological consistency. In the case of the antinomian question, we shall see in the following chapters how successfully Luther's heirs were able to make up for his limitations in addressing the life of sanctification, and where they may have come too close to undermining Luther's theological cornerstone: justification by grace through faith.

⟨⟩ CHAPTER TWO

Philipp Melanchthon

On February 19, 1546, Philipp Melanchthon announced to an assemblage of students at Wittenberg, "Alas, gone are the horsemen and the chariots of Israel!"[1] Luther was dead. The words he chose were a commentary not only on his mentor but on himself as well, as he was echoing the prophet Elisha at the time when Elijah was taken up into heaven (2 Kings 2:12). Like his Old Testament counterpart, Melanchthon knew there was much reforming work still to be done, and he was surely praying for a double measure of the Spirit which had led Luther through such tumultuous times.

This comparison of Elijah and Elisha with Luther and Melanchthon has persisted since the sixteenth century. The image of the great prophet Elijah, constantly embroiled in political turmoil and being accompanied by his younger, less well-known protégé, was bound to elicit comparisons to the two most important Lutheran reformers of the sixteenth century. When Master Philipp joined the Wittenberg faculty in 1518, one year after the famous posting of Luther's theses, he was only twenty-one years old. Although trained within the humanist tradition, Melanchthon quickly fell under the spell of Luther's radical message of grace. And while his reputation as an exceptional linguist was already being established, it would be his theological works which would bring him fame, renown, and controversy during his own lifetime and down to the present day. In the years that followed he would make good use of his intellectual gifts by providing unparalleled expression to the faith that Luther had been describing. At the same time, like Elisha, Melanchthon would always play second fiddle to his mentor in their reforming agenda, yet never depart from his mentor and hero until the latter was taken from this earth.

However, even before Luther's death, Melanchthon believed that continuing the Reformation agenda would necessitate certain changes in the direction of the movement.[2] Luther's reactive approach to whatever was the

---

[1]*CR* 6:59.
[2]See James Michael Weiss, "Erasmus at Luther's Funeral: Melanchthon's Commemorations of Luther in 1546," *Sixteenth Century Journal* 16.1 (1985): 91–114.

issue of the moment could not bear the increasing weight that the growing evangelical institution was supporting. From the beginning, Melanchthon was aware that a more formal, systematic structure needed to be established without the excesses which Luther's bold rhetoric sometimes created. Luther himself had recognized this, as we shall see below, acknowledging Melanchthon's gifts in this area. His appreciation for his younger colleague's meticulous, logical, and organized mind was immense: "Philipp has done in dialectics what nobody else has done in a thousand years."[3] However, the latter's timidity did cause Luther concern at times as well.[4]

In our discussion of the influence of the antinomian question in relation to Melanchthon's theology, our task in this chapter is twofold. First, we need to elucidate how Melanchthon's concern with possible antinomian excesses in sixteenth century German society was responsible for many of his theological innovations as well as his deviations from Luther's theological program. Secondly, we will consider these contributions in terms of their effectiveness in responding to various concerns related to the antinomian question as well as their faithfulness to the fundamental principles of Luther's theology.

A Brief History of Melanchthon Scholarship

The self-assigned task of many students of the Reformation during the nineteenth and twentieth centuries was to rescue Luther from Lutheranism. Karl Holl, Wilhelm Pauck, and Paul Althaus, to name but a few, have been in agreement that the theology of Luther suffered various alterations by the time the Formula of Concord was presented in 1580 and has been none the better as a result. Clearly something went wrong; and when something goes wrong there is usually the need to find a scapegoat.

More often than not, the accusing finger has been leveled at Melanchthon. Germany's *praeceptor* has held the unenviable dual role of hero of the Reformation (as author of the *Augustana* and *Apology*) and favor-

---

[3]*LW* 54, 156; *Tischreden* No. 1545.
[4]The source of this timidity lay in a concern not for his own safety but for the well-being of society as a whole. His well-known fear of war, then, was a result not of fear for his own life, but of his awareness that war brings with it terrible suffering. This important distinction is brought out by Heinz Scheible, who relates: "In his personal life Melanchthon was courageous. For example, in Wittenberg there was always student unrest. In 1512 the rector of the University was even murdered by a student seeking revenge. Whenever such rioting occurred, Master Philipp would go out into the street and confront the heated crowd. Once someone even brandished a pike in his face!" ("Luther and Melanchthon," *Lutheran Quarterly* 4 (Autumn 1990): 326.

ite whipping-boy for the various controversies during his own lifetime,[5] as well as various other theological aberrations within Lutheranism down to the present day. While the controversy continues regarding the extent to which he corrupted Luther's thought, with some arguing he only maintained a respectful disagreement of theological opinion with the elder reformer,[6] he has remained blameworthy in many people's minds for the role he played in intellectualizing the Christian faith.

Attention to this aspect of Melanchthon's influence on Lutheranism was highlighted in a 1947 article that appeared in *Concordia Theological Monthly*. In "The Melanchthonian Blight," Richard R. Caemmerer Sr. argued that Melanchthon had reduced much of the content of Christian faith to information. He protested that Melanchthon "describes the process of conversion in terms which revolve largely in the domain of simple information...he was too wrapped up in his own educational method to observe that he asked his Christian to be content with a rational apprehending and application of information."[7]

Caemmerer has certainly not been alone in this concern. From the same seminary, three years later, a young Jaroslav Pelikan presented a similar argument in his first book, *From Luther to Kierkegaard*.[8] This intellectualization of the Christian faith has also been asserted by Bernhard Lohse and Heinz Scheible, although Scheible assesses its significance quite differently, as we shall see. While Melanchthon's tendency to reduce faith to knowledge is largely agreed upon, the reasons for this predilection are not.

What we find in Caemmerer's article and Pelikan's early book is a reiteration of earlier charges that it was Melanchthon's humanist background that was to blame for this theological aberration. While Master Philipp was able to produce his earlier works—of which some are presently canonized in the Book of Concord—under the direction and influence of Luther, his love

---

[5] No one has taken Melanchthon to task more seriously, and more unfairly in my opinion, for these sixteenth century controversies than F. Bente in his *Historical Introductions to the Book of Concord* (St. Louis: Concordia Publishing House, 1965), first published in *Concordia Triglotta*, 1921.

[6] Karl Holl, 'Die Rechtfertigungslehre in Luthers Vorlesung über den Römerbrief mit besonderer Rücksicht auf die Frage der Heilsgewißheit,' in *Gesammelte Aufsätze zur Kirchengeschichte*, 3d ed., 3 vols. (Tübingen: J.C.B. Mohr/Paul Siebeck, 1923), 1:126–29. Holl is best known among those who have argued for the corrupting influence of Melanchthon on Luther, while a more contemporary defense of the former may be found in Heinz Scheible, "Luther and Melanchthon."

[7] Richard R. Caemmerer, Sr. "The Melanchthonian Blight," *Concordia Theological Monthly* 18, no.5 (May 1947), 329.

[8] Jaroslav Pelikan, *From Luther to Kierkegaard* (St. Louis: Concordia Publishing House, 1950).

affair with humanism proved too strong in the end, drawing him back under its banner with its optimistic view of the human will, corrupting his later thought. Thus, Caemmerer argued that Melanchthon's "Humanistic heritage and his educational preoccupation combined to produce the un-Lutheran but potent oversimplification of Christian knowledge as information."[9]

It can indeed be demonstrated without a great deal of difficulty that Melanchthon, later in his career, elevated doctrine and knowledge to a degree not found in his earlier writings.[10] Likewise, a noticeable shift in his discussion of the human will is also discernible from his earlier writings to those of his later years. However, to argue that Melanchthon made a reversion, or backslid into the humanistic heritage of his upbringing and early education, requires either a leap of faith or significant psychological wrangling, especially when Melanchthon himself insisted repeatedly that his theological perspective was constant through these years.

In light of this, more scholars recently have rejected this reversion theory. Timothy J. Wengert offers a strong rebuttal to adherents of the earlier school of thought. He takes Wilhelm Maurer to task for suggesting that Melanchthon "lurched" back and forth between Erasmus and Luther.[11] Likewise, he rejects a similar point by Ekkehard Mühlenberg, who suggested that Melanchthon, later in his career, tried to synthesize their positions.[12] Rather, Wengert argues that, between the two men, "[Melanchthon] was hardly caught in the middle. He rejected the substance of Erasmus' arguments, decried his characterization of Luther, and took him to task for his immoderate behavior."[13] Wengert further rejects the notion that Melanchthon ever underwent a crisis of conversion from humanism to Lutheranism from which he felt the need to partially revert. He agrees with Siegfried Wiedenhofer, who insists, "[W]hat can be said from a biographical perspective is this: a break between a humanistic and a reformational phase in Melanchthon's self-understanding is not ascertainable."[14]

---

[9]Caemmerer, "Melanchthonian Blight," 328.

[10] See Werner Elert, *The Structure of Lutheranism*, trans. Walter A. Hansen (St. Louis: Concordia Publishing House, 1962).

[11] See the section, *Melanchthons Verhältnis zum Humanismus* in Wilhelm Maurer, *Der junge Melanchthon zwischen Humanismus und Reformation*, 2 vols. (Göttingen: Vandenhoeck and Ruprecht, 1967,1969) II:223–29.

[12] Ekkehard Mühlenberg, "Humanistische Bildungsprogramm und reformatorische Lehre beim junge Melanchthon," *Zeitschrift für Theologie und Kirche* 65 (1968): 431–44.

[13] Timothy J. Wengert, *Human Freedom, Christian Righteousness: Philipp Melanchthon's Exegetical Dispute with Erasmus of Rotterdam* (New York: Oxford University Press, 1998).

[14] Siegfried Wiedenhofer, *Formalstrukturen humanistischer und reformatorischer Theologie bei Philipp Melanchthon*, 2 vols. (Frankfurt: Peter Lang, 1976), 1:111.

In light of the doubtful correlation between the shift in Melanchthon's theological writings and an alleged reversion to humanism, an explanation needs to be offered for the fact that the *praeceptor*'s writings did undergo changes during his career as a reformer. It is my contention that the primary underlying reason for this shift was not some subconscious motivation that steered Melanchthon's writings, but a very conscious decision on his part to provide a theology that he believed would be more effective in bringing about the changes in religious life in Germany that he and Luther desired to see. The primary reason for his changing theological course, then, was his concern over the threat of antinomianism. It was this very practical concern, rather than some sinister humanist undercurrent in his thought, that explains much of his developing theology and suggests the reason why it took the turns which it did.

Melanchthon's concern over antinomianism was twofold. First, Lutheran theology, with its emphasis on grace, made it too easy for hypocrites and those weak in faith to find an excuse for a libertine lifestyle. Luther had observed the same thing, pointing out:

> Thus under the papacy people used to perform those foolish and meaningless works, neither commanded nor demanded by God, with the utmost pleasure, diligence, and zeal, and at great cost. We recognize this same zeal for meaningless things in the sectarians of our day and in their disciples, especially the Anabaptists. But in our churches, where the true doctrine of good works is set forth with great diligence, it is amazing how much sluggishness and lack of concern prevails.[15]

The second concern that the reformers had to contend with was the charges from the Catholics that the Lutherans were neglecting good works. Johann Eck never tired of insisting that the Lutherans were living lives of libertine excess. When encouraging piety in the lives of the Catholic faithful, he warned them, "they are not to turn aside or draw back from good works (something the Lutherans, haters of all good, do) and especially that they exercise works of piety not toward apostate monks and nuns fornicating and committing adultery under the honest title of marriage, but toward the Catholic poor."[16] Any attempt to achieve eventual reunion, or even respectability, was going to have to address the charges of men like Eck.

Thus, it was the two sides of the antinomian concern that fueled much of the theological work of Melanchthon, especially in his later years. His desire to see both a safe and secure Lutheran church and a morally renewed Germany forced him to tackle this two-pronged problem in his writings,

---

[15] *LW* 27:53.
[16] Johann Eck, *Enchiridion of Commonplaces*, trans. Ford Lewis Battles (Grand Rapids: Baker Book House, 1979), 55.

especially since his earlier work could be cited as evidence that he had contributed to this same antinomianism.

It is ironic, as we shall see, that it was this very concern that led him to make theological changes that others would later argue contributed to a weakening of Luther's thought and subsequently a church with less religious conviction and piety. Whether and to what extent that is truly the case is beyond the scope of this work. Nonetheless, the shift in theology that Melanchthon permitted himself to make was designed to minimize religious apathy. It would be sad if his good intentions were forgotten. It would be even sadder if his contributions had actually fostered such libertinism.

The Influence of Humanism

Various arguments about what went wrong with Luther's reforming theology in the centuries, or even decades, following his life have focused on Melanchthon and his humanist influence. While the twentieth century was witness to the greatest number of critiques of Melanchthon's role in this "decline" of Lutheran orthodoxy,[17] we can find references to the deleterious effects of his humanist influences much earlier than that. In fact, we find references to Melanchthon's intellectualizing tendency and its relation to humanism present even in Luther himself. Wilhelm Pauck, who emphasizes these scattered references, sees this humanism as a major source of the tension between the two men. "Now it is very instructive to see that Luther thought he knew wherein this difference in attitude between himself and Melanchthon consisted. He believed that his friend's anxiety was derived from his scientific-humanistic way of thinking." Additionally, "[H]e maintained that his friend's anxiety and fear must be attributed to his philosophy and to his humanistic scholarship."[18]

---

[17] See Ken Schurb, "Twentieth-Century Melanchthon Scholarship and the Missouri Synod," *Concordia Theological Quarterly*, 62, no. 4 (1998): 287–307.

[18] Wilhelm Pauck, "Luther and Melanchthon," *Luther and Melanchthon in the History and Theology of the Reformation* (Philadelphia: Muhlenberg Press, 1960), 29–30. That Luther did indeed ascribe humanism as a cause for Melanchthon's fearfulness, and thereby his subsequent theological twists and turns, is attested to in the following letter which Luther wrote to him from Coburg four days after the *Augustana* was presented to Charles V: "You are so terribly concerned about the end and issue of this affair, because you cannot comprehend it. But if it were possible for you to comprehend it, I for one should not want to have any part in it and still less I should want to be the one who started it. God has placed it under a certain basic concept which is not available to you either in your Rhetorics or your philosophy, and it is called faith. This basic concept includes all things that are visible and not apparent (Hebr. 11:3). Whosoever wants to make them visible, apparent, and comprehensive as you do, gets care and sorrows as his reward as you do." WA Br. V; 406, 54 (29 June 1530).

In the following century Jakob Boehme argued even more directly that Melanchthon, whom he referred to as *"Graecus"* and *"Aristotelicus,"* was to blame for various distortions of Lutheranism.[19] Likewise, around the turn of the eighteenth century, the radical Pietist Gottfried Arnold was arguing that Melanchthon had reintroduced Aristotelian thought into Lutheranism, though Luther had rejected it, thereby importing an element of academic quarreling that was proving to be more and more divisive.[20]

When we reach the twentieth century, these earlier claims are proclaimed anew. Pauck, as we have seen, looked at Luther's own assessment of the reason for Melanchthon's anxiety at Augsburg and concluded, "[I]n his theology, Melanchthon gave to Luther's understanding of the gospel a humanistic-scientific form which, in respect to its basic presuppositions, was foreign to Luther's spiritual outlook."[21] Likewise, we have already discussed how Pelikan, one of Pauck's students, was equally eager to find the source of Melanchthon's theological waywardness in his humanist allegiances, as were Caemmerer, Maurer, Mühlenberg, and others.

The evidence for such influences, and the shift back toward Erasmus which Mühlenberg points to, is often said to be found in Melanchthon's discussion of the human will in the early and late editions of his *Loci*.[22] In the early 1521 edition, we find such extreme statements on human will as, "Since all things that happen, happen necessarily according to divine predestination, our will has no liberty."[23] Likewise, a few pages later, "If you relate human will to predestination, there is freedom neither in external nor internal acts, but all things take place according to divine determination."[24] It is little wonder that Luther, who would later pen *The Bondage of the Will*, could scarcely find enough good things to say about this early work of Melanchthon. "You cannot find anywhere a book which treats the

---

The same day, in a letter to Justus Jonas, he remarked, *"Philipp is tortured by his philosophy and nothing else."* WA Br.V; 409, 18.

[19] See F. Ernest Stoeffler, *The Rise of Evangelical Pietism* (Leiden, Netherlands: E.J. Brill, 1965), 202.

[20] See F. Ernest Stoeffler, *German Pietism During the Eighteenth Century* (Leiden: E.J.Brill, 1973), 178.

[21] Pauck, *"Luther and Melanchthon,"* 22. See also his introduction to the *Loci* of 1521, where he argues, *"this preoccupation with a 'theology of definitions' was a result of his humanistic studies and particularly of his admiration for Erasmus and his dependence upon him."* Philipp Melanchthon, *Loci Communes Theologici* (1521) Ed. Wilhelm Pauck (Philadelphia: The Westminster Press, 1969), 11.

[22] See Maurer, *Der junge Melanchthon*, 2:244ff. (*"Die Anthropologie der Loci"*) for a discussion of the relationship between the early Melanchthon's anthropology and his descriptions of the human will.

[23] Melanchthon, *Loci* (1521), 24.

[24] Ibid., 30.

whole of theology so adequately as the *Loci communes* do.... Next to Holy Scripture, there is no better book."[25]

However, by 1555 Melanchthon's reformulation and expansion of the *Loci* appeared to be presenting a different theology. Remarks such as, "Even in this corrupted nature God has allowed such freedom with regard to external motions of the body.... As far as external works are concerned, there remains in man a free will,"[26] have contributed to the suspicions of historians like Maurer and Mühlenberg that Melanchthon underwent a substantive shift in his theology back in the direction of Erasmus. At the same time, we need to acknowledge that Luther himself later softened some of his harsh polemic in his *The Bondage of the Will*. Elsewhere he could also admit: "We have, of course, in a certain sense a free will in those things which are under us. For the divine mandate has constituted us lords of the fishes of the sea, of the fowls of the air, and of the beasts of the field."[27] When this is coupled with the fact that Melanchthon continued within the later *Loci* to explain, "Further, it is also true that we still do not have enough power to keep God's law; we cannot begin inward obedience in our hearts without divine help and without the Holy Spirit,"[28] it is apparent that the shift in language between the early and late *Loci* on the subject of human will is nothing one does not find paralleled, to some extent, in Luther as well. The reason for the shift, as we will see below, is important. The shift itself, however, cannot tell us anything about an internal change in Melanchthon's theological orientation.

When we turn to his writing *On the Soul*, we find in Melanchthon's later work a greater appreciation and utilization of the philosophical perspective of the Greeks. The optimistic depiction of the nature of the human will stands in such stark contrast to what he had written in the early *Loci* that Pelikan sees a break, at least implicitly, in Melanchthon's allegiance to Luther. "Melanchthon's *de anima* pays lip service to the Christian and even to the Lutheran doctrine of sin, but by the psychological pattern that it sets up, the natural mind is given an opportunity to function both within and without the context of divine grace."[29] However, even if we turn to the very late *Liber de anima* of 1553, in which we find a very detailed discussion of the abilities and functions of the rational mind, the essential teaching of

---

[25] *WA TR*, Vol.V, No. 5511.
[26] Melanchthon, *Loci* (1555) trans. Clyde L. Manschreck (New York: Oxford University Press, 1965), 53.
[27] *WA* 42, 64.
[28] Melanchthon, *Loci* (1555), 57.
[29] Pelikan, *From Luther*, 27.

Luther on the nature of the soul is still present. That is, the human being, while able to perform laudatory, outward, civil acts, is still completely unable to merit or achieve anything good in the eyes of God. Citing the exemplary life of Cato, Melanchthon argues, "Cato loved virtue, but not on account of God; neither did he say that he was in God's care, nor did he love God. This gradation is to be observed, so that the difference between philosophy and gospel may be clearer."[30] Again, nothing could be clearer, nor is there anything hiding between the lines when Melanchthon writes, "The will is averse to God, it does not fear God."[31] Pelikan allows himself to be drawn into this notion of a reversion in Melanchthon's theology because of a failure to acknowledge that Melanchthon was writing for different audiences with different concerns at different points during his career. While we acknowledge that Luther's spirited writings were generally oriented toward specific issues while Melanchthon wrote more system-atically, it would be an error to rush to conclusions about a change in the theology of the latter without paying attention to his ranging contexts as well.

Melanchthon was aware of this apparent theological disparity between Luther and himself, but he believed it amounted to nothing more than appearances. He would write:

As you know, I formulate some things less harshly concerning predestination, the assent of the will [to grace], the necessity of our obedience [after justification], and mortal sin. I know that on all these issues Luther is in fact of the same opinion. But the uneducated people love his coarse formulations too much, because they do not perceive what context they belong in. I do not want to pick a fight with them. They are entitled to their opinion.[32]

The question remains, if this observable shift was not due to a revived humanist influence in his thought, what was functioning as the impetus for such a change? One clue presents itself in another difference between the early and late editions of the *Loci*. Not only was his discussion of human nature making a shift, but his understanding of the place of God's law was changing as well. In the 1521 edition, Melanchthon could write, "But [the law] is abrogated by the new preaching, now that the message concerning his Son is begun...and all that is commanded is that we embrace that Son."[33] Three decades later, after he had discovered the third use of the law, he would write, "As he created us to be like him in eternity, the law cannot be

---

[30] Melanchthon, "On the Soul," in *A Melanchthon Reader*, trans. Ralph Keen (New York: Peter Lang Publishing, 1988), 271.
[31] Ibid., 276.
[32] *CR* 3:383.
[33] *Loci*, (1521), 122.

effaced."[34] The two statements appear, as much as any two statements concerning the role of free will, to be at odds. However, we understand that Melanchthon meant to convey that, in regard to our justification, the law is "abrogated," while in regard to the life of faith it can never be "effaced." The change in emphasis which occurred during those three tumultuous decades, in regard to his discussion of the law, is most certainly connected to the change in emphasis regarding the human will. It was the knowledge that his earlier claims regarding the impotence of the will and the abrogation of the law might become, and in some cases had become, an excuse for ethical and religious apathy on the part of his listeners and a perfect target for the slings and arrows of his opponents in Rome that motivated him. In the later *Loci,* after a discussion of the relation of works and free will, he explains this very factor in influencing his thought. "And if this freedom [of the will] were not in men, then all worldly law and all education of children would be in vain. However, it is certainly true that through worldly law and the education of children God wants to force men into honorable customs, and such pain and work are not totally in vain."[35]

Moreover, historians have observed the subtle steps that took place along the way from the first to the last edition of the *Loci.* Wengert, in his discussion of Melanchthon's 1532 Commentary on Romans, explains where he had already begun to make changes in his language. Beginning with a criticism of Origen, who had failed to distinguish between civil and God-pleasing righteousness, Melanchthon sought to answer the charges of his Catholic opponents. Moreover, Wengert argues that his targets here were not the moderate, reforming Catholics, like Erasmus, but the more polemical Eck and the authors of the Confutation.[36] He continues to explain how Melanchthon's other primary concern, that believers not be led into apathy or discouragement, fed into his discussion of the human soul in this text as well. Thus we see in this intermediate step along the path of Melanchthon's career a self-conscious move toward personal responsibility motivated out of a fear of antinomianism—both the accusation and its actual presence.

Much of this concern appeared as a result of his work in the various visitations of the churches throughout Germany. Melanchthon, who took part in more of these trips than Luther, was greatly concerned with the libertinism he discovered. Moreover, even from the beginning, his efforts to address these abuses were met with resistance. Much later he would write Georg Buchholzer about what he found during those early days of the Reformation.

---

[34] *Loci,* (1555), 198.
[35] Ibid., 54.
[36] Wengert, *Human Freedom,* 142.

"During the inspection of churches [in 1527] we [Melanchthon and law professor Jerome Schurff] discovered many kinds of ineptitudes.... When we tried to emend these things, I also got my ears boxed, so that afterwards others attacked me."[37] In fact, it was as a result of his Visitation Articles that Agricola became further incensed with what Melanchthon was writing about the law and repentance, and this very issue would function as a prelude to the later antinomian controversies. Nonetheless, Wengert describes the function of the Visitation Articles' discussion of free will as being directed towards those who might take advantage of the implications of the Lutheran teaching that describes the impotence of human beings to please God:

> Regarding free will, the Latin version set its sights on those whose teaching on the will's bondage was interpreted by the masses as permitting license. Against them Melanchthon invoked the distinction between civil and spiritual righteousness and insisted that despite sin and the devil, it was within human powers (by God's grace and aid) to do good according to civil righteousness.[38]

We find, then, in the visitations that Melanchthon undertook, as well as in the Visitation Articles which followed, a real concern that earlier statements that could be used to encourage a spirit of antinomianism had to be reworked and reconsidered. It was this concern, rather than some desire to return to the intellectual life of humanism, that was responsible for his later statements concerning the relative freedom of the will, and, as we will see further below, the changing understanding of the law.

Wengert quite adeptly presents his conclusion, with which I must agree:

> [T]hese changes had nothing directly to do either with the original conflict with Erasmus during the 1520s or with Erasmus's theology. Although some of these changes meant that Melanchthon had created a much wider space for the human will and showed a greater openness to positions echoing Erasmus's criticisms from the *Hyperaspistes*, the causes for these changes rested in the inner logic of Melanchthon's own theology and in the theological environment of the early 1530s.[39]

At the same time, we should not completely overlook the influences of humanism on the life and thought of Melanchthon. As a student of the classics, he was truly inspired by the works of the Greeks. His use of dialectics, philosophical distinctions, and his discussions of ethics were significantly influenced by Aristotle. At the same time, although he made more use of that "rascally heathen" than Luther, it can in no way be argued that Melanchthon's philosophical presuppositions led to any of the

---

[37] *MBW* 6654; *CR* 7:1144f; Nov. 28, 1552.
[38] Wengert, *Human Freedom*, 140.
[39] Ibid., 147.

theological aberrations we might find in his writings. As Robert D. Preus points out, the same presuppositions were held by Melanchthon's arch-nemesis among the Gnesio-Lutherans, Matthias Flacius, as well.[40]

Where humanism did considerably influence Melanchthon's theology was in its insistence on inculcating virtue in the lives of the people. As Philipp Schaff points out, the reason he taught and studied theology was for the purpose of promoting civil virtues and piety in his readers and listeners.[41] We see this clearly in a letter he wrote to Joachim Camerarius: "I never wanted to become engaged in theological work for any other reason than that I might contribute to the improvement of life."[42] From this, it is a short step to see the reason for his personal concerns with the problems of antinomianism. For Melanchthon, theology was not so very tied up with the *Anfechtung* of the individual and the personal road to justification, as it was for Luther, but very much oriented toward the improvement of the life of the community. Thus we see that humanism did not corrupt Melanchthon's theology with some overly-optimistic notion of human nature, but that it oriented his concerns toward the well-being of the Christian community, which thereby led him to take the libertine implications of the revived Pauline theology most seriously.

The Intellectualization of Faith

That Lutheran theology, specifically the doctrines of justification and sanctification, were presented by Melanchthon differently than Luther cannot be denied; Melanchthon did indeed demonstrate a tendency to intellectualize the faith. On the one hand, Pelikan takes Melanchthon to task for this "blight" on Lutheranism. Unlike Luther, who he believes held a more holistic view of religious faith, "the constitutive aspect of faith in the theology of Melanchthon is assent—not the response of the total individual to the Father of our Lord Jesus Christ, but agreement with a set of revealed truths."[43] On the other hand, we find in Scheible the argument that all the fundamental traits of his thought were in place during Luther's lifetime and did not cause the latter considerable concern, which invites the question of whether later generations should have been so critical. While Pelikan goes overboard in his Melanchthon-bashing, which was not uncommon at the time he was writing

---

[40] Robert D. Preus, *The Theology of Post-Reformation Lutheranism: A Study of Theological Prolegomena* (St. Louis: Concordia Publishing House, 1970), 81.
[41] See Philipp Schaff, *History of the Christian Church*, vol. 7 (Grand Rapids: William B Eerdman's, 1910), 7:189.
[42] *CR* 1:722.
[43] Pelikan, *From Luther*, 33.

his book, I believe Scheible overstates his claim a bit as well. Certainly it is true that Melanchthon's theology had a more intellectual component from the beginning, which did not appear to overly concern Luther. At the same time, however, we need to acknowledge that Melanchthon's writings did undergo a shift over the years, as we have seen in the different editions of the *Loci* discussed above. The root cause for this intellectualized faith cannot be found, at least directly, in humanism, but rather in Melanchthon's growing concern with the antinomian question and its related phenomena. Luther's radical insistence on grace had served the dawning Reformation well in its ability to paint the differences between the parties in the starkest colors. However, the abuse of Christian freedom which some of Luther's more extreme statements could afford needed to be curtailed, and Melanchthon believed this could be accomplished only by reining in some of the rhetorical excesses of earlier years. Above and beyond this, Melanchthon was by nature a more reserved character who preferred to tread lightly where others might storm ahead with little concern for breaking diplomatic ties that might prove helpful in the future.[44]

Temperament and Task

The first key to understanding Melanchthon's intellectualization of the Christian faith and its relation to the antinomian question is understanding both his temperament and his chosen task. Philipp Melanchthon was not another Martin Luther; his personality was completely different from that of the confrontational monk who relished a good fight. Melanchthon much preferred to avoid confrontation, polemics, and name-calling in favor of simply explicating the positions of the reformers and attempting to find common ground where it existed. As Schmauck points out, "the spirit of Melanchthon was not that of a witness or confessor, but that of a scholar and teacher, a definer, a discriminator, and a systematizer."[45]

Furthermore, this difference in temperament and the way in which it directed his younger colleague's theological work was not unknown to Luther. The elder reformer understood that he himself was generally oriented toward specifics, while his younger colleague was more concerned with the broader picture. That is, Luther's approach to theology usually took the form

---

[44] Melanchthon was not afraid of a fight when the situation required it, but even then his tactics were different; he was always the diplomat: "Philipp stabs, too, but only with pins and needles. The pricks are hard to heal and they hurt. But when I stab I do it with a heavy pike used to hunt boars." *LW* 54, 50; *Tischreden* No. 348.

[45] Theodore E. Schmauck and C. Theodore Benze, *The Confessional Principle and the Confessions of the Lutheran Church* (Philadelphia: General Council Publication Board, 1911), 587.

of attacking a single issue, frequently allowing himself to make extreme statements which would come back to haunt him, while Melanchthon tried desperately to contain the expanding movement's theology in a systematic framework. In 1531 he would write, "Small and insignificant things affect me greatly, but not the big things. For [I] think, 'That is too high for you; you cannot grasp it, so let it go.' Philipp does just the opposite. My concerns do not affect him at all; the great concerns of state and church do. Only personal cares weigh heavily on my mind. In this way the gifts are different."[46] Similarly, Luther understood the respective "gifts" which they had been given as instrumental in carrying out the task of the Reformation. "I am the coarse woodsman who must blaze and prepare a new trail," he could write. "But Master Philipp comes neatly and quietly behind me, cultivates and plants, sows and waters with joy, according to the gifts that God has richly given him."[47] That Luther viewed Melanchthon's reserved, systematizing theological approach as of major benefit for the Church is made clear in his noteworthy praise of the latter's work. In September of 1529, in a letter to Justus Jonas, he wrote, "All the Jeromes, Hillarys and Macariuses together, are not worthy to unloose the thong of Philipp's sandal. What have the whole of them together done which can be compared with one year of Philipp's teaching, or to his one book of Common Places? I prefer Melanchthon's books to my own, and would rather have them circulated than mine."[48]

That Melanchthon's personality was more that of an academic than a heroic confessor cannot be denied. That his concerns were likewise oriented in the direction of a systematic exposition of the faith Luther expounded was not a liability, but, as the "coarse woodsman" believed, a complement to the groundbreaking work which Luther was undertaking. That this work had a more intellectual taste was indeed a product of his temperament. That it may be blamed, in part, for the overly intellectualized nature of later Lutheranism may indeed, to some degree, be valid. However, this would be more of an accident of history; perhaps even a necessary accident that followed from the essential systematizing work which he undertook, rather than a character flaw or theological limitation on the part of the younger reformer who "cultivates and plants, sows and waters with joy."

Furthermore, it should be obvious that one writing a more systematic exposition of faith will describe it in more intellectual terms than one writing reactive tracts and treatises. Melanchthon was concerned with detailing the specifics of faith within a concrete, Lutheran framework, and thereby needed

---

[46] *WA TR* Vol. 1, No. 80.
[47] *WA* 30(2):68-69.
[48] *WA Br* Vol. 5, No. 1472.

to respond to and defend against the various criticisms from Rome as well. It can hardly be surprising, then, that his work has a more intellectual flavor than, say, Luther's sermons or polemical treatises.

Forensic Justification

Beyond his temperament and the nature of his task, Melanchthon was nevertheless responsible for additional theological innovations that contributed to the intellectualizing of the faith. Most noticeably was his emphasis on forensic justification. This understanding of the redeeming work of Christ on the cross would appear to *reinforce* the tendency toward antinomian attitudes insofar as it focuses the discussion of salvation even more acutely on the work of Christ; and we do indeed find just that complaint in the next few centuries arising from the Pietist camps. As we shall see, however, Melanchthon's emphasis on this model of redemption was part of a larger plan to respond to those who were criticizing Lutheran theology's potential moral laxity.

While the Christian tradition which Luther and Melanchthon inherited maintained a number of complementary models of justification (e.g., that of Anselm in his *Cur deus homo* being the most well-known, but also those of Peter Abelard, the medieval mystics, and remnants of the ransom theories of the early Church),[49] we find in the mature Melanchthon a conscious move toward a single model of redemption: forensic justification. As Wengert points out, by 1534 the various metaphors for human salvation used by Melanchthon had been narrowed to just this one.[50] The edition of his *Scholia* published that year not only introduced the third use of the law, but demonstrated a shift toward a single model of justification as well, which became, according to Wengert, "the bedrock of his explanation of that doctrine."[51]

Melanchthon's reasoning was twofold. First, as Carl E. Maxcey points out,[52] there was the need to respond to people like Osiander, who were appropriating the teaching of the infusion of the divine life in Christ and proceeding down various heterodox roads with their conclusions. Secondly, and of more importance for this discussion, there was the need to formulate a theological system with which to respond to the charges of men like Eck, who continued to raise the specter of the antinomian question. By insisting

---

[49] See Maurer, *Der junge Melanchthon*, 2:338ff.
[50] Timothy J. Wengert, *Law and Gospel: Philipp Melanchthon's Debate with John Agricola of Eisleben over* Poenitentia (Grand Rapids: Baker Books, 1997), 178f.
[51] Ibid., 178.
[52] Carl E. Maxcey, *Bona Opera: A Study in the Development of the Doctrine of Philipp Melanchthon* (Chicago: Nieuwkoop B De Graaf, 1980),78.

on the single model of forensic justification, Melanchthon was not only excluding any notion of our own value or worth in the work of redemption, but
providing more clarity to the many convoluted discussions of human
salvation. While forensic justification in and of itself may perpetuate the
problem of antinomianism, when it is coupled with two other aspects of
Melanchthon's thought it becomes part of a model which is able, as we shall
see, to uphold both the absolute priority of God's grace as well as the
believer's responsibility to respond with a life of piety.

The first necessary complementing factor consists of a more specific
definition of faith. Yes, it is through faith that humanity receives the imputed
righteousness of Christ; we need to be very clear, however, about our understanding of what that faith is. From early in his career, Melanchthon never
tired of insisting that faith is more than agreement with doctrinal statements.
His *Loci* of 1521 criticized the papists for this tendency. "It is well known
that the common run of Sophists define faith as the assent to what is set forth
in Scripture; therefore, they say that even the godless have this faith."[53] This
criticism is echoed through his various works, being clearly conveyed in the
confessional *Augustana*[54] and *Apology*[55] as well. Thus, for Melanchthon, the
first thing one needs to have in appropriating the doctrine of forensic
justification is a definition of faith that looks beyond mere historical knowledge and challenges one to see whether the *"faith"* one has is indeed the
heartfelt trust in the Gospel which Luther had explicated so well.

The second factor in Melanchthon's theology that must be appropriated
alongside his insistence on forensic justification is the third use of the law.
While we will return to the specifics of this innovation later, it will suffice
here to point out that for Melanchthon the teaching of justification through
faith must be accompanied by the preaching of the law to the redeemed. He
is insistent that the preacher does not simply preach law followed by gospel,
but continues on with the responsibilities of the people of God. Lutheran
theology does not end, for Melanchthon, with the absolution. It is no coinci-
dence that he introduces the third use of the law at the same time that he is
focusing the conversation over redemption on forensic justification. Wengert
summarizes the importance of this new emphasis on forensic justification,
arguing:

---

[53] *Loci* (1521), 89. Cf. Maurer, *Der junge Melanchthon*, 2:368ff. ("Wortglaube und
Gesitglaube").
[54] *The Augsburg Confession*, XX, 23.
[55] *The Apology of the Augsburg Confession*, as in *The Book of Concord*, trans. Theodore G.
Tappert (Philadelphia: Fortress Press, 1959), e.g., 113.

> To eliminate absolutely every notion of merit from the definition of justification, even that of Augustine, Melanchthon narrowed his metaphors to one, the forensic declaration of forgiveness of God 'gratis propter Christum'.... However, this definition left Melanchthon and the Reformers open to the charge of antinomianism or libertinism.... So while eliminating human works from God's declaration of righteousness, Melanchthon asserted that the law continues in terms of obedience.[56]

Melanchthon's insistence on the single model of forensic justification did indeed contribute, unfortunately, to the intellectualizing of the Lutheran faith. It may indeed be true that this more cerebral faith may be behind the "sterile" theology that many Lutherans have bemoaned over the centuries. It is both ironic and sad, considering that Melanchthon's intention was to respond to the sixteenth century's growing penchant for moral apathy, that this has been his legacy. However, the fault cannot be completely laid at the door of Master Philipp. The intellectualism that springs from the teaching of forensic justification is possible only when Melanchthon's other two complementary points are neglected. We see this, for example, in the case of Pietism. While the forerunners of Pietism in the sixteenth and seventeenth centuries (e.g Philipp Nicolai, Johann Gerhard, and Johann Arndt) revived the discussion of the *unio mystica* in response to the narrow forensic doctrines of orthodoxy, later Pietism, of the Spener-Halle school, made more of an unwitting return to Melanchthon. For figures like Spener and Francke, the answer to the rampant impiety in society was not to neglect the Anselm-inspired Lutheran doctrine of justification, but to narrow the definition of faith and insist on the necessity of good works.[57] That is, they complemented the preaching of forensic justification with the insistence that faith is something more than the promises made in baptism and the recitation of the creed, and that the law needs to be preached to the redeemed in the form of moral instruction. As a result, they found themselves, as one might expect, under attack from the same orthodox positions with which Melanchthon had been confronted two centuries before.

The Third Use of the Law

Of Melanchthon's theological peculiarities, there are some in which the influence of his concern over the antinomian question is not immediately apparent, as we have seen in his intellectualizing of the Christian faith. In others Melanchthon's concern over abuses of Christian freedom are more

---

[56] Wengert, *Law and Gospel*, 205.

[57] See further my article, "Not By Accident: The Christology of Lutheran Pietism," *Covenant Quarterly* 60 no. 1(2002) 34–44.

obvious. His introduction of the third use of the law obviously belongs to this category.

As noted above, it was in the *Scholia* of 1534 that we find the first written record of Melanchthon teaching the law's third use. As the Reformation began to take hold through different regions of Germany and around the Baltic, it was becoming more apparent that the spontaneous good works that the reformers had hoped to see springing from the lives of the faithful were rather slow in coming. Melanchthon's earlier confrontations with Agricola at the time of the first visitations convinced him that the people needed more prodding to live lives worthy of the great calling of the gospel. The third use of the law, then, picked up where the proclamation of the gospel left off. As Wengert points out, Melanchthon, "having placed the gospel at the end of the movement in Christian life, now felt compelled to discuss what happens after justification."[58] If the preaching of the law is limited to the theological use—as the mirror which shows us our sins—what then becomes of the redeemed sinner who remains *simul iustus et peccator*? As discussed in the previous chapter, the believer knows that the law no longer condemns, and so, while the second use of the law remains after justification, it has lost much of its power to curb behavior. The condemning voice of the law is reduced to a whisper for the redeemed; the believer knows that sins have been forgiven, salvation attained, and the danger of condemnation has largely passed. The earlier hope of both Luther and Melanchthon that justified sinners would spontaneously live lives of virtue without any need for a law to tell them what to do was later realized by both men to have been a bit optimistic. Melanchthon's answer was to explicate the role that the law plays for the redeemed. "The third use of the preaching of the law is concerned with those saints who now are believers.... Although God now dwells in these and gives them light, and causes them to be conformed to him, nevertheless, all such happens through God's word, and the law in this life is necessary, that saints may know and have a testimony of the works which please God."[59]

While Melanchthon's formal introduction of a third use for the law was a theological innovation of sorts, we have already seen that precedent for it could be found in Luther. Moreover, the Lutheran reformers were hardly the first theologians to suggest that the law could be used to instruct Christians in aspects of daily living. Nonetheless, Master Philipp's insistence that the law serves this pedagogical function was an important step for Lutheranism. As we have seen, Luther had cast the law in quite a different light with his

---

[58] Wengert, *Law and Gospel*, 163.
[59] *Loci* (1555), 127.

insistence that whatever accuses us of our own sinfulness is law. Melanchthon's reworking of the uses of the law in the 1530s reclaimed the law's work as instruction, placing it alongside, but in an inferior position to Luther's existential law. Luther's acknowledgment of this contribution meant that the law would be acknowledged to have more than a single use and function; the law does instruct as well.

Melanchthon's brainchild was not an isolated incident—a detached broadening of Luther's discussions of the law—but a conscious effort to respond to what he perceived as a neglect of law in Lutheran theology and practice. His encounters with Agricola on the one hand, and his opponents in Rome on the other, convinced him that it would be necessary to reinforce the importance of the law in the developing evangelical movement. Properly speaking, the third use of the law is not an answer to the antinomian question. Nonetheless, it is an attempt to curb abuses of Christian freedom that were springing from what some were calling an overemphasis on grace. By underlining the importance of preaching the law to believers, Melanchthon was trying to make up for this imbalance. The third use of the law does not answer the question, "Why do I, as a believer, need to be concerned about following these rules?" Rather, it bypasses this concern, seeking to improve the behavior of Christians through a different means. Master Philipp believed (as did Freud, in relation to the superego) that more exposure to the law would manifest itself in more obedient behavior. This was, after all, underlying Luther's notion of the first use of the law. Thus, the third use would assure that more preaching of the law would reach the people in the pews. In this way Melanchthon hoped to minimize some of the libertinism that was finding root in Luther's theology. This further underscores what was presented above, that Melanchthon's concern was not simply to answer what we are calling the antinomian question, but the broader and greater task of improving the moral conduct of society at large.

While it is impossible to determine the direct effects of this theological innovation within the Lutheran territories of the sixteenth centuries (and we will leave it to the social psychologists to determine how exactly the teaching of rules affects behavior), we do know that Melanchthon made a valuable contribution to the preaching of the law, insisting that it held a place of importance in the lives of believers as well as unbelievers. The legacy of the third use of the law has been a constant reminder that the preaching of the law holds an essential place among the faithful. Even when the third use is understood to be no more than that of the second use for believers, as we saw in Werner Elert's discussion of this use of the law in the previous chapter, it still functions as a demand that the law needs to be preached to sinners and saints; this was Melanchthon's great concern.

More Reasons for Good Works

In order to encourage his readers even more in the direction of good works, Melanchthon did not stop with telling them what to do through the third use of the law. Knowing how the human mind works, he understood that the antinomian question itself needed to be responded to as well. Melanchthon had a response; one that he believed would not compromise the gospel or the principle of *sola fide*. Answering his critics in Rome through the *Apology,* he would insist, "Therefore we praise good works and require them, and we show many reasons why they should be done."[60]

Taking a page from Luther, Melanchthon would insist that engaging in either virtuous or vicious behavior carries with it significant temporal consequences. On the one hand, God does chastise Christians, as a father corrects his children when they stray too far. Citing the example of David and Bathsheba, he reminds us, "Although obedience is for the glory of God, and not principally for fear of punishment, nevertheless God has revealed terrible punishments respecting it, so that we may know his will and earnestly desire to show obedience."[61] On the other hand, as the fourth commandment reassures us, there are temporal blessings that God is eager to share with us as a reward for abiding by His word. Along these lines, Melanchthon directs us to consider Matthew 10:41 as well.[62] Melanchthon's concern with abuses of Christian freedom, once again, is what best explains his reminders that good works obtain temporal favor from God while sins may bring temporal chastisement. What is more, as Maxcey has pointed out,[63] this insistence on the reasons for and causes of good works are more pronounced between the years 1535 and 1541; this being, as we may recall, the same time when the third use of the law was introduced, forensic justification was being insisted upon, and he was making a shift in his discussion of the human will. As we saw in the previous chapter, Luther had likewise insisted that human moral behavior carries with it temporal reper-cussions. During these crucial years of the Reformation, however, Melanch-thon felt compelled to emphasize this position more than Luther had in his

---

[60] *Apology,* 134.
[61] *Loci,* (1555), 182.
[62] "Anyone who receives a prophet because he is a prophet will receive a prophet's reward, and anyone who receives a righteous man will receive a righteous man's reward."
[63] Maxcey, *Bona Opera,* 293.

continued efforts to respond to the libertinism that the Lutherans were both accused of and engaging in from time to time.

Moreover, if these temporal rewards and punishments were not sufficient impetus for changing one's ways, Melanchthon could remind his readers that there is no doctrine of the perseverance of the saints in Lutheranism. Lest one forget, "It is highly necessary to know that there are distinctions in sins, that some sins remain even in the saints in this life, and that some sins grieve and repel the Holy Spirit, causing some men to fall from grace, who, if not again converted, fall into eternal punishment."[64] Like Luther, Melanchthon insisted that the sins we commit can indirectly have eternal consequences. While this approach is certainly effective, and would certainly pass muster with Luther, one is forced to ask if perhaps Melanchthon went too far with this approach. He continues, "However, as long as we do not will to follow these evil tendencies with action, but painfully strive against them and believe that these sins are forgiven for the sake of *Christ*, and that we are clothed through *Christ*, we remain holy."[65] Unfortunately, these words force us to ask ourselves whether we have striven enough, placing a great deal of responsibility for our salvation in our own actions. Luther had acknowledged that the old nature prevents Christians from striving for righteousness with all their heart, mind, and strength, and yet they are being told here that they remain holy in the eyes of God only if they "painfully strive" against sin and refuse to act on the evil tendencies that still reside in their nature. While Luther had also argued that our salvation is secure as long as one struggles against sin, Master Philipp has raised the bar substantially with this striking language. His approach may be effective in making some take the life of faith more seriously, but those with tender consciences may fear that they have not done enough to obtain their salvation. Here we find Melanchthon's concern for Christian piety potentially leading to an undermining of the believer's trust in the graciousness of God, insofar as such Herculean efforts on the part of the redeemed sinner appear to be required to keep hold of one's salvation. By the same token, we do not want to overstate this criticism. The same author of Article IV of the *Apology* certainly understood the importance of justification by grace alone. What may best be gleaned here is that Melanchthon's zeal for the life of sanctification could lead him occasionally to make careless remarks, just as Luther's enthusiasm for the doctrine of justification could affect his better judgment at times as well.

---

[64] *Loci*, (1555), 183.
[65] Ibid., 184.

The Majorist Controversy

The Majorist Controversy, in which Melanchthon was indirectly involved, demonstrates most clearly the influence of his concern with the antinomian question. While the controversy with Georg Major took place in the early 1550s, Melanchthon had been involved in a nearly identical polemical exchange two decades before. Bente explains his relation to this controversy: "Though not personally mentioned and attacked by the opponents of Majorism, Melanchthon must be regarded as the real father also of this controversy. He was the first to introduce and to cultivate the phrase: 'Good works are necessary to salvation.'"[66] Indeed, the Majoristic Controversy, which centered on this claim, was foreshadowed by statements made by Melanchthon in the 1530s. In his *Loci* of 1535, he argued that good works are "necessary for eternal life (*necessaria sunt ad vitam aeternam*)." This was a significant step beyond what he had written in the *Apology*, where he had responded to the authors of the *Confutation*, explaining "Of course, good works are necessary. We say that eternal life is promised to the justified, but those who walk according to the flesh can retain neither flesh nor righteousness."[67]

This later statement, that good works are necessary for salvation, played a recurring role in Lutheran theology long after Melanchthon stopped using it. It was revived by Major and Justus Menius later in the same century, as well as by the Pietists at Halle in the following centuries. However, during the 1530s, it is easy to perceive that Melanchthon's reason for introducing such a controversial statement was his fear of antinomianism. As indicated above, the date at which it appears parallels his introduction of the third use of the law, refocused discussion of human will, and analyses of rewards and punishments. The antinomian issue was at the heart of his reasoning for making this claim. It is possible to document that Melanchthon made this connection quite consciously. In 1556, while the Majorist Controversy was raging, he specifically referred to the Antinomian Controversy of two decades before as the reason for his previous controversial statement. He wrote to Flacius:

> But concerning necessity, I confess that the furies of the antinomians attacked me twenty years ago when a court preacher [Agricola], to applause of the entire audience, said, 'Das Muß ist versalzen (the must/mash [of the law] is oversalted).'

---

[66] Bente, *Historical Introductions*, 112.
[67] *Apology*, 160.

> And how I say that these propositions are true and eternal, I have explained enough.[68]

That is, when the antinomians, led by Agricola, were downplaying the importance of the law, he had responded to their arguments by making greater and greater claims about the importance of good works. Agricola's writings were, in Melanchthon's mind, getting out of hand. For example, Agricola had gone so far as to write, "God's Word says, 'When you sin, be happy. It is to have no consequence. Sin does not condemn you; for good works do not save you, but rather faith in Jesus Christ alone.'"[69] For Melanchthon, who was always very concerned with the implications which theological statements had for society in general, it was necessary to rebuke Agricola for this irresponsible language. Comments like those of Agricola could have devastating consequences for those trying to maintain good order and piety in society. It was this impetus that forced Melanchthon to go so far as to argue, as we have seen, that good works are actually necessary *for salvation*.

Years later, after changing his tone and language, Melanchthon refused to recant his earlier statements, to the consternation of his opponents. A few years before his death, in December of 1557 or early 1558, he wrote that the phrase *"new obedience is necessary"* was indeed to be held, but that the qualifying *"for salvation (ad salutem, zur Seligkeit)"* was not necessary due to its possible misinterpretation.[70] He even counseled Major against its use.[71]

It is clear that Melanchthon's motivation here was the fear that statements which denied the necessity of good works would perpetuate abuses of Christian freedom on the part of the people. On the surface of things, it would appear that Melanchthon's position was quite at odds with Luther, who had insisted in 1521, "Surely there will never be any peace, if it is necessary to have good works, and no one in his whole life knows that he has them."[72] Schaff weighs in against Melanchthon, concluding that, "He gave up...solifidianism for the necessity of good works."[73] This may be a rash judgment, but Schaff has not been alone. At the end of this drama, we find Melanchthon forced to abandon his attempt to reformulate theological language in regard to the necessity of works. In December of 1553, he conceded, "New obedience is necessary;...but when it is said: New obedience is

---

[68] *CR* 8:842.
[69] *Colosser*, J.vii.v, as in Wengert, *Law and Gospel*, 35.
[70] *CR* 9:407.
[71] See Bente, *Historical Introductions*, 114.
[72] *LW* 32, 193.
[73] Schaff, *History of the Christian Church*, 371.

necessary to salvation, the Papists understand that good works merit
salvation. This proposition is false; therefore I relinquish this mode of
speech."[74] It would be a mistake, however, to conclude from this statement
that Melanchthon had lost the battle. While he was unsuccessful in importing
this controversial phrase into orthodox Lutheran theology, his efforts did
have the effect of redirecting discussions in Lutheranism away from the
radical statements of Agricola, and toward a greater concern with the
importance and necessity of works. His repeated reminders of the reason for
this proposed statement kept the dangers associated with the *sola fide*
doctrine fresh in the minds of his readers.

As to the question whether Melanchthon truly gave up solifidianism by
virtue of his position in this controversy, it would be difficult to conclude
that he personally made such a theological shift. Nowhere did he argue that
these good works were a cause of salvation, only that their presence was
necessary for salvation. It is a subtle but important distinction. He was not
simply arguing that good works are necessary as a sign of salvation, with
which no one at that time would disagree, but that they were actually
involved with a believer's justification. As we discussed in the previous
section, for both Luther and Melanchthon the Christian must be actively
involved in the internal struggle of putting the sinful flesh to death (which we
can understand, in part, as good works[75]). Without this good work, the
forgiveness of sins can be lost. That is to say, if the Christian fails to actively
pursue piety, thereby putting the old Adam to death, faith weakens and may
be abandoned. As a result, in a manner of speaking we may say that good
works are necessary for salvation; they do not contribute to salvation directly, but they are involved with the retention of faith, which is, of course,
necessary for salvation. At the same time, this ambiguous statement can also
be understood to suggest that the good works are the cause of salvation. That
Melanchthon understood this distinction but held to the former interpretation
should be apparent from his concession in 1553 quoted above. He was
willing to concede that the statement should not be used, not because it was
false but because of its possible misinterpretation. Despite the objections of
Bente and Schaff, while we may judge Melanchthon's language to be
imprudent, it can still be judged to have been consistent with Luther's
theology.

---

[74] *CR* 8:194.
[75] See further Maurer, *Der junge Melanchthon*, 2:382, on the topic of mortification and good
works.

The Synergistic Controversy

The Synergistic Controversy, the final controversy in which Melanchthon was involved that we will discuss here, is again most easily explained by his concern with this antinomian issue. The controversy itself, one may recall, focused on the question of whether the human being plays any active part in her conversion to faith, or whether she is completely passive. Melanchthon, clearly deviating from Luther on this point, declares:

> We should not think that a man is a piece of wood or stone, but as we hear the word of God, in which punishment and comfort are put forth, we should not despise nor resist it. We should immediately rouse our hearts to earnest prayer, for the Lord Christ says, 'How much more will your heavenly Father give his Holy Spirit to you if you ask him! [76]

This peculiarity on Melanchthon's part has been, not surprisingly, blamed on his humanist background. Pelikan, discussing Melanchthon's role in this particular controversy concluded, "Melanchthon's humanism had led him to ascribe to the human will a more active part in conversion than Luther had believed to be in keeping with the monergism of divine grace, as taught in the New Testament."[77] Likewise, Preus finds the explanation for Melanchthon's doctrinal deviancy of his later years in the humanism which he "never became free of; and we have the full-blown result of this in his synergism."[78]

While it is true that the spirit of humanism was consistent with Melanchthon's rejection of what Schaff called the "Stoic fatalism" of Augustine and Luther, the leap from correlation to causation is one that Pelikan and Pauck make too quickly. The more reasonable explanation, as Schaff has pointed out, is his concern for the necessity of good works.[79] The implications that follow if we as human beings play no role in our conversion were a real source of concern for Melanchthon. If one is as passive as a stone or piece of wood, as Flacius was insisting, then there is no point in pursuing one's own salvation. Flacius admitted and affirmed that his position of monergism did indeed "exclude all efficaciousness and operation of the natural will in conversion."[80] This was unacceptable to Melanchthon, who insisted that Flacius's position would lead to Manichaean fatalism. Indeed this was exactly the charge of the party in Rome. Likewise, Erasmus expressed the same concern in his *Hyperaspistes,* which one may recall was a response to the extreme position of Luther in *The Bondage of the Will.* As Wengert

---

[76] *Loci,* (1555), 60.
[77] Pelikan, *From Luther,* 44.
[78] Preus, *The Theology,* 82.
[79] Schaff, *History,* 371.
[80] As in Bente, *Historical Introductions,* 139.

points out, Melanchthon's reasons for reviving the notion that one cooperates in one's conversion "has less to do with some internal predilection for synergism than with his increasing desire to answer the objections of and build bridges to the so-called reform Catholic party, on the one hand, and with his fear of theological statements that could be used to support antinomianism, on the other."[81] The antinomian question and its theoretical consequent, libertinism, continued to nag at Melanchthon, pushing him in this case to an outright rejection of Luther's position on the reception of grace.

When we look at Melanchthon's own words in discussing this issue, we are able to confirm that this concern was the reason for his change in theological direction. In the *Loci* of 1535—a date surely standing out in the mind of the reader by this point—Melanchthon began to discuss the three concurring causes of the conversion of a person: the Word of God, the Holy Spirit, and the faculty of the human will. Even if the will is involved ever so weakly, for Melanchthon it still plays a part, and he is perfectly clear as to the reason for insisting on this:

> We do not say this to ensnare the consciences, or to deter men from the endeavor to obey and believe, or from making an effort. On the contrary, since we are to begin with the Word, we certainly must not resist the Word of God, but strive to obey it.... We see that these causes are united: the Word, the Holy Spirit, and the will, which is certainly not idle, but strives against its infirmity.[82]

He continues to express this concern in his *Loci* of 1548, where he again conveys his concern over antinomian or Manichaean apathy, writing:

> I therefore answer those who excuse their idleness because they think that free will does nothing, as follows: It certainly is the eternal and immovable will of God that you obey the voice of the Gospel, that you hear the Son of God, that you acknowledge the Mediator. How black is that sin which refuses to behold the Mediator, the Son of God, presented to the human race! You will answer: 'I cannot.' But in a manner you can, and when you sustain yourself with the voice of the Gospel, then pray that God would assist you, and know that the Holy Spirit is efficacious in such consolation. Know that just in this manner God intends to convert us, when we, roused by the promise, wrestle with ourselves, pray and resist our diffidence and other vicious affections.[83]

When we consider the Synergistic Controversy in relation to the antinomian question, two things are certain. First, the motivation for Melanchthon's position is found in his concern regarding antinomianism, not his previous association with humanism. Second, it was a clear break with

---

[81] Wengert, *Human Freedom*, 145.
[82] *CR* 21:376.
[83] *CR* 21:659.

Luther. While Master Philipp insisted that the will was involved ever so weakly, this remained a qualitative break with Luther's monergism. The question for us remains as to what importance this esoteric discussion has within the more practical discussions of Christian morality. Was Melanchthon's synergism a positive way of responding to the antinomian question? Was the condemnation he received from the Gnesio-Lutherans deserved? What is the relevance of this apparently obscure, sixteenth century theological debate today, if any?

The concern about removing any act of the human will from the process of justification was not entirely misplaced. If human beings are believed to be as passive as blocks of wood or lumps of clay, this can certainly become an excuse for apathy, disinterest, or even worse: Johannes Janssen conveys the story of a young man in St. Gall who beheaded his brother and attributed the act to God, explaining to his parents that the act was "in fulfillment of the heavenly Father's will;" he himself had been merely a passive agent of the act. Similarly, in Esslingen, a man trampled his wife to death, declaring, "Now is the Father's will accomplished."[84] Admittedly, these are probably acts that would likely have taken place without any expression of Luther's monergism. The excuses offered by these men, however, do provide evidence that the implications of the theology of Luther and the other reformers were trickling down to the laity. If these two extreme accounts of fatalistic reasoning have reached us almost five hundred years later, it is reasonable to surmise that similar excuses for less atrocious behavior were not difficult to find at the time that Melanchthon was noticing a penchant on the part of his compatriots for abusing the implications of Luther's theology. With his pastoral heart and concern for public order, we can hardly be surprised that he decided that one way to rein in these excesses was to insist that the human will did indeed play a part in an individual's conversion. Any support for this type of fatalism needed to be corrected or removed.

The problem, as many of Melanchthon's colleagues perceived, was that this approach seriously compromised Luther's theological premises. More was at stake than this simple disagreement: Luther said that individuals play no role in their justification while Melanchthon argued that they provide a minimal assent to the forgiveness they receive. For Luther, despite his unwillingness to convey his theology systematically, there existed an intimate relationship between every theological premise and his insistence on the absolute graciousness of God. His belief in God's monergism in justification could not be placed aside without undermining the fundamental

---

[84] Johannes Janssen, *History of the German People at the Close of the Middle Ages*, trans. A.M. Christie (St. Louis: B. Herder, 1908), 4:114.

principles of his theology. "If God's mercy is to be praised, then all [human] merits and worthiness must come to naught."[85] Luther believed that even natural reason is able to discern that God is a merciful creator.[86] Christians especially must acknowledge that salvation has been initiated and completed by God alone through Christ. More is at stake here than an overly optimistic perception of human nature. To Luther's way of thinking, insofar as an individual claims to play a role in his own justification, that person is usurping God's function as creator, attempting to claim a place as co-creator with God of human salvation. Luther had spelled this out already in 1517, writing:

> It is characteristic of God (*es ist Gottes Natur*) to make something out of nothing. Hence God cannot make anything out of him who is not as yet nothing.... Therefore God receives none but the forsaken, heals none but the ill, gives sight to none but the blind, quickens none but the dead, makes pious none but the sinners, makes wise none but the ignorant,—in short, He has mercy on none but the miserable, and gives grace to none but those who are in disgrace. Whoever, therefore, is a proud saint, wise or just, cannot become God's material and receive God's work within himself, but remains in his own work and makes an imaginary, seeming, false, and painted saint of himself, *i.e.*, a hypocrite.[87]

When the sixteenth century Lutherans condemned Melanchthon's synergism,[88] and when contemporary Lutherans continue to have trouble with the "decision-theology" found in many American evangelical circles (e.g. Billy Graham's altar calls), there is more at stake than the theological minutiae involved with either consenting to one's salvation or being a passive recipient. Luther was adamant that when all worth is stripped from human efforts and when God is acknowledged as the sole provider of every good thing, then faith, trust, and gratitude toward the Creator reach their peak; at that moment the individual understands God's mercy. Any claim on the part of a sinful human being to have played a role in the divine work of justification can result only in diminished reverence and love of God. While Melanchthon would never have claimed that the human will plays any causal, worthy, or meritorious role in the reception of the forgiveness of sins, even his minor concessions to human participation, as when he wrote, "the will of man, which does not resist the divine voice…somehow, with trepidation, assents,"[89] were sufficient to demonstrate his difference with Luther and bring about the condemnation of men like Flacius.

---

[85] *WA* 1,161.

[86] *WA* 56, 177.

[87] *WA* 1,183f.

[88] See the Formula of Concord, Solid Declaration, Article II.

[89] Bente, *Historical Introductions*, 130f.

It is easy to sympathize with Melanchthon in his attempt to curb the abuses of a society that would use Luther's theology as a loophole to justify apathy, inaction, or even outright sin. Luther's concern, however, had not been to construct a theological institution that had as its primary goal civil peace and justice but to offer the pure gospel message of God's absolute mercy and grace to individuals within society. Admittedly there would be those who would abuse the freedom they heard described therein, but in no way did Luther ever believe himself to have the right to curtail the freedom of the gospel, the very word of God, in order to deal with the indiscretions which came from its misuse.

Conclusion

The key to understanding Melanchthon's theology, his use of language, his changes in emphasis, and his deviations from Luther is not to be found in his humanist background. Rather, his interest in humanism only points us to the overarching concern behind his academic and theological work: the improvement of society. By providing various responses to the antinomian question and related abuses of the gospel, he hoped to contribute to this goal. At the same time, however, we need to acknowledge that religion for him was more than a means to improve public piety. Melanchthon was as concerned with the individual appropriation of the gospel message of forgiveness and the hope for life eternal as any of the reformers. Added to this, however, was a mighty concern for piety and peace throughout Europe. It was this concern that motivated him to face head-on the antinomian question as it was being leveled at the adherents of Lutheranism both by Rome as well as those in society at large who saw in the new doctrine the opportunity to abuse the freedom of the gospel.

It has been a failure to understand both the place of the influence of humanism as well as his concern regarding the antinomian question that has made Melanchthon such a difficult figure to understand for later generations. Attempts to explain his work through vague psychological diagnoses have failed to account for the complexity of this man's theological career. Any attempt to understand him without significant treatment of this concern can only offer an inadequate account of his life and work.

While Melanchthon's various attempts to respond to the various forms of the antinomian question tended to land him in trouble with those who sought to maintain Luther's strong stand on solifidianism, some of his theological innovations did provide helpful responses to his critics in Rome, the moral cynics in Germany, and the pastors trying to guide their flocks. By expanding on principles that were inherent in Luther's thought (i.e. a third use for the law, temporal rewards and punishments, the sin against the Holy Spirit), Melanchthon provided tools to keep the morally-challenged on the straight and narrow, while remaining faithful to his mentor. At other times, his enthusiasm in seeking a morally-upright Lutheran society led him to what would be declared heterodox positions, positions which did indeed compromise the principles he had so eloquently expressed in the *Augustana*. Melanchthon cannot be judged innocent of violating Luther's solifidianism. In the end, however, perhaps his best response to the antinomian question, and the one closest to the spirit of Luther, can be found near the end of his *Loci* of 1555, written five years before his death. Here he writes: "At this point someone might say, 'Shall we let the flesh indulge in every sensual pleasure? Shall we not restrain ourselves with work, fasting and similar exercises? Shall we cease being chaste, moral, and temperate?' Answer: Anyone who loves God's word already knows the answer."[90]

---

[90] *Loci*, (1555), 251.

ℂℛ CHAPTER THREE

Philipp Jakob Spener

"Dear Christian reader, that the holy Gospel is subjected, in our time, to a great and shameful abuse is fully proved by the impenitent life of the ungodly who praise Christ and his word with their mouths and yet lead an unchristian life that is like that of persons who dwell in heathendom, not in the Christian world."[1] With these words Johann Arndt began his monumental work *True Christianity*. The year was 1605 and Lutheranism had become more or less established in Germany. Despite the hopes of previous generations, however, evangelical doctrine was not bringing about the desired reformation in personal piety among the people of Northern Europe; perhaps they were even worse. The seventeenth century was quickly discovering that "faith alone" meant just that for a great number of new Protestants; "faith" was existing all by itself and the good works that were supposed to follow were seriously lacking. A few pastors and theologians decried the present libertine spirit, but voices like those of Arndt, Johann Gerhard, John Valentine Andreae, and Theophilus Grossgebauer were for the most part, as Theodore Tappert describes them, "voices crying in the wilderness."[2]

Shortly after Arndt published *True Christianity*, Europe was ravaged by the Thirty Years War, plunged into decades of bloodshed, hunger, and moral depravity. As John McIntosh has pointed out, by the last phase of the war political ambition superseded any previous religious concern, bringing in its wake an even greater moral breakdown. Clergy were able to excuse their "laxity and licentiousness" by appealing to the Lutheran position on *adiaphora* (which we will discuss later in this chapter). The fragmented political structure, in imitation of the French at that time, moved in the direction of absolutist ideas of the power of government. With civil rulers coveting more and more power, the church was often forced to fall in line under the direction of its political protector. Article 28 of the Augsburg

---

[1]Johann Arndt, *True Christianity*, trans. Peter Erb (New York: Paulist Press, 1979), 21.
[2]Theodore G. Tappert, introduction to *Pia Desideria*, trans. Theodore G. Tappert (Philadelphia: Fortress Press, 1964), 7.

Confession, which had sought to limit the authority of civil rulers, was fading into memory and Christian piety was but one of its casualties.[3] F. Ernest Stoeffler was right to insist, "It is difficult to overestimate the catastrophic effect of the Thirty Years War upon the German people.... Perhaps even more important than the material loss was the effect of the war upon the moral fibre of the people."[4]

In 1635, shortly before the end of the war, Philipp Jakob Spener was born at Rappoltsweiler in Alsace, the son of a devout father—councilor to one of the dukes of Rappolstein—and a mother equally committed to her faith. From an early age, young Philipp was deeply committed to his own faith and its practice. As an adult, when asked about youthful indiscretions he could recall but one: at the age of twelve he had been persuaded to join in a dance with his peers. However, shortly after the dancing had begun he fled the dance floor filled with anxiety and regret, never to return.[5] During these early years, in addition to reading the Bible, he was fond of a number of books written by English Puritan authors who were critical of the Christianity of the day. His favorite book, however (after the Bible, of course), remained Arndt's *True Christianity*.

In 1651 Spener began his studies at the University of Strassburg under the direction of Johann Conrad Dannhauer, Sebastian Schmidt, and Johann Schmidt—three men as committed to orthodoxy as to the practical religious needs of the Church. During his planned year abroad, his *Wanderjahr*, Spener actually found himself outside the empire for two years because of an illness that waylaid him in Geneva in 1565. It was while he was in this stronghold of Reformed theology that he met the famous Jean de Labadie, who was stirring up Europe with his hopes for a reformed and renewed Christianity and attracting attention because of his small devotional gatherings. Spener spent some time at Labadie's services and even produced a translation into German of his *Manual de Priere* ("Manual of Prayer"). However, if Spener's doctoral committee and Stein's theological analysis can be believed, he returned home from his time abroad, contrary to the suspicions of many, a convinced Lutheran.[6]

While Spener's career would take him to some of the highest clerical posts in Germany, it is not the specifics of his pastoral work at Franckfurt-

[3] John McIntosh, "Proposals for Godliness in the Church," *The Reformed Theological Review* 35, S-D (1976): 79–88.
[4] F. Ernest Stoeffler, *The Rise of Evangelical Pietism* (Leiden, Netherlands: E.J. Brill, 1965), 180f.
[5] See K. James Stein, *Philipp Jakob Spener: Pietist Patriarch* (Chicago: Covenant Press, 1986), 42.
[6] Ibid., 63ff.

am-Main, Dresden, and Berlin that concern us here.[7] Rather, in this chapter it is his theological contributions, as they relate to the antinomian question, which shall direct our discussion of this highly influential figure in Lutheran theology.

Far more so than in the previous chapter, it is easy for the student of Spener to see where and how the antinomian question influenced his theology. He was living at a time, possibly more so than at any other time, when Lutheran orthodoxy had been firmly established and was vigorously defended throughout Germany. And yet, perhaps more than at any other time as well, vice reigned throughout the empire under the guise of Christian freedom. For one who firmly believed Luther's gospel, it was a most sad state of affairs. "If we limit ourselves to our Evangelical church, which according to its outward confession embraces the precious and pure gospel, brought...[by] that blessed instrument of God, Dr. Luther...we cannot turn our eyes upon it without having quickly to cast them down again in shame and distress."[8]

One of the key problems, which Spener correctly identified, was the abuse of that freedom which Luther had described so eloquently during the previous century. It was the abuse, not the freedom, to which he pointed in order to explain the sad state of affairs. Luther had done his job well; it was the godless who had corrupted his meaning. The fundamental problem was clear. Faith had come to be understood in such a way that salvation was assured to those who verbally confessed the gospel regardless of the state of their hearts or how they lived their lives.

> How many there are who live such a manifestly unchristian life...and yet pretend to
> be firmly convinced that they will be saved in spite of all this! If one asks on what
> they base their expectation one will discover, as they themselves confess, that they
> are sure of this because it is of course not possible to be saved on account of one's
> life, but that they believe in Christ and put all their trust in him, that this cannot fail,
> and that they will surely be saved by such faith. Accordingly they have a fleshly
> illusion of faith (for godly faith does not exist without the Holy Spirit, nor can such
> faith continue when deliberate sins prevail) in place of the faith that saves.[9]

The question for Spener, as for all of the Pietists, was a simple one. How does one make *bekennende Christen* into *tätige Christen*, confessing Christians into active Christians? Spener was unique among the German

---

[7]For those looking for a biography of Spener in English, Stein (cited above) is the only real option. In German, Paul Grünberg's three volume *Philipp Jakob Spener* (Göttingen: Vandenhoeck & Ruprecht, 1893–1906), reprinted as the first three volumes in *PJSS*, remains the unsurpassed authority.

[8] *PD*, 40.

[9] *PD*, 64.

Pietists and their sixteenth century predecessors in that he was the first to offer a specific plan and agenda, and for this reason he is considered by many to be the Father of German Pietism, if not of Pietism as a whole. Spener described this simple plan in a little work entitled *Pia Desideria*, an occasional piece that has undergone countless printings and is read around the world by seminarians, clergy, and students of religion to this day. It requires no penchant for exaggeration to agree with Johannes Wallmann that between the publication of the Formula of Concord in the sixteenth century and Schleiermacher's *Reden über die Religion* in the nineteenth, no other work matches the importance in church history of this small piece by Spener.[10]

With good reason, Wallmann and Peter Erb declare that the dawn of the Pietist awakening can be given the precise date of Sep. 8, 1675, the date Spener's *Pia Desideria* was published;[11] the full title of which read: *Pia Desideria, or a Heartfelt Desire for a God-pleasing Reform of the True Evangelical Church, Together with Several Simple Christian Proposals Looking Toward this End*. Originally penned as an introduction to a republication of Arndt's sermons, Spener's short work laid out what he believed to be the problems in the church as well as a detailed program that would help effect their solution. In so doing, Wallmann tells us, Spener unleashed the Lutheran Pietist movement.[12] The response was enthusiastic. There was an immediate call for the work to be printed as an independent booklet, and within four years of its initial release Spener had received more than three hundred letters supporting his agenda, alongside the published support of fellow theologians and clergy.[13]

While written early in his career, the rather short *Pia Desideria* contained the fundamentals of Spener's lifelong plan for the renewal of his beloved Lutheran church. According to Stoeffler, it was in this text that the "essence of what Spener thought and hoped to accomplish was adequately summed up."[14] For this reason, along with the fact that the *Pia Desideria* is the most familiar and accessible of Spener's works today, this chapter will follow the outline of this text in discussing Spener's theological contribution to understanding and responding to the antinomian question. The six

---

[10] Johannes Wallmann, "Postillenvorrede und *Pia Desideria* Philipp Jakob Speners," in *Der Pietismus in Gestalten und Wirkungen* (Bielefeld: Luther-Verlag, 1975), 466.

[11] Peter C. Erb, "Pietist Spirituality: Some aspects of Present Research," in *The Roots of the Modern Christian Tradition*, (Kalamazoo: Cistercian Publications, Inc., 1984), 250.

[12] Wallmann, "Postillenvorrede," 466.

[13] See John Pustejovsky, "Philipp Jakob Spener," *Dictionary of Literary Biography* (Detroit: Gale Research Inc., 1996) 164:321–329.

[14] Stoeffler, *Evangelical Pietism*, 232.

proposals found in the text represent the foundation of Spener's plan to address the excesses he saw in the evangelical church. Using these proposals, then, to guide us through his work, we will consider the various approaches that Spener took to the perennial theological problem we have undertaken to address. Admittedly, this is something of a false construct, as not every proposal Spener made was dealing directly with the antinomian question. As a result, certain of these proposals—the early ones in fact—will receive more attention than others. I do believe, however, that each of the six topics addressed by Spener in this text can direct us to elements of his thought that do bear directly on the questions we are asking in this project. Thus, I do not want to claim that Spener's only concern in *Pia Desideria* was the antinomian question. Nevertheless, I would insist that this issue can be found in the background of each proposal he made in this, his brief *tour de force*.

Proposal One

"Thought should be given to a *more extensive use of the Word of God among us.*"[15] It was fitting for Spener to begin his program of Christian renewal with reference to the Holy Scriptures. Not only did he, like the orthodox party of his time, hold the Bible to be the source and norm of all theology and the moral foundation for the Christian life,[16] but also, in the hierarchy of theological disciplines, biblical or exegetical theology was placed right at the top.[17] In relation to the antinomian question, the importance of the Christian scriptures is not difficult to see. The Word of God, for Spener, as for Luther and Melanchthon, contains a twofold message: law and gospel. Moreover, the word of God is not merely a religious text but a medium of the Holy Spirit.[18] Therefore, the believer who encounters the law in the Word of God is moved to true repentance as she looks into the mirror of God's demands for her life. This true repentance precludes any cynical scheming that might consider finding a backdoor to a continuing life of sin; true repentance desires an end to sinning, not an excuse for more. Likewise, the gospel message conveyed through the Word of God creates gratitude in the heart of the believer. The one who truly receives this message cannot in the same moment of thankfulness attempt to "pull a fast one" on Christ, who has laid down his life on behalf of the sinner. Granted there is no perfect repentance or unadulterated gratitude among believers in the church militant, but Spener

---

[15] *PD*, 87.
[16] See further *PJSS*, Grünberg, I, 388.
[17] See further Martin Brecht, *Geschichte des Pietismus* (Göttingen: Vandenhoeck & Ruprecht, 1993), 1:372.
[18] See *PD*, 63, 87.

was convinced that *"more extensive use of the Word of God"* would surely make a substantial difference in the lives of its hearers. More than we find in Melanchthon, Spener insisted on the importance of constant exposure to the message of the Bible—a commitment that Luther had held as well. To accomplish this, Spener had a few specific suggestions.

The Bible as Information

It is not sufficient to merely hear the Word of God or to read it for oneself; it must be reflected upon, contemplated, and personally appropriated. In relation to this, Spener stressed the difference between *buchstäblichen und lebendigen Erkenntnis* (literal and living knowledge) of the truths of Christianity. Elsewhere he distinguished between *historische und lebendige* (historical and living) faith, of which, he taught, it is only the latter that saves.[19] Spener believed that most Christians hold only this former faith, a knowledge of the facts of salvation that lacks the saving power that comes with true faith and understanding of the gospel. Thus, for faith to be complete, it must contain three elements: 1.) *Erkentnus oder Wissenschaft* (realization), 2.) *Beifall* (approval), and 3.) *Zuversicht oder das Vertrauen* (confidence).[20] Unfortunately, few individuals have the three elements that make up genuine saving faith. The majority of the people in congregations only have a literal knowledge of Christianity that does not penetrate to their hearts through the working of the Holy Spirit. While they may subscribe to the same tenets of faith as the truly faithful, they are loyal only to the *fides quae creditur* (the faith in which we believe) rather than the *fides qua creditur* (the faith by which we believe).[21] As Spener expressed himself in a sermon entitled, *"On the Office of the Holy Spirit"*:

> It is true, my dear person, the Lutheran faith is the true faith. It is the true doctrine
> which one should believe. However, this does not yet save you if the faith by which
> you accept such doctrine and therefore such heavenly light is not also in you.
> Indeed, you say, 'I likewise also believe in God and console myself with the merits
> of Christ; upon these I will live and die.' This is well spoken. I grant that true faith
> is in you. I only remind you of the words of Paul, 2 Corinthians 13:5: 'Examine
> yourselves; whether you are in faith; prove yourselves.'[22]

It should be clear from these references that Spener did not denigrate the importance of knowledge of the Christian faith in his insistence on its internal reality, unlike some of the more radical Pietists who followed him. It is not only that genuine belief *wants to learn* the articles of faith; there must

---

[19] *PJSS* II.2, 221.
[20] Ibid., 215.
[21] See further Stein, *Spener,* 171, and Grünberg, *PJSS,* I Grünberg, I, 444f.
[22] *PJSS* III.1, 583f.

be a *real understanding* of the work of Christ for true faith to exist.[23] Of course the exposition of the Christian faith requires more than the *Verkonfessionalisierung*, or rigid confessionalizing which the orthodox party had been accused of. Knowledge of doctrine must be accompanied by personal acceptance and trust in the faith proclaimed, i.e. personal appropriation. "Again, you hear the Word of God. This is good. But it is not enough that your ear hears it. Do you let it penetrate inwardly into your heart and allow the heavenly food to be digested there, so that you get the benefit of its vitality and power, or does it go in one ear and out the other?"[24]

Spener made concrete plans to assist believers and non-believers alike in allowing the law and gospel to penetrate into their hearts, to help them inwardly digest the claims that Christianity has made. Consider his "Meditation on the Suffering of Christ,"[25] in which he lays out a wonderful program for personal piety based on a threefold meditation on the sufferings of Christ. First, it is necessary to reflect on the *necessity* of Christ's suffering to remind oneself of one's sins. Second, whereas Christ's suffering was *sufficient*, the believer needs to reflect on the "deep use and fruit" that is gained from it. Third, insofar as Christ's suffering was a *holy suffering*, "we must look upon it with the same heartfelt intention to follow the example of that obedience in every way."[26] Thus, Spener provided his readers a specific plan by which they may not only renew their familiarity with the biblical account of the sufferings of Christ, but also may internalize and appropriate the message in a way that he believed would strengthen faith and the desire to live a pious life.

Likewise, in his attempt to help his audience make fruitful use of the time they spend reading the Word of God, he made sure to emphasize the importance of prayer. "We are to close off our reading with prayer so that the Holy Spirit might also hallow what we have read and seal it in us that not only do we hold the Word in our thoughts but that the Spirit's power might impress itself into our soul and that we might hold the Word in a good heart and bring forth fruit in patience."[27] Spener understood that the power of the Word of God lies not only in its message but in the medium of the Holy Spirit who brings that message to the reader. However, the Spirit does not bring the Word of God to a passive Christian, merely infusing the power of faith. No, the believer has already been a passive recipient of the grace of

---

[23] *PJSS* II.1, 293.
[24] *PD,* 66.
[25] *Selected Writings,* 76ff.
[26] Ibid., 78.
[27] Ibid., 72.

God at the initial point of justification. Throughout the rest of his life he must cooperate with the Spirit so that his salvation may be worked out with fear and trembling. Spener could not countenance the notion that the Bible is a magical book which, when its words are read, miraculously confers the grace of faith on the individual. While Luther taught the same thing, it is true, as Erich Beyreuther has pointed out, that the connection between the Word of God and the Spirit is stronger in Spener than it is in Luther. As Beyreuther explains, Spener was combating the *"lazy faith"* of his time.[28] The problem in the seventeenth century was that the orthodox had come to focus on the *content* of the biblical message to such a degree that conversion had become an intellectual process. Spener wanted to return attention to the will.[29] Through Spener's emphasis on the role of the Spirit in relation to scripture he was again able to conceive of the power of the Word being a spiritual rather than a cognitive phenomenon, correcting a misinterpretation of Luther—a misinterpretation that, as we saw in the first chapter, was repeated in many post-Kantian Luther studies. With this focus on the will rather than knowledge in faith, it is easy to understand why Spener insisted on prayer accompanying the reading of the Bible. If the power that resides in the Bible is primarily knowledge, the reader comes to trust in herself to understand the Word of God. However, if the Bible's power lies in its ability to change one's will, as Spener insisted, then the reading of Holy Scripture becomes a spiritual exercise, rather than intellectual. For this reason the believer needs to pray that the Spirit would assist in the changing of the will, for that is a task which God alone can perform.[30]

The Bible is indeed the source and norm of Christian life and doctrine. Nonetheless, Spener wanted to insist that we understand in this statement not only that it contains information that can save humanity, but that it holds the power to change the human will through the working of the Holy Spirit. Therefore he deemed it necessary that his audience understand that the reader of Scripture should not be a passive recipient of its power, but must cooperate with the Spirit through meditation and prayer in order that those who hear its message might enjoy the full effect of the Word of God. Where this is more fully accomplished, pious living and good intentions are bound to follow. Then who would even conceive of asking the antinomian question?

---

[28] Erich Beyreuther, *Geschichte des Pietismus* (Stuttgart: J.F. Steinkopf Verlag, 1978), 121.

[29] See further *PJSS*, Grünberg, I, 436.

[30] In connection with this, it becomes clear how the Pietists could claim that it was the orthodox who were Pelagian, for they were trying to afford faith (and subsequently salvation) through the exercise of their intellect alone.

Catechesis

While in his first call at Frankfurt, Spener decided that catechesis and the accompanying liturgical act of confirmation were in serious need of a revival. He decided at that time to do his part to encourage their active use, not only in Frankfurt but in the village churches connected with the city as well. Admittedly this was not a concern that sprung from Spener's own theological imagination. As Wallmann has pointed out, there was in the Alsatian tradition a particular importance attached to *Katechismus-unterrichts,* instruction in the catechism, already present. Spener's view that the teaching of the catechism "is not of less worth than the sermon" may have found its origin during his student years at Strassburg.[31]

What he did introduce was the idea of the senior pastor of a church as prestigious as Frankfurt doing the instruction himself. Wallmann describes how not a few parishioners in Frankfurt were surprised when the Senior and a doctor of theology took on this task; there were those in Dresden years later who took offense at this as well.[32] But Spener was undeterred. Catechesis was a passion of Spener, to which testifies the publication of his lengthy *Einältigen Erklärung* (*Simple Explanation*) of Luther's catechism and his *Catechismus-Predigten* (*Catechism-Sermons*).

Spener's style and content in catechesis was also somewhat unusual for his day. In 1678 he identified three points that are necessary in catechetical instruction: 1.) That one pay attention more to the meaning than to the words, 2.) That the catechesis should be based on the Bible, especially the New Testament, and 3.) That everything should address praxis.[33] His insistence on attention to *meaning* rather than *words* was one contributing factor in his decision to use the vernacular rather than Latin in instruction, a move for which he was attacked by various orthodox clergy.[34] Likewise, Spener found more harm than good in the practice of memorizing large portions of the Bible and catechism, believing that it caused an intellectual overload and stood in the way of simply reading and meditating on the meaning of the text. He firmly believed that piety came as a result of *reflection* on the Christian faith, the faith described by Luther, not simply *hearing* the words spoken. The edifying work of the Holy Spirit through the medium of Holy Scripture does not simply happen by allowing the ears to hear it, this being

---

[31] Johannes Wallmann, *Philipp Jakob Spener und die Anfänge des Pietismus* (Tübingen: J.C.B. Mohr / Paul Siebeck, 1970), 208f.

[32] Ibid., 210.

[33] Ibid., 212.

[34] For Spener's defense of this practice see Koppel S. Pinson, *Pietism as a Factor in the Rise of German Nationalism* (New York: Octagon Books, 1968), 164f.

the dangerous teaching of *opus operatum* found in the Roman church. Rather, the Word must be inwardly digested so that the hearer receives the full benefit of its power.[35] "Insofar as piety is concerned, its practice is often reduced to the requirements that children learn by memory and repeat prayer formulae, but their words have an empty ring and are repeated without thought or understanding for they do not know what the significance of those words is and are not required to follow then through in life."[36]

Spener appears to have become aware of this need for a less cognitive approach to catechesis in 1677. It was in that year that the alchemist Merkerius von Helmont paid Spener's catechism class a visit. While von Helmont was impressed with what he saw, he shared his host's concern with making the information that the students were receiving more than simply knowledge of truth claims. He asked Spener three times, "But how are we going to bring the head into the heart?" This crucial question led Spener to reflect on how best to help children appropriate their lessons. Memorization was subsequently limited to the questions and answers in Luther's *Small Catechism* and certain essential Bible verses.[37]

Collegia Pietatis

Spener's most well known contribution to the life of the church, his *collegia pietatis*, or conventicle groups, was the cause of considerable attention during his lifetime. Part and parcel of Lutheran Pietism, these were vigorously attacked by his orthodox opponents, whose fears turned out in many cases to be justified. While the small groups experienced varying amounts of support and incrimination, the nature and design of Spener's model was geared toward the very Luther-an goal of familiarizing the laity with the Word of God and the subsequent increase in piety that should follow from that. Beyreuther, in discussing these meetings, explains that behind Spener's entire undertaking stood the deep concern over the dangerous menace of a crisis of faith into which Europe had slid at that time.[38]

In a sermon he gave on October 3, 1669, six years before the publication of *Pia Desideria,* Spener commented, "How much good it would do if good friends would come together on a Sunday and instead of getting out glasses, cards, or dice would take up a book and read from it for the edification of all or would review something from sermons that were heard."[39] The following

---

[35] See *PD*, 66f.
[36] Spener, from his "On Hindrances to Theological Studies," 1680, as in *Pietists: Selected Writings,* ed. Peter C. Erb (New York: Paulist Press, 1983), 65f.
[37] See Stein, *Spener*, 81.
[38] Beyreuther, *Geschichte*, 95.
[39] *PD*, 10.

year Spener began meeting in his home twice per week, on Sundays and Wednesdays, with such small groups. These assemblies came to be known as *collegia pietatis* (gatherings for piety) or *"Frankfurt conventicles."* The gatherings would begin with prayer, continue with the reading of a selection from a sermon, the New Testament, or some other edifying literature for discussion, and end with the singing of a hymn. While both men and women were allowed to attend, they did not sit together, nor were women permitted to speak. In 1675 the use of non-biblical readings was discarded and only the Word of God was read in the meetings. By 1682 the groups were attracting hundreds of interested participants, necessitating a move from Spener's home to one of the city churches.[40]

The idea for such gatherings did not come from Spener. Precedent for them was found throughout Europe, and even, as we shall see, in Luther himself. Actual meetings were taking place throughout both the Lutheran and Reformed countries at a time when loose ecclesiastical control allowed such gatherings to exist unchecked. A Dutch movement known as the Collegiants, begun by the Van der Kodde brothers, combined Reformed theology with mystical elements in their small gatherings. While there was no overt connection with Pietism in this early group, there were those Reformed Pietists who did make their way in and out of these groups.[41] More immed- iately, the followers of the Frenchman Labadie, already mentioned above, had been gathering in small groups for years. While the degree to which Spener's *collegia pietatis* found their inspiration in Labadie's conventicles is open to debate, it would be hard to deny the significant impact of Labadie's work on the young Spener (who had spent considerable time in Geneva).

Within Lutheranism as well, the idea of small devotional groups was hardly a late seventeenth century innovation. Martin Bucer had published a tract entitled *Verteidigung der sogenannten Collegiorum Pietatis* (*Defense of the So-called Pious Groups*) defending this practice in sixteenth century Lutheran Strassburg. Various groups of this nature had existed throughout evangelical Europe during the seventeenth century, including a conventicle connected to a Lutheran congregation in Amsterdam, which Spener had become aware of as a student.[42] These devotional groups were nothing new to the Protestant peoples of Europe, and so Spener can hardly be credited with their introduction. However, his contribution in regard to these

---

[40] See further Stein, *Spener*, 86; Pustejovsky, *"Philipp Jakob Spener,"* 325; Ted A. Campbell, *The Religion of the Heart: A Study of European Religious Life in the Seventeenth and Eighteenth Centuries* (Columbia: University of South Carolina Press, 1991), 84f.

[41] See further Stoeffler, *Evangelical Pietism*, 176ff.

[42] See further, Stein, *Spener*, 86.

conventicles is hardly of secondary importance. It was Spener who concretized their formulation, proposed their widespread implementation, and
readily stressed their importance. Pinson correctly points out that there
"undoubtedly were private gatherings before Spener.... But it was Spener
who made it the central institution of Pietist religious organization and
life."[43]

The idea behind the conventicles was simple. The more time that people
spend reading and reflecting on the Word of God, the stronger their faith will
become and, as a result, the more pious their behavior will be. The forum of
the small group would allow them more time to reflect on the lessons, ask
questions, and discuss the meaning and implications of the text under
consideration. "In a short time they would experience personal growth and
would also become capable of giving better religious instruction to their
children and servants at home."[44]

As was noted in the previous paragraphs, the focus of the groups came to
be on reading the Bible itself. While other edifying literature certainly
communicates the good news of salvation, Spener remained very focused on
the Bible itself as the very Word of God through which the Holy Spirit is
active. Years later, in Dresden, after two young theological students created
another group dedicated to the study of the scriptures, a *collegium
philobiblicum*, Spener reacted negatively to the group's "scientific society
flavor" and minimal focus on the practical use of the Bible's teaching.[45] For
Spener, the all-important study of the Bible should never become an
intellectual exercise; it must remain a practical activity oriented toward the
Christian life. In speaking of the *collegia pietatis*, Spener declared, "The
Word of God remains the seed from which all that is good in us must grow.
If we succeed in getting the people to seek eagerly and diligently in the book
of life for their joy, their spiritual life will be wonderfully strengthened and
they will become altogether different people."[46]

Spener's experiment with the conventicles enjoyed mixed success. As
we have already seen, what began as a small gathering of the faithful in
Spener's home soon blossomed, forcing the group to seek a larger meeting
space. As news of the group spread, similar groups were proposed in other
cities. Between the years 1670 and 1674, Spener found himself in dialogue
with colleagues in the free cities of the nearby Schwäbisch-Fränkish region
of Germany about starting similar groups. Likewise, his work drew the

---

[43] Pinson, *Pietism*, 112f.
[44] *PD*, 90.
[45] Stein, *Spener*, 114ff.
[46] *PD*, 91.

attention of those in Augsburg, Windsheim, Rothenburg, Schweinfurt, Nürnberg, Ulm, and Regensburg.[47] In 1677, the faculty at the University of Tübingen gave their stamp of approval to Spener's suggestion that *collegia pietatis* be established for students of theology. Perhaps the greatest testimony to the success of these groups is their continued prevalence today. Nearly every Protestant church in the United States today (and not a few among Roman Catholics) has weekly Bible studies, cell groups, or devotional gatherings. Pious gatherings for the purpose of reading the scriptures and mutual edification are as commonplace as baptismal fonts, and generally more visible. While we do not want to place all of the credit for this phenomenon with Spener, it would be a mistake not to see him as a chief architect of their design.

If there was success in the practice of *collegia pietatis*, there was also excess. From the very beginning there were concerns and criticisms of these extra-ecclesial organizations. Many among the orthodox opponents of Pietism saw a great danger in the new conventicles. The separatist mentality of those in these groups, when coupled with their own tendencies toward self-righteousness, created a vile mix in the eyes of those seeking to hold the Lutheran church to its traditional moorings. Jean Labadie himself had abandoned his earlier orthodox Calvinism in favor of a more radical, separatist enthusiasm, and there were those in Lutheranism who feared the same could happen in Germany *en masse* thanks to Spener's proposals. The fears were not unfounded. In 1676, Johann Jakob Schütz, a member of Spener's original *collegium,* refused to receive the Eucharist because of the "unworthy" parishioners who were receiving it alongside him. Schütz eventually even stopped attending worship altogether. In 1675, a number of the Pietists in Frankfurt declared the majority of the clergy to be unworthy of their calling. They proceeded to state their preference for receiving the sacrament in their meetings, thereby avoiding Communion with the many unworthy congregants who were not part of their group. By 1682 they had officially separated from the church. At other Pietist conventicles begun by Spener, the simple and practical study of the scriptures gave way to readings from the Book of Revelation and mystical works by Oetinger, Hahn, Bengel and others. The interests and overtones of the group "lent themselves to all sorts of mystical *Schwärmerei* [spiritual enthusiasm]."[48] The groups appeared to be getting out of hand, abandoning Spener's original plan for modest reflection on and discussion of law and gospel in the Bible, and becoming elitist clubs for religious enthusiasts. The orthodox party's fears were in

---

[47] Beyreuther, *Geschichte*, 93.
[48] Pinson, *Pietism*, 51.

many cases being realized. We can hardly be surprised, then, when we discover that the Saxon government, on March 10, 1690, issued an edict that forbade conventicles as well as the promotion of Pietism by any faculty or students.[49]

Spener shared the concerns of his orthodox opponents in this regard. He recognized that what began as a fruitful and well-intentioned venture was in many cases getting out of control. In 1685 he published a work, *Der Klagen über das verdorbene Christenthum mißbrauch und rechter gebrauch* (*The Abuse and Proper Use of the Complaints Concerning Corrupted Christianity*) in which he argued that those who are able to see the weaknesses of the church are obligated to stay within its ranks and serve. Furthermore, in the spirit of Luther and Augustine, he insisted that sharing the sacraments with those who are unworthy does not minimize the efficacy or value of the Eucharist. We can also understand from this why Spener felt moved to distance himself from the later writings of Labadie, clarifying that he approved only of the Frenchman's tracts written during his time in Geneva and not the more separatist works he published in the Netherlands.[50] His willingness to clarify his position and rebuke those who were abusing the conventicle system was appreciated by those who otherwise opposed his Pietist agenda. Valentin Löscher, the vigorous but fair opponent of all things Pietist, confessed, "It must be said to his credit that Dr. Spener endured very well in this first test. He not only withdrew from these separatists, but he also worked against them, although with too little zeal."[51]

Summary

What one finds here is a vigorous attempt on the part of Spener to reinvigorate the Christian community not only through increasing the use of the Bible in worship, catechesis, and weekly meetings, but through a renewed emphasis on appreciating the meaning of the Word of God. Spener's insistence that the reading of the scriptures needs to be accompanied by meditation, reflection, questioning, and prayer lent itself to a more complete program for Christian renewal which was designed to assist believers in their life of faith.

The reader can certainly perceive that in most of the suggestions that Spener made in regard to the use of the Word of God, there is a strong compatibility with the thought of Luther. His insistence that the Bible needs

---

[49] See Stein, *Spener*, 118.

[50] *PJSS* XV.1, 245f.

[51] Valentin Ernst Löscher, *The Complete Timotheus Verinus* (Milwaukee: Northwestern Publishing House, 1998), 1:17.

to be in the vernacular and in the hands of the people comes straight out of the work of the Reformer. The need to personally appropriate the claims of Christianity and not simply parrot them is, likewise, a constant theme in Luther. Even the conventicles find precedent in Luther who, in 1526, discussed an institution "which a truly Evangelical Church should have [and] would not be held in a public place for all sorts of people, but for those who mean to be real Christians and profess the gospel with hand and mouth. They would gather together to pray, read, baptize, receive the sacrament, and do other Christian works."[52]

As discussed above, and as Grünberg has pointed out, Spener regarded the authority of scripture as more spiritual than mechanical. He focused more on its content than on its form.[53] This concern for and emphasis on the spiritual aspect of the Word of God was part of a plan to enliven the message of Christ, to move it from the realm of the intellect to that of the will. Whether or not he remained loyal to the fundamentals in Luther's theology is not an easy question to answer. At the very least, this theological direction of Spener's cannot be understood as compromising Luther's emphasis on *sola fide*. Moreover, as we saw in the first chapter, there has been perpetual disagreement as to what sort of balance between the intellect and the will vivified by the Holy Spirit adequately reflects Luther's thought. What is agreed upon is that Luther held these two components together. Insofar as Spener attempted to move theology away from sterile intellectualizing about the claims of Christianity without minimizing the importance of knowledge of the tenets of faith, it would be difficult to imagine that his position fell far from that of the "blessed instrument of God, Dr. Luther."

Proposal Two

"Our frequently mentioned Dr. Luther would suggest another means, which is altogether compatible with the first. This second proposal is *the establishment and diligent exercise of the spiritual priesthood.*"[54] It was in 1520 that Luther developed and expressed his doctrine of the priesthood of all believers. Most clearly articulated in his polemic of that year, *To the Christian Nobility of the German Nation Concerning the Reform of the Christian*

---

[52] *LW* 53:63f. One of the crucial differences between Luther's plan and Spener's *collegia pietatis* was in Luther's suspicion that his own proposal was a dangerous one. He predicted that, "If I should begin it myself, it may result in a revolt. For we Germans are untamed, crude, boisterous folk with whom one ought not lightly start anything except under the compulsion of a very great need." *LW* 53, 64.
[53] *PJSS*, Grünberg, I, 409.
[54] *PD*, 92.

Estate, Luther wanted Christians to understand the full extent of the benefits that come with being a child of God. Rome had for too long hobbled the spiritual life of believers by placing all authority, power, and privilege in the hands of the clergy while laity were reduced to observers of the power of God with certain moral responsibilities. Luther's insistence that all Christians share the privilege of being priests before God, able to approach the throne of grace with confidence, was intended to empower others as much as it had empowered him.

Later Lutheranism unfortunately lost sight of this spiritual advantage. The priesthood of all believers was, more or less, returned to the clergy alone. Lutheran parishioners came to be as passive and uninvolved in the spiritual functions of the Church as they had been under Rome. It was much easier for everyone involved if those with the clerical collars were to take on the sole function and responsibility of shepherd to the flock. Luther's aspiration for an invigorated body of believers was settling back to the reality of a comfortable hierarchy between pastor and parish. Helmut Blume, in describing the life of the Lutheran worshipper in the late sixteenth century, describes the changes that had taken place. "From responsible member of the congregation and participant in the service, the individual proceeded to entertained listener and private worshipper, from 'doer of the Word' to 'hearer alone'—and beyond that to contemplative observer."[55] The Thirty Years War did even more damage to whatever remained of the role of the laity as spiritual priests within the community. Donald Nevile explains, "After the restoration of peace, the Lutheran Church emerged from the ashes, but its worship showed an even more severely mechanical and legalistic character."[56]

Spener's intention in the mid- to late-seventeenth century was to revive Luther's concept of a spiritual priesthood. With his forebear he believed that the Roman Church's stark delineation between the roles of laity and clergy was actually demonic. "Indeed, it was a special trick of the cursed devil that things were brought to such a pass in the papacy that all these spiritual functions were assigned solely to the clergy."[57] Luther had well understood the importance of all Christians sharing in the spiritual functions that belong to the Church, maintained, of course, within an organized and structured

---

[55] Helmut Blume, "The Age of Confessionalism" in *Protestant Church Music* ed. Helmut Blume (New York: W.W. Norton & Co., 1974), 149.
[56] Donald Nevile, "Pietism and Liturgical Worship: An Evaluation," *Consensus* 16, no.2 (1990): 91–106.
[57] *PD*, 93.

framework.[58] However, while Luther focused on the *benefits* that this afforded believers, Spener wanted his parishioners to remember the *responsibilities* that followed as well. The greatest of these, in Spener's mind and writings, was the spiritual responsibility of accountability. "Let us therefore be diligent in investigating ever more deeply our own shortcomings and those of the rest of the church in order that we may learn to know our sickness, and then with a fervent invocation of God for the light of his Spirit let us also search for and ponder over remedies."[59] With this call for self-examination and mutual accountability, Spener hoped to invigorate the spiritual lives of those in his congregations. By holding the mirror of the law more directly in front of our fellow believers and ourselves, he believed, we come to recognize more clearly our own iniquity, the great gift of the forgiveness of sins, and where our lives need to change. Greater accountability is not an answer *per se* to the antinomian question. It does, however, lead a person to consider the implications of what one sees in oneself. Self-examination can reveal the sin in one's life that is being forgiven; it may also reveal a problem with one's saving faith itself.

The first function of self-examination, as mentioned above, can be to strengthen faith through the increased awareness of one's sin and one's dependency on the grace of God. This aspect of Spener's plan preempts the antinomian question. The stronger one's faith, the more nonsensical such a proposition becomes. Spener wanted Christians to take very seriously the requirement to diligently search their hearts. It is not enough merely to engage in good deeds. One must follow such acts of love with an honest examination of one's motives in order to differentiate between what is done out of self-interest and what is done out of love for God.[60] Stein explains that the motivation must match the deed for one to identify genuine acts of love. "Significant in Spener's appeal for diligent love of neighbor and for avoidance of self-love was his stress on motivation. Christians were to test their impulses toward doing good works by sharing them with a trusted confessor, reporting regularly on how opportunities to practice Christian love were taken or neglected."[61]

While Spener's discussions of self-examination and determining one's motives appear at times to suggest the possibility that one can purify one's intentions through hard work, Spener would have denied this. While much of what he writes on this subject can lend itself to this rather optimistic view of

---

[58] Ibid.
[59] Ibid., 37
[60] Ibid., 96.
[61] Stein, *Spener*, 100.

human potential—one with which Luther would have had strong disagreements—Spener insisted that the more one grows in faith and awareness of oneself, the more sin one discovers. Spener's own self-examination did not lead him to greater self-congratulation. "On the contrary, I recognize more and more how deficient I myself am."[62]

Spener firmly believed that a greater awareness of one's sin would bring about more dependency on God and recognition of what behavior one needs to change. Thus, self-examination is one way to combat the over-inflated estimation of one's own moral worthiness that exists among many believers. At the same time, however, he had serious reservations about the practice of private confession. For confession to function as a truly life-changing event within the Christian life the sinner has to be truly penitent. The danger always exists that the confessor may grant absolution to one who has not truly repented, thereby offering false security to a false Christian.[63] Private confession can easily become a vehicle of libertinism insofar as all that is required for absolution from the pastor is a confession of sins and the desire for forgiveness. True repentance can never be assured and so the danger of false security—the foundation of the antinomian question—remains. Nonetheless, as one might expect, Spener certainly did not call for the abolition of the confessional, although he continued to view it with a suspicious eye.[64]

If self-examination can motivate a person to a life of piety through gentle encouragement, it can also do so through fear. Spener did not only envision his parishioners being accountable for their moral weaknesses, but for the condition of their faith as well. This latter concern was a much more serious consideration, as it calls into question one's salvation. Self-awareness and humility are one side of the coin of personal accountability; the other is the fear of damnation.

Spener did not think of the situation in which one might lose one's faith as a mere theoretical possibility. Rather, he believed it to be an extremely common phenomenon. Insofar as he was a loyal Lutheran, he insisted that infant baptism conveys genuine rebirth, the forgiveness of sin, and saving faith. In Lutheran Germany, of course, the vast majority of children were welcomed into the Church through baptism at a very early age. The reason that the truly faithful were so few in number among adults was that most people lose, or reject, the faith given them as infants. Whereas small children do not have the mental capacity to resist God's grace, they truly receive the

---

[62] *PD*, 45.
[63] *PJSS*, XI.1, 85.
[64] Stein, *Spener*, 141.

blessings of the sacrament. However, those who do not live a life of service to God as required by their baptism lose the saving faith that they had received; and this is the condition of most of Christendom.[65] This being the case, Spener wanted to be clear that one cannot rely on one's Baptism alone for assurance of salvation. The adult who was baptized as an infant needs to constantly reflect on whether or not her life manifests the work of the Spirit. If this is lacking, she needs to consider what might be hindering or undermining her faith, or whether there is any faith still present.

In relation to this discussion of self-examination, Spener described different types of sins. A fuller understanding of the specific nature of one's sins, Spener believed, would allow his congregants a deeper insight to the state and condition of their faith—if they indeed still have such faith. In his *Catechismuspredigten* (Catechism sermons) of 1689 he discussed this very important aspect of his thought in a section entitled, *von der Sünde* (on sin).[66] Here he began by reestablishing that sin broadly conceived can be divided into two types: original sin and actual sin. Original sin is the cause of all other sins and remains within the Christian believer until the moment of death. Actual sin is doing what God forbids, or not doing what he commands. In these definitions he remains very close to Luther. However, as this section unfolds, we find him going much further than Luther in discussing the phenomenon of sin in human life.

Spener goes on to explain that there are two types of actual sin: sins of weakness (*Schwachheit-sünde*) and sins of malice (*Boßheit-sünde*).[67] Sins of weakness are those that do not rule (*herrschen*) a person. They are done either in ignorance or in haste, without thought or intention when emotion takes over or one is temporarily swayed by some other persuasion. Spener explains that the man who commits such a sin of weakness does not remain in it, or, when he realizes what he has done, has no pleasure in his behavior, wishes it had never happened, and is truly sorry in his heart. These sins, Spener explains, are found among the faithful and the pious, and even the greatest Christians struggle with them; Romans 7 and Galatians 5:17 are cited as evidence for this. Sins of weakness, as genuine sins, still deserve eternal punishment, but are covered by the blood of Christ when committed by Christians.

Sins of malice, on the other hand, are much more serious business. These are sins that are performed consciously, having been premeditated, and do not result in any sorrow on the part of the sinner. Also called willful sins

---

[65] *PJSS*, III.1, 87.
[66] *PJSS*, II.2, 166ff.
[67] Ibid., 172ff. See also *PJSS* II.1, 266.

(*Müthwillige-sünde*), Spener believed that these sins are common only to the unregenerate (*Unwiedergebohrnen*). Subsequently, when one who has faith commits such sins, both the Holy Ghost and divine mercy are lost. He becomes like one who was never baptized and is now in need of a new conversion with heartfelt repentance for saving faith to be restored.[68] Already in 1677 he had explained that such sin is the *todt-sünde,* or deadly sin, for which one becomes the subject of God's anger and condemnation.[69]

While one reason for this delineation of actual sins was the need to explain the admittedly difficult passages of I John 1:8 and 3:6,8,9, Spener had more ambitious intentions with this formulation. With this twofold understanding of actual sin, Spener believed he could more effectively respond to the libertine, false faith that was filling his parishes and his countrymen with false security. Of course, Spener would maintain, the faithful commit sins throughout their earthly pilgrimage. However, these are only sins of weakness for which they immediately experience sorrow and regret. Those who are consciously committing sins without any intention to change are demonstrating that their faith is not genuine. When he poses the question, "Can you have true faith which serves sin and does not with vigorousness make a great effort toward divine blessedness?" he answered with an emphatic *"No!"*[70]

By dividing actual sins into those of weakness and malice, he gives the most direct response we have yet encountered to the antinomian question. He answered Paul's interlocutor by explaining that he will indeed continue to sin by accident and in moments of weakness. However, if he makes the conscious decision to violate the law of God, he is demonstrating that he has no conscience about rejecting the Word of God and the testimony of the Holy Spirit. Such an act is either the rejection of true faith or an indicator that it has already been rejected. In his own version of the antinomian question, Spener asks, "Can someone read the scriptures, put their trust in Christ, and still serve sin?" He answered, "Yes, it happens all the time." It is in the following question that Spener shoots down the hopes of the libertine. "Is that not then a true faith? [Answer]: No. It is only an historical, dead faith and a fleshly security."[71]

While Spener offers in these definitions of sin a bold and innovative response to the antinomian question, he has also made an equally bold deviation from the theology of Luther at the same time, albeit probably

---

[68] Ibid. 174ff.
[69] *PJSS*, II.1, 268.
[70] Ibid. 294.
[71] Ibid., 296.

unwittingly. Luther could not be clearer in his treatise *Against Latomus*[72] that there is only one type of actual sin. While some of his comments suggest that he allows for this type of delineation of sins, as when he writes, "Thus sin in us after baptism is in its nature truly sin; but only according to substance, and not in its quantity, quality, or action, for it is wholly passive," such a conclusion would be inaccurate.[73] One needs to note that Luther refers here to sin after baptism, not sin committed by the faithful. The difference in language is subtle but important. When Luther speaks of the power of baptism, he is referring to the declarative power of Christ that transforms our status in the eyes of God. Thus, his point in the quote above is that after baptism sin loses its power to declare the sinner guilty, not that it becomes a lesser type of sin. This point is brought out more clearly later in the same treatise when he writes about this sin, "but now it is sin without wrath, without the law, dead sin, harmless sin, as long as one perseveres in grace and his gift. As far as its nature is concerned, sin in no way differs from itself before grace and after grace; but it is indeed different in the way it is treated."[74]

As we saw in the first chapter, when Luther argues that the regenerate are *simul iustus et peccator*, he is saying that they are *extrinsically righteous* and *intrinsically sinful*, not a combination of the two, not *partly* righteous and *partly* sinful.[75] To do so removes the focal point for the assurance of salvation from God's Word of promise to human behavior. When Spener forces his readers to look to their own moral conduct as the sign of whether or not they are saved, he runs the serious risk of creating new Pharisees on the one hand and terrifying consciences on the other. By Spener's own admission, those who are more mature in faith become more aware of their sins. Luther would insist, then, that these are also the ones who are most likely to recognize their own willful sinfulness—a sinfulness that Luther insisted all Christians continue to suffer with until they join the Church triumphant.

Stein is right on target when he admits that, "In some sense Spener had a less firm grasp on the ontological reality of sin."[76] As Stein explains, this optimistic view of the moral life of the redeemed was fueled by Spener's

---

[72] "First of all, do not doubt that 'sin' is used in Scripture in a single very simple way, not in many different ones." *LW* 32, 195. And again, "one sin is no more a sin than is another." Ibid., 202.

[73] Ibid., 207.

[74] Ibid., 229.

[75] See further, Alister E. McGrath, *Iustitia Dei*, Second Edition (Cambridge: Cambridge University Press, 1998), 209.

[76] Stein, *Spener*, 262.

desire "to prevent the enervation of Christian discipleship through the teaching of 'cheap grace.'" In so doing, Spener erred on two fronts. First, he supposed that actual sin can be divided into two types, with the regenerate only committing the less serious of the two sins. This would have been completely unacceptable to Luther, for whom the power and reality of sin, both in believers and unbelievers, was essential to his theology. Secondly, by insisting that conscious sinning results in the rejection of faith and the loss of mercy, he weighs down consciences in a way that likewise would have resulted in the unleashing of Luther's furious pen during the previous century. It is true that Luther maintained a place for self-examination, which could certainly lead one to conclude that faith is no longer present. However, for Luther this self-analysis would focus more on whether one was fighting the battle and less on whether the battle was being won. When Christians come to trust in their own moral conduct rather than the promise of God for their salvation, the principle of *sola fide* is placed in serious jeopardy.

Proposal Three

"[T]he people must have impressed upon them and must accustom themselves to believing that *it is by no means enough to have knowledge of the Christian faith, for Christianity consists rather of practice.*"[77] This third proposal may have been the most shocking to those with strong orthodox Lutheran sensibilities. Can Spener be saying that works are necessary above and beyond the confession of faith that Christians make? It was this very issue that was the center of theological concern during Spener's time, and ambiguous statements, like this one, were fueling the controversy.

In the seventeenth century, Löscher wrote, "Spener's zeal not to leave souls in the sleep of carnal security, but to promote the earnestness of piety, was by all means praiseworthy. [However, he] employed many incautious ways of speaking about active faith (which he had taken from Arndt, Tauler, and the other mystics) as if this were the kernel of our Christian doctrine of God."[78] Spener was determined, then, to combat the "carnal security" that he believed had infected the Lutheran church. Insofar as one of his primary attacks on this contented moral degradation was an insistence that faith be living and active—especially active!—he invited much suspicion toward his teachings on faith and works.

Spener's concern that faith always be accompanied by obedience to God—the two being as interconnected as the sun and its rays—was of course

---

[77] *PD*, 95.
[78] Löscher, *Timotheus Verinus*, 16.

nothing new in Lutheranism. In the *Pia Desideria* he was able to quote the venerable Dr. Johann Gerhard:

> Those who are wanting in love of Christ and who neglect practice of piety do not obtain the fuller knowledge of Christ and more abundant gift of the Holy Spirit. Hence to obtain a genuine, living, active, and salutary knowledge of divine things it is not enough to read and search the Scriptures, but it is necessary that love of Christ be added, that is, that one beware of sins against conscience, by which an obstacle is raised against the Holy Spirit, and that one earnestly cultivate piety.[79]

Spener insisted repeatedly that for faith to be genuine it must manifest itself in good works. He believed that too many of his contemporaries wanted to enjoy the blessings of grace while refusing to uphold their end of the bargain by living a life of obedience. The problem with this approach to the Christian life is not so much that the contract is voided when the person refuses to obey, but that the refusal to obey is an indicator that the person does not have the requisite faith to receive God's blessings. Spener explains that where you have half a Christian—the one who receives the forgiveness of sins, but in whom there is no obedience—you have no Christian at all.[80] The obedience is not necessary in order to receive salvation, as if obedience is a reason for the gift, but must necessarily be present if the grace and gift of God's mercy are truly present. Spener does indeed maintain that one can differentiate between true and false faith based on whether or not works are present,[81] although he would encourage his listeners to be more concerned with themselves than their neighbors in this regard.

Regarding the statement of Melanchthon and the Majorists, discussed in the previous chapter, that "good works are necessary for salvation," we find Spener shying away from this language.[82] He did not want to use this expression for the same reason that Melanchthon eventually avoided its use as well; it holds too much potential for misunderstanding. Additionally, insofar as Spener insisted that he was an orthodox Lutheran, he could not overtly contradict the Book of Concord. As a result, the language of good works being necessary for salvation was put aside. He did, however, use language remarkably close to that of Melanchthon and Major, maintaining that pure teaching *and* a holy life are both necessary for salvation,[83] or that "good works are completely necessary."[84] In the end, it is safe to conclude that

---

[79] *PD*, 106.
[80] *PJSS*, XI.2, 693.
[81] *PJSS*, II.1, 299.
[82] *PJSS*, II.2, 193.
[83] *PJSS*, Grünberg, I, 452.
[84] *PJSS*, II.2, 192.

Spener would have agreed with Melanchthon that while this volatile statement may indeed be correct, properly understood, its potential for offense and abuse is large enough that it is better to avoid it altogether. The reason that he never made the same controversial claims as the early Melanchthon is simply that Spener was writing after 1580, the year the confessionally binding Book of Concord was released, while Melanchthon's works were all prior to that monumental year. Had Spener been a contemporary of Melanchthon, it would be difficult to imagine him opposing the *praeceptor's* early statements on the necessity of good works for achieving salvation.

Nonetheless, there were certain statements made by Spener that do not appear to jibe with his claims to adherence to the theology of Luther. For example, he would insist that, "Therefore, because faith is necessary, so also are works necessary."[85] While he did not say specifically "for salvation," the parallelism suggested in this sentence, while it does not repeat the forbidden words of Major, certainly suggests the same thing. Or consider what was written in the *Pia Desideria*: "Nor is it enough to be baptized, but the inner man, where we have put on Christ in Baptism, must also keep Christ on and bear witness to him in our outward life."[86] When this is compared with all that Luther said about the sufficiency of baptism, it is easy to see where the suggestion that Spener had abandoned the theology of *sola fide* could come from. Spener was fully aware of this, regretting that "those who zealously cultivate such godliness can hardly escape being suspected as secret papists, Weigelians, or Quakers."[87]

However, while some of the more vitriolic opponents of Pietism, like Johann Friedrich Mayer of St. James Lutheran Church in Hamburg, insisted that Spener had abandoned the message of the gospel, probably forfeiting his salvation in the process, Spener continued to insist on his own orthodoxy and commitment to the theology of Luther. And indeed there is much in his writings that even the most hard-core orthodoxist could take pride in.

When Spener writes about the initial justification of the sinner, he is very clear that this is entirely the work of the Spirit; the individual can never merit such a blessing or even the offer of grace. Moreover, sharing Luther's rejection of contemporary notions of free will, he could also insist, "[W]hen it comes to our believing and loving God, the human will is impotent. Luther had spoken correctly about the *servum arbitrium*, the 'bondage of the

---

[85] "*Also / weil der glaube nothwendig ist / so sind auch die werke nothwendig.*" Ibid., 193.
[86] *PD*, 117.
[87] Ibid., 47.

will.'"[88] While the unredeemed sinner has the freedom to go to church and listen to the sermon, like King Herod who chose to listen to the words of John the Baptist, still, the will is powerless to bring itself to faith.

If Spener held to such a Luther-an understanding of grace and salvation, one might ask, then, why he was so often the subject of vitriolic polemic that questioned his orthodoxy. The key to understanding Spener's more extreme statements about the necessity of works for salvation lies in his focus on the practical life of the Christian rather than the scholastic minutiae which concerned the Lutheran Orthodoxists. That is to say, Spener, when discussing faith and works, spoke about their relationship to the life of the believer as it is lived today, not at the initial point of justification. The point in time at which one is justified is over in an instant, and it is from that point on that the believer actively participates in the Christian life in cooperation with grace. As Grünberg explains, by combining justification and sanct-ification, and by talking about the latter as a process, he redirected focus from the one time event of justification to the present status of one being justified. Much of the misunderstanding and fighting that took place between the Orthodox and the Pietists is based on a failure to appreciate this differ-ence in emphasis. Spener's more radical statements about justification do fit into Luther's theological parameters once one understands that he is talking about *ein Akt, der immer fortgesetzt wird* (an act which is continual). It is within this framework that Grünberg believes Spener's words "we must walk in the light, if the blood of Christ is to purify us" must be understood.[89] And it is for this reason that Spener can discuss the absolute necessity of fighting sin in our lives, even citing Luther for evidence that the old Adam must be put to death if we are to inherit eternal life.[90]

For this reason, we may affirm that Spener remained very much within the boundaries of Luther's emphasis on *sola fide* within his discussion of faith and works; and we would be in very good company in doing so. Bey-reuther quotes Emanuel Hirsch with approval, who wrote, "Spener, making a conscious decision with untouchable honor and clarity, advocated the ortho-dox Lutheran teaching of justification."[91] Likewise, Martin Brecht insisted that Spener retained a Melanchthonian theory of justification, although he focused more on the role of the creation of the new man within that model.[92] Grünberg concurs, explaining that Spener is orthodox in speaking of works

---

[88] *PJSS* III.1.2, 1006f.
[89] *PJSS*, Grünberg, I, 449.
[90] *PJSS*, II.2, 218f.
[91] Beyreuther, *Geschichte*, 120.
[92] Brecht, *Geschichte*, 375.

as the necessary fruit of genuine faith; the difference with the Orthodox party is found in his emphasis on the necessity of love following from genuine faith.[93]

At the same time, Spener did express himself rather differently than orthodox Lutherans before him. Grünberg points out how Spener had insisted that Christians have *der ganze Christus* (the whole Christ) as the object of their faith. Jesus is not only to be the high priest who intervenes on our behalf, but the king who rules our lives and the prophet who proclaims the father's will as well. Half [or one third] of Christ is not the true Christ, Spener would insist.[94] And while one would not wish to carry this reasoning too far into the doctrine of justification, we can appreciate the point Spener was trying to make. Christ should be more to a Christian than a free ticket to absolution.

Spener's contribution to the antinomian question in his discussions of the role of faith and works was not insignificant. As with his first proposal, he was able to further clarify that faith is something more than knowledge of doctrinal positions. It is a living and active phenomenon which must manifest itself in good works and deeds of love if it is a genuine, saving faith. Moreover, by shifting discussions of justification from the initial moment of reconciliation to the ongoing life of faith, he succeeded in reminding his listeners that the Christian life can never be a passive event. It is not something that simply happens to Christians, but that which Christians help make happen. Cooperation, participation, and obedience are required for one to finish the good race. Admittedly, he was not always clear about this focus in his writings, lending himself to errant perceptions and accusations. However, in the end one would have to conclude that Spener's theological writings on the subject of faith and works were essentially loyal to that of Luther while even importing some new and fresh language into the discussion in his ongoing attempt to close up the moral loophole suggested in the antinomian question.

Proposal Four

"Related to this is a fourth proposal: *We must beware how we conduct ourselves in religious controversies* with unbelievers and heretics."[95] This proposal helped earned Spener a reputation as an indifferentist and dangerous ecumenist, although by contemporary definitions of those words

---

[93] *PJSS*, Grünberg, I, 451.
[94] Ibid., 445f.
[95] *PD*, 97.

we could by no means consider him as such. His willingness to consider non-Lutherans as brothers and sisters in Christ made him a theological pariah in the eyes of many of his orthodox contemporaries,[96] for whom polemics were the center of their theological agenda. Many at that time, however, found Spener's attitude refreshing:

> Controversies are not the only or the most important thing, although knowledge of them properly belongs to the study of theology. Not only should we know what is true in order to follow it, but we should also know what is false in order to oppose it. However, not a few stake almost everything on polemics. They think that everything has turned out well if only they know how to give answer to the errors of the papists, the Reformed, the Anabaptists, etc.[97]

We see, then, that Spener was not interested in removing theological polemics from the life of the Church, but placing them in a secondary role to the life of faith. He was most interested in inculcating humility and good doctrine in his churches, so that while the teachings of Luther would be respected, taught, and defended, they would not become an occasion for pride or encourage a mentality that emphasized a shrewd intellect and the desire for the conquest of an opponent.[98] Especially in our very ecumenical age, it is easy for us to sympathize with Spener who, during his career, repeatedly raised the question, "What good is it if our audience is free from all papist, Reformed, and Socinian errors, while at the same time having a dead faith."[99]

At the same time, there needs to be some appreciation for the reasons behind the extreme confessional approach among the Orthodox in the sixteenth and seventeenth centuries, with their rather intolerant approach to theological difference. As Albrecht Ritschl argues, the early, developing Protestant churches needed time to develop internally before actively engaging the ideas and theologies of the world around them. Like certain plants that initially grow abnormal, misshapen leaves to protect the young seed, the young Lutheran church needed these extreme protective measures to protect it while it developed its own form, structure, and identity. Later,

---

[96] Even the radical Pietist Gottfried Arnold received such a commendation from Spener. Löscher later regretted, "Dr. Spener does say that he wishes Arnold's *Ketzer-Historie* had never been published in that way. Yet he calls him a brother in the Lord." (*Timotheus Verinus*, 1:24) This was the type of duplicity that the orthodox at that time could not understand. In this same volume, Löscher labels as "indifferentism" the practice of those who recognize "papists, Calvinistic Reformed, and all kinds of enthusiasts as brothers in Christ and treat them as such." (Ibid., 1:52)

[97] *PD*, 49.

[98] Ibid., 100.

[99] *PJSS*, XIII.1, 294.

when the seed has grown hardy enough to survive in its environment, it sprouts more healthy, normal leaves that help it flourish in the world. "In comparison to the plant's own leaves, these protective leaves appear to be stunted or deformed, but at the same time they are indispensable and salutary for the first period of the plant's life."[100] Whether or not Spener would have agreed entirely with this model is uncertain. However, he clearly believed that the time for the mature leaves of Lutheranism to sprout and grow had come in the seventeenth century.

Spener believed that too much interdenominational conflict had been brought into the pulpit. The Orthodox had imported all manner of polemic into the life of the church without appreciating that not all theological errors have the same seriousness.[101] Many of the fierce controversies that erupted over theological minutiae, he believed, were not helpful but destructive for the Lutheran community. There was a certain need to distinguish between articles of faith that had *Nothwendigkeit* (necessity) and those that had *Entbehrlichkeit* (dispensability). Not every error in doctrine leads to damnation.[102]

Despite Spener's insistence that controversies and polemics should be minimized in theological writings, seminaries, and the parish, he was far from indifferent about matters of doctrine. Despite his willingness to consider people with highly controversial positions as brothers and sisters in Christ, he would hardly be confused with an ecumenist today. Pinson points out that Spener never went so far toward ecumenism as did Gottfried Arnold, who had the audacity to confess that there were positive elements in Roman Catholicism.[103] Moreover, Stein, who likewise rejects the notion that Spener was an active ecumenist, points out that Spener did not support the various union efforts that were attempted during the seventeenth century by people like Gottfried Leibnitz. Neither did Spener consider discussion of reunion with Rome to be worth pursuing; rather he considered it to be meaningless and dangerous.[104]

When analyzing Spener's zeal for religious tolerance, then, we must be careful to consider his statements within their historical context. When he criticized his contemporaries by quoting Gregory Nazianzen ("We are all godly people for this one reason that each one of us condemns the rest as

---

[100] Albrecht Ritschl, "'Prolegomena' to the *History of Pietism*," in *Three Essays*, trans. Philip Hefner (Philadelphia: Fortress, Press, 1972), 135.
[101] *PJSS*, II.2, 222f.
[102] See *PJSS*, Grünberg I, 415f.
[103] Pinson, *Pietism*, 85.
[104] Stein, *Spener*, 213.

godless,"[105]), he is by no means claiming that polemics, controversy, and condemnation of heresy have no place in the Church. His was a time during which these three practices had been elevated to an unacceptable level of practice and prominence, leading to theological arrogance and intolerance in secondary matters. This was a time during which the Duke of Braunschweig had declared that if his son became a Calvinist, he would declare that it was Satan himself who had sired him.[106] This was a time during which Lutherans believed that the Roman Catholics and Reformed possessed neither true doctrine or even the genuine sacraments.[107] This was a time during which Spener's unwillingness to grant that "anyone should be inflicted with worldly punishment for advancing erroneous blasphemy of God" drew condemnation from the orthodox, although he was partially excused for later advising that some "coarse seducers" should be imprisoned.[108] Spener was trying to find some middle ground. On the one hand, the Church needed polemicists to fight for the purity of doctrine. On the other, this should be reserved for serious theological difficulties, not tossed around as if for sport.

It may appear that this fourth proposal of Spener's does not fit very neatly into our discussion of the antinomian question. Perhaps so, but there are still some very important principles at work here that do bear directly on our concern regarding libertinism in Lutheranism. Behind much of Spener's criticism of the treatment of religious controversies lay a theme we have already discussed under his first proposal. The Christian faith must be about more than the intellectual component of religion. When theological controversies are placed center-stage in the life of the Church, it is the cerebral side of faith that receives undue emphasis. Additionally, polemics of this type always focus on what another is doing wrong. When this practice is overemphasized there can be little room left for the preaching of the law to the individual in the pew. While it may be true that the gospel message may be more clearly articulated, expressed, and refined through theological debate, this will frequently take place at the expense of the law. It is for this reason that religious controversies so easily lead to Pharisaism. Within this environment, as we saw in the quote from Gregory above, the more one condemns others, the more holy one believes oneself to be. This stands quite apart from Luther's model for the Christian life that begins with one's own *Anfechtung*, one's own struggle with sin, error, and temptation, not the struggle with someone else's. As a result, we can see why later Pietists

---

[105] *PD*, 49.

[106] Stoeffler, *Evangelical Pietism*, 184.

[107] Stein, *Spener*, 212.

[108] Löscher, *Timotheus Verinus*, 199f.

would actually accuse the Orthodoxists of Pelagianism. They alleged that it was the latter group who was trying to reach God through their own works, their own intellectual efforts.[109]

This being said, we must not forget that Spener found considerable room in the life of the Church for religious controversies.

> Before us are the holy examples of Christ, the apostles, and their successors, who engaged in disputation—that is, vigorously refuted opposing errors and defended the truth. The Christian church would be plunged into the greatest danger if anybody wished to remove and repudiate this necessary use of the spiritual sword of the Word of God, insofar as its use against false teachings is concerned.[110]

For Spener, as for most of the Pietists, there is a time and place for polemics, debate, and controversy. Sound doctrine is important. It is essential for the life of the Church, and there should always be people who fill this role within the community of the faithful.[111] A neglect of the intellectual defense of Christian doctrine would be an even worse tragedy for Spener than its overuse. Being deeply committed to the theological tradition that he inherited, he argued that incorrect teaching of the article of justification is a major cause of human depravity.[112] Good doctrine must be defended against those who would undermine the teaching of men like Luther. For Spener, then, this practice has a very important place among God's children, as long as it is remembered that it exists alongside their other duties. He agreed with Arndt, whom he quoted, "Purity of doctrine and of the Word of God is maintained not only by disputation and writing many books but also by true repentance and holiness of life."[113]

When we weigh Spener's fourth proposal against the standard of Luther and his doctrine of *sola fide*, it would be difficult to find much of what Spener wrote to be at odds with the position of the Reformer. Certainly the two men had different temperaments, interests, and approaches to theology. However, this difference cannot lead us to conclude theological disparity. Just as Spener insisted that the Church needs those who will engage in vigorous debate with the enemies of the gospel, Luther recognized that Christians need pastors and theologians who will commit their lives primarily to feeding the sheep with which they have been entrusted. Neither man argued that polemics should be the focus of everyone serving in the Church. As Spener pointed out, it was Luther who wrote, "Truth is lost not

---

[109] Ibid., 71.
[110] *PD*, 99.
[111] Ibid., 108.
[112] *PJSS*, XIII.1, 438f.
[113] *PD*, 99f.

by teaching but by disputing, for disputations bring with them this evil, that men's souls are, as it were, profaned, and when they are occupied with quarrels they neglect what is most important."[114] As for ecumenism, it is difficult to say. Luther certainly stuck to his guns when he met with members of other Protestant churches, uttering some pretty strong words to emphasize their differences. It is unlikely that he would have approved of Spener's reluctance to condemn some of what was being written during the seventeenth century. He would have judged it imprudent, but it was certainly not a decision that led Spener outside the boundaries of Luther's thought.

Proposal Five

"Since ministers must bear the greatest burden in all these things which pertain to a reform of the church, and since their shortcomings do correspondingly great harm, it is of the utmost importance that the office of the ministry be occupied by men who, above all, are themselves true Christians and, then, have the divine wisdom to guide others carefully on the way of the Lord."[115] It is much easier, of course, for a layperson to indulge in a libertine lifestyle when she sees her pastor doing the same thing. If the clergy do not answer the antinomian question with a resounding, "No!," in both their words and deeds, one can hardly expect the laity to do so. In quoting John Chrysostom, Spener impressed upon his hearers the importance of a good example from those in positions of authority in reforming the life of the Church: "Just as you know, when you see a tree whose leaves are faded and withering, that there is something wrong with the roots, so, when you see that the people are undisciplined, you must realize that no doubt their priests are not holy."[116]

We have already discussed how the moral life of the people in Germany had undergone serious degradation as a result of the Thirty Years War. At times, Spener seemed to be living amidst the worst of it. According to Stein, the birthplace of the Reformation was not only exempt from such vice, but the center of much of it:

> In addition, church life throughout Saxony seemed worse off than other places. Sunday desecration, the drunkenness of leading and common people alike, libertinism in sexual relations, neglect of the poor, begging, and large numbers of lawsuits all reflected, at best, a formal and coarse Christianity. The parish clergy,

---

[114] WA 40³, 361.
[115] *PD*, 103.
[116] Ibid., 44.

more generally committed to orthodoxy than to piety, seemed unlikely to promote an increase in faith and morals.[117]

If one hoped to see an increase in the piety of individual believers, and if people were going to stop abusing the freedom they believed they had in the gospel, then the clergy were going to have to do more than give orthodox sermons on Lutheran doctrine and condemn all the cases of heterodoxy they came across. Saxony had always been a stronghold for orthodox Lutheranism, but that was proving not to be enough to change the lives of the people. During his time in Saxony, Spener lamented: "Nowhere has the stiff orthodoxy, the scholastic treatment of dogmatics, the passionate polemics, the unfruitful method of preaching struck such deep roots as here."[118] If virtue and piety were to be restored, it was going to have to begin with the pastors, who were far from innocent of the sinful condition of the society in which they lived. In the *Pia Desideria* he bemoaned, "[W]e preachers in our estate need reformation as much as any estate can ever need it."[119] He was convinced that when pastors and professors alike lived in a manner worthy of imitation by those who looked to them for spiritual guidance, much good would be accomplished. A firm believer in the power of example, Spener knew this was an essential step toward the reforming of Christian society and the lives of individual believers.[120]

While this principle is hardly one on which there could be much disagreement, the matter was not so simple as encouraging clergy to behave like gentlemen. Of course all could agree that pastors should not be frequenting brothels, drinking to excess, or failing to control their tongues. This was never in dispute between the Orthodox and the Pietists, although its urgency may have been. Rather, it was the questions of *adiaphora* that split Lutherans. All could agree on the importance of piety; the question was what constituted a life of piety. What was one to do with those ambiguous moral decisions, the behavior neither commanded nor forbidden in the Bible?

Unlike the Adiaphora Controversy of the sixteenth century, that which took place in the seventeenth century between the Orthodox and the Pietists found the former group maintaining that the "indifferent" things need not be insisted upon. When it came to activities like the theater, dancing, playing cards, and drinking bouts, the Pietists tended to view these social functions as sin; there is no *adiaphora* in the realm of morals, they maintained. Behaviors like dancing are not motivated by the Holy Spirit, and therefore it should

---

[117] Stein, *Spener*, 110.
[118] Ibid.
[119] *PD*, 45.
[120] Ibid., 104.

be apparent that they only serve the sinful desires of the human heart. As a result, they are sin.

The Orthodox, on the other hand, fancied a position much closer to the majority of Lutherans today, albeit one that may lend itself more to abuses of Christian freedom. Valentin Löscher was among those who insisted that some of the activities forbidden by the Pietists, like dancing, were not necessarily sinful. This could be said only if they were misused. At the heart of the disagreement was the question of human desires originating in the realm of nature. While the Pietists generally regarded these with suspicion, the Orthodox believed that human motivation toward worldly pleasures was generally a good. It is only when they are abused that these desires become sinful.[121]

While Spener certainly shared the world-denying tendency of other Pietists, his distaste for those things considered *adiaphora* was based not on a theological premise that led him to believe that they were sinful, but on his desire to avoid any appearance of sin. If drinking bouts led to drunkenness, or even had the appearance of impropriety, he would oppose them. As Stein explains, "Spener's spartan attitude was partially predicated upon his adherence to usefulness (*Nützlichkeit*). He was opposed to anything that wasted time, money, or opportunity to do good.... [However], [w]ith regard to 'middle things,' as then *adiaphora* were also known, Spener was rather hesitant to condemn. When he did speak out, it tended to be on the basis of pastoral counsel rather than on scriptural mandate."[122] Thus, Spener's concern with avoiding bad precedents, appearances, and idleness led him to oppose many of the same activities as his Pietist contemporaries and heirs. However, in contradistinction from them, this opposition was based more on concerns about abuses of Christian freedom and less on any disavowal of all worldly desires.

When held to the measuring rod of Luther's message of the gospel and its freedom, there are certain conclusions we can reach regarding Spener's fifth proposal. It is certainly safe to say that Luther would have found much to applaud in Spener's insistence that clergy be above reproach in regard to moral conduct. While not the first item on the Reformer's agenda during the previous century, it would be false to conclude that Luther would have let such libertine excesses among the clergy go unchecked in the seventeenth century had he still been around to comment. Regarding *adiaphora*, Luther would have clearly fallen in the Orthodox camp on the subject of the bless-

---

[121] See further F. Ernest Stoeffler, *German Pietism During the Eighteenth Century* (Leiden: E.J. Brill, 1973), 70.

[122] Stein, *Spener*, 234f.

ings of worldly pleasures, as any casual reader of Luther's *Table Talk* cannot
help but notice. He would surely have rejected the suggestion of later Pietists
that there are no *adiaphora* in spiritual and moral matters. Only those things
forbidden in Scripture can be considered sin. However, as stated above,
Spener based his opposition to these middle things not on a different doctrine
of sin, but on a desire to rectify an antinomian moral complacency. As for
Spener's loyalty to his predecessor, one could suggest that the ever-reaction-
ary Luther would have been disturbed by the extreme claims of later Pietists
about *adiaphora,* in which case he would have opposed Spener's moral
crusade. However, if he found himself more troubled by the coarse lifestyle
of those Christians who bore his name, he would have applauded Spener's
work. The potential for both responses lies in Luther's theology. On this
point, the difference between Spener and the Orthodox was one more of
emphasis than any qualitative theological difference.

Proposal Six

"[I]t should be pointed out to students that everything in their sermons
should have edification as the goal.... [T]hat *sermons* be so prepared by all
that their purpose (faith and its fruits) may be achieved in the hearers to the
greatest possible degree."[123] As with catechesis, Spener was convinced that
the more exposure believers have to the Word of God, the stronger their faith
will become; and the stronger their faith becomes, the more they will desire
to pursue lives of piety in gratitude to God. Moreover, it is not sufficient just
to hear sermons preached based on the Scriptures, for sermons must convey
all of God's message: law and gospel, "faith and its fruits," faith as gift and
responsibility. When preachers preach as they should, making sure to stress
both justification and sanctification, misconceptions about what the doctrine
of *sola fide* implies will be cleared up; the antinomian question will simply
dissolve.

Since Luther's death, evangelical sermons had tended to erode in their
sense of urgency, personal responsibility, and the use of plain language directed at the people in the pews. At the same time, preachers putting on airs,
impressing with their knowledge and rhetoric, were on the rise. As Stoeffler
explains, "the Orthodoxist, who characteristically waited for God to deal
with men, could afford to display his erudition in the language of the schools
while he awaited for divine action. The Halle [i.e. Pietist] preacher, on the
other hand, who felt himself to be God's chosen agency to rescue the sinner

---

[123] *PD*, 115.

from the fires of hell, had to use a more persuasive approach."[124] Thus, a combination of the increased emphasis on objectivity, institutionalization, and the misconstrued *ex opere operato* interpretation of Luther's theology led the Lutheran church to a point where preaching had become overly formal, academic, and sterile. As Stoeffler goes on to explain, the Protestant scholastic's understanding of Word and Sacrament, "which radically de-emphasized human effort in the appropriation of salvation," led to an overly intellectualized understanding of faith.[125] As a result, preaching tended to focus on the objective understanding of what God had done for sinful humanity. The role and contribution of the individual believer was then seriously lacking in orthodox homiletics.

For Spener, not only did the sermon need to be re-crafted; it was to become a central part of worship. Grünberg explains that Spener did not really think about the organic connection of the sermon to other parts of the liturgy. He saw *Gottesdienst* (divine service) chiefly as *Predigtgottesdienst* (a divine preaching service).[126] And so, while Spener placed the sermon at the center of worship in his ongoing attempt to increase public piety, it should be noted that his re-crafting of preaching did not entail an overemphasis on the law in order to improve morals. He insisted time and again that it is the love of God, as revealed in the gospel, which moves people to live righteously. In his first sermon in Dresden, he explained to his congregation, "My chief work shall be the gospel, because I know that it is the only way to salvation. On the other hand, a hundred years of law sermons can convert no one, for no law has been given that can give life."[127] As Grünberg explains, Spener's concern for the gospel led him to very Christocentric preaching, which Luther had so skillfully done before him, but had been lost in much of evangelical preaching.[128]

In another move to recapture the legacy of Luther, one finds Spener moving back to the Bible as the source and norm for preaching. In the seventeenth century, the individual pastor would have done very little exegesis of the Scriptures himself. The accepted belief at that time was that the Lutheran Confessions had adequately captured the teachings of the Bible. As a result, independent exegesis was not necessary. Spener disagreed. As mentioned above, Sebastian Schmidt had made a profound impression on Spener at the University of Strassburg, where he taught the young man a

---

[124] Stoeffler, *German Pietism*, 49.
[125] Ibid., 52.
[126] *PJSS*, Grünberg II, 32.
[127] *PJSS*, IX.1.2, 1005f.
[128] *PJSS*, Grünberg II, 46.

great deal about biblical exegesis. Quite simply, preaching was to be based on the Word of God as found in the Bible.

The form of his preaching was simple as well. He insisted, "[T]he pulpit is not the place for an ostentatious display of one's skill. It is rather the place to preach the Word of the Lord plainly but powerfully."[129] Elaborate displays of learning had no place in a Sunday sermon. Clarity and simplicity were the hallmarks that Spener sought in his preaching, as he frequently appealed to the lost ideal of "apostolic simplicity," or the *pristina piscatoria simplicitas.*"[130] Even today, readers of Spener cannot help but notice how direct and understandable his writings are, more so than many of the scholars who seek to sing his praises. The essence of this concern is found in a sermon from 1663, which Grünberg summarizes: "How will we bring the unlearned masses to heaven when our sermons are more art than edification? *Schlecht und recht ist das Allerbeste und Festeste* (crass and correct is the best and most sound)...."[131]

At the same time, Spener's attempt at apostolic simplicity could make for some very boring preaching. His sermons could be up to two hours long; there were few illustrations or parables, little drawn from the history of the Church, and no personal experiences or impressions. While these sermons frequently made use of long quotes from Luther, Chrysostom, Augustine, and other Church fathers, there was very little drawn from classical literature. Described as having a doctrinaire-didactic tone throughout, Spener's sermons not only would be boring to congregations in the twenty-first century, they were boring to many of his contemporaries as well. He suffered not only from what Stein calls a lack of appreciation for good humor, but a "lack of excitement in his delivery.... At the age of sixty-seven, he confessed that he never felt worn or weak from preaching because he had exhausted neither his body nor his spirit with passionate emotion."[132]

Lastly, aside from a return to the Bible and simplicity in style, Spener made one additional important homiletic innovation during his career. At a time during which the Sunday Gospel reading was the requisite lectionary selection for the sermon, Spener bucked tradition once again. During Advent of 1676 he began preaching a series of Sunday sermons based on the epistles of Paul. Being convinced that the Gospel readings provided less material for the much-needed emphasis on piety and sanctification, he allowed himself to make use of the epistle readings as sermon texts. Incidentally, with the

---

[129] *PD*, 116.
[130] See *PJSS*, Grünberg I, 400.
[131] *PJSS*, Grünberg II, 36. See further *PJSS*, III.1, 486.
[132] Stein, *Spener*, 268.

exception of a number of sermons based on 1 John, he later reversed his position, once again only preaching on the Sunday Gospel texts.

As for our study here, this temporary opposition to the Lutheran use of the lectionary provides us with a very good insight into the mind and theology of Spener. First, we may remark how his move to the epistle texts underscores his commitment to stressing piety in the Christian life from the pulpit. Interestingly, Luther had complained in the previous century that these epistle selections from Paul were not chosen from the more gospel-centered portions of the Apostle's writings.[133] Thus, we see in Spener a decided shift toward the law in his preaching and theology, a tendency most certainly not present in Luther. At the same time, as we have seen, Spener was clear that the focus of any and every sermon needs to be the gospel.

Conclusion

This last example, regarding the lectionary, can serve as a telling indicator of the essence of most of the differences between Luther and Spener. Aside from Spener's discussion of sins of malice and sins of weakness, the fundamental differences between the two come down to a relative emphasis on the law or the gospel. If we are then to ask whether Spener's accentuation of the life of sanctification was faithful to Luther's insistence on *sola fide*, we find ourselves in a difficult position. Certainly Spener maintained formal allegiance to this principle. He rejected Majorism, synergism, and any notion that human beings contribute to the earning of their salvation. At the same time, his stress on the third use of the law, coupled with his doctrine of sin, led him to make some statements that could, at the very least, carry implications that were contrary to Luther's theology. The fact that the two men emphasized different sides of the law and gospel dichotomy cannot, however, be grounds for any allegation of theological inconsistency between the two. Luther was an occasional writer as much as Spener, and the two were writing at very different times. While any projection of what Luther would have said had he been around in the seventeenth century is speculation at best, and projection at worst, it is safe to say that disagreement between the two on this point could exist within the framework of Luther's theology of grace. As we saw with Melanchthon, it is possible to remain loyal to Luther's theology while maintaining a respectful disagreement on particulars.

We may also see at this point that Spener's approach to the antinomian question was quite different from that of Melanchthon. The earlier Philipp was more interested in fine-tuning the theological system of the young

---

[133] *LW* 53, 23f.

evangelical movement in order to close the moral loophole of libertinism. His discussions of a third use of the law, forensic justification, the necessity of works for salvation, and synergism clearly convey that he was first and foremost a theologian. His responses to the antinomian question were theological. Spener, on the other hand, was always a pastor first; and his approach to theological difficulties reflects this. When we look to the Father of German Pietism for his contribution in addressing the antinomian question his suggestions betray his practical nature. Spener was a man who was very closely connected to the laity in the pews of his churches, and hence his proposals were of a kind that would make an immediate difference in the lives of his parishioners: catechesis, Bible studies, and meditations on the suffering of Christ. In fact, when Pastor Spener dabbled theologically with the problem of antinomianism, we find a doctrine of sin that clearly contradicts Luther. Spener's greatest contribution to the life of the Church was his understanding of how to help Christians grow in their faith as individuals, a theme taken up with a vengeance in the nineteenth century by Søren Kierkegaard, although with a very different approach to the problem, as we shall see.

ℂℛ CHAPTER FOUR

Søren Kierkegaard

In 1843 Søren Kierkegaard let it be known in Denmark that "in the world of spirit cheating is not allowed."[1] This was, however, exactly what Lutheran Denmark was attempting to do, as far as Kierkegaard was concerned. Like Spener before him, this melancholy Dane was greatly concerned with the lack of religious seriousness and piety among the citizens of his native land; the confidence in their own justification was standing in the way of their sanctification. The ludicrousness of Danish Christendom was apparent to everyone: "I suppose no one could get permission to earn his living by keeping a whorehouse unless he could produce proof that he was baptized."[2] How absurd it is, he believed, that one could commit one's life to God and then make no changes in one's conduct—at least six days out of the week. As mentioned above, Kierkegaard held very similar concerns to those of Spener: How does one emphasize that the Christian life necessarily involves sanctification? How do we respond to the antinomian question? At the same time, as we shall see, his understanding of the root of the problem and his chosen response differ significantly from those of the father of German Pietism.

In large part, we can say that Kierkegaard answered the antinomian question with poetry. His lyrical accounts of the nature of repentance, faith, and love were designed to paint such a magnificent picture of the Christian life as to remind the reader of her own dismal approximation of these virtues, if she held them at all. By engendering such humility, Kierkegaard hoped to eliminate spiritual complacency, the chief architect of antinomianism. Moreover, this work needed to be carried out over and against the accommodating mediocrity of the Danish church that had reduced Christianity to a comfortable and occasional habit that everyone was born into and could carry out with minimal effort. "My task," Kierkegaard tells us, "has continually been to provide the existential-corrective by poetically presenting the

---

[1] *Fear and Trembling*, trans. Howard V. Hong and Edna H. Hong (Princeton: Princeton University Press, 1983), 80.
[2] As in Walter Lowrie, *Kierkegaard* (New York: Harper and Brothers, 1962), 532.

ideals and inciting people about the established order, with which I collaborate by criticizing all the false reformers and the opposition, who simply are evil—and whom only ideals can halt."[3]

While this poetic, indirect approach to theology made up the majority of Kierkegaard's writings, it is true that in the last year of his life he discarded this maieutic tactic in favor of some rather shocking direct communication. He tells us in a little piece entitled *What Christ Judges of Official Christianity,* published in 1855, "I began by passing myself off as a poet, subtly aiming at what I thought was the truth about official Christianity." The year before his death witnessed a significant shift. "Then this poet suddenly changed; he—if I may say it this way, threw away his guitar and—took out a book called *The New Testament of Our Lord and Savior Jesus Christ.*"[4] Despite this change, whether we speak of Kierkegaard's early pseudonymous writings, later Christian writings, or his final stinging assault on Christendom, a common theme is always present in his work. Nearly every page of his copious legacy conveys the extreme demands of Christianity. Whether he is describing the rigors of the ethical life, the offense which faith creates, or the conduct God requires of a Christian, Kierkegaard wanted his reader to know that Christianity is anything but easy.

One element of Kierkegaard's approach, which differentiates him from the other figures treated here, has to do with what he believed to be the source of Danish antinomianism. He was convinced that this problem did not spring from the laity perceiving a moral loophole in the preaching of orthodox clergy; the preaching itself conveyed antinomianism. Unlike Melanchthon and Spener, who were concerned that orthodox preaching might leave out or minimize sanctification, Kierkegaard believed that the preaching itself offered a message that was contrary to the Word of God in the New Testament. Melanchthon and Spener argued that an incomplete portrayal of the law and gospel could have negative moral implications for society. Kierkegaard insisted that the message heard in Danish churches was not simply incomplete, it was inaccurate. Christianity had been diluted in various ways to the point that what was heard from the clergy on Sunday mornings was not Christianity at all. Perhaps with the Pietists in mind, Kierkegaard expressed through the mouth of Johannes de Silentio, "In the old days, people said: It is too bad that things do not go in the world as the preacher preaches. Maybe the time will come, especially with the aid of philosophy, when they can say: Fortunately things do not go as the preacher preaches, for

---

[3]*Pap* X[4] A 15; as in *SKJP* 1:331.
[4]*The Moment and Late Writings*, trans. Howard V. Hong and Edna H. Hong (Princeton: Princeton University Press, 1998), 129, 130.

there is still some meaning in life, but there is none in his sermons."[5] The problem was not that the clergy tolerated an abuse of Christian freedom, but that they communicated it themselves in their sweet, sentimental expressions of the life and work of Jesus—an image of Jesus that Kierkegaard could find nowhere in his own New Testament.

Kierkegaard's dissatisfaction with the Lutheran clergy of his day was held in an unusual tension with his feelings toward the reformer himself. Admittedly, his familiarity with the writings of Luther was limited; primarily he read sermons in Danish translation.[6] His feelings toward Luther, however, did not share any such modest limit. For a theologian who had read so little of the reformer, Kierkegaard held some very strong opinions. His initial impressions were positive. Regin Prenter, in his analysis of the relation between the two theological giants, points to an entry in Kierkegaard's journal from 1847 where he appears surprised at the essential agreement between himself and Luther on the subject of the existential appropriation of the gospel. Kierkegaard remarks, "How strange! The category 'for you' (subjectivity, inwardness) in the conclusion of *Either-Or* (only that truth which edifies is truth to you) belongs to Luther."[7] The Danish poet had found an ally in the German reformer—an ally in his battle against the church that bore the latter's name and to which the former belonged. In Luther, Kierkegaard found inspiration for his own insistence on the subjective reception of the message of the god-man.

The honeymoon, however, did not last. Kierkegaard came to the conviction that the responsibility for the battle he was fighting could largely be placed at the feet of Luther. While Luther's theology may have been a correct exposition of the Word of God, he was offering a corrective for his own time. He forgot that his reactive words would become concretized into a new system. Today's corrective can easily become tomorrow's norm. In 1854 he explained, "Luther's emphasis is a corrective—but a corrective made into the normative, into the sum total, is *eo ipso*, confusing in another generation (where that for which it was a corrective does not exist). And with every generation that goes by in this way it must become worse, until the end result is this corrective, which has independently established itself, produces characteristics exactly the opposite of the original."[8] As we shall see more clearly later on, Kierkegaard did not take the more charitable approach of

---

[5] *Fear and Trembling*, 29n.
[6] See Regin Prenter, "Luther and Lutheranism," in *Bibliotheca Kierkegaardiana* vol.6 (Copenhagen: C.A. Reitzels Boghandel, 1981).
[7] Regin Prenter, "Luther and Lutheranism," 123f.
[8] *Pap* XI[1] A 28; as in *SKJP* 1:333.

blaming later generations for not appreciating the reformer's context but placed the blame squarely on Luther's shoulders.

Unlike the other theologians considered in this project, Kierkegaard had no inhibitions about criticizing, blaming, and lambasting Luther for what he perceived to be failures on the part of the father of Protestantism. As we will see, however, these attacks should not necessarily be perceived as indicators of any essential theological difference between the two men. Kierkegaard believed that both he and Luther were correctives, offering opposite correctives during two very different times. Kierkegaard would have been the first to admit that he was deeply indebted to the work of Luther and the other reformers in bringing the gospel to light three centuries before. Nevertheless, he was sure that Luther's lack of foresight had brought devastating implications to Protestant Europe. This ambiguous relationship may be illustrated in a quote from Luther that Kierkegaard offers in his *Book on Adler*. Here he tells us, "the world continually remains, as Luther says, like a drunken peasant, who, if you help him up on one side of the horse, falls off on the other side."[9] Kierkegaard stands opposite Luther, complaining that his partner has been pushing too hard, while at the same time recognizing that the *essential* fault lies with the drunken peasant who allows himself to be pushed back and forth without making the effort to find balance himself.

What then is to be done? How does one correct for the flawed Christianity of nineteenth century Denmark? The approach to the dilemma that Kierkegaard chose to undertake is articulated by the pseudonymous Johannes Climacus, who describes his own task in the *Postscript*:

> So there I sat and smoked my cigar until I drifted into thought. Among other thoughts, I recall these...Wherever you look in literature or in life, you see the names and figures of celebrities...who know how to benefit humankind by making life easier and easier, some by railroads, others by omnibuses and steamships, others by telegraph, others by easily understood surveys and short publications about everything worth knowing, and finally the true benefactors of the age who by virtue of thought systematically make spiritual existence easier and easier and yet more and more meaningful— and what are you doing?
>
> At this point my introspection was interrupted because my cigar was finished and a new one had to be lit. So I smoked again, and then suddenly this thought crossed my mind: You must do something, but since with your limited capabilities it will be impossible to make anything easier than it has become, you must, with the

---

[9]*The Book on Adler*, trans. Howard V. Hong and Edna H. Hong (Princeton: Princeton University Press, 1998), 157f. n.

same humanitarian enthusiasm as the others have, take it upon yourself to make something more difficult.[10]

Christian faith and life, or what Climacus here calls "spiritual existence," had been reduced to the level of a casual enterprise—something undertaken with the greatest of ease. Theological and philosophical advances had rendered Luther's *Anfechtung* unnecessary. There was no more need for a dark night of the soul; spiritual existence could be had at bargain prices. When faith is so easy to come by, the antinomian question will appear with considerable regularity. In order to avoid both the false notion that Christianity is an easy task as well as the rampant abuse of Christian freedom, Kierkegaard set out to explain to the world that Christian faith is the most difficult task of all. In so doing, he hoped to make others see that what was posing as Christianity was not the authentic "Christianity of the New Testament." He intended to demonstrate thereby why genuine believers will not and cannot lead lives devoid of sanctification—or, what he often called the "imitation" of Christ. If Christianity seems easy, he would tell us, perhaps it is not genuine Christianity. Thus, in order to respond to our antinomian cynic, Kierkegaard began by considering the presuppositions behind the antinomian question and then inquiring into their validity.

For one to argue, "I am saved by faith, not works, and therefore may do as I please," implies that the individual truly believes. The father of Existentialism would here suggest, "Examine yourself, now—for this you have the right to do; but you really do not have a right to allow yourself, without self-examination, to be duped by 'the others' or to dupe yourself into believing that you are a Christian—so, then, examine yourself."[11] Kierkegaard preempts the argument by questioning whether or not the individual does indeed have faith. To determine whether this is the case, Kierkegaard could return to what Luther had said is required for an individual to have saving faith. There are three questions that one must answer. (1) Have I repented of my sins? (2) Have I trusted in Christ for the forgiveness of sins? (3) Do I still have this faith? If the individual can honestly answer "yes" to these three questions, she may be assured that she is justified in the eyes of God. Kierkegaard, in helping others to see that Christian faith is not a walk in the park, not only reminds his reader of these three questions, but also seriously calls affirmative answers to them into question. He explains through his various works that each of these three stages, if you will, involves immense

---

[10]*Concluding Unscientific Postscript to Philosophical Fragments*, trans. Howard V. Hong and Edna H. Hong (Princeton: Princeton University Press, 1992), 186.

[11] *Practice in Christianity*, trans. Howard V. Hong and Edna H. Hong (Princeton: Princeton University Press, 1991), 39.

existential investment. It is not enough to be able to identify or define the elements of Christian faith; they must be experienced. "The learned Christians argue about what Christianity actually is, but it never occurs to them to think otherwise than that they themselves are Christians."[12]

Kierkegaard's response, then, to the antinomian question involves an analysis of the presuppositions that stand behind it. In so doing, the individual will become, he hoped, more concerned with whether or not he has saving faith than with whether he can get away with various moral indiscretions. Additionally, Kierkegaard hoped to encourage spiritual maturity in his reader through this call for self-examination, as greater faith is another essential tool in helping one respond to the antinomian question for oneself. Thus, while there is a logical questioning of the presuppositions behind the antinomian question, there is also the psychological effect of creating concern and humility, compelling the reader to seek refuge in God's grace and thereby forestalling the pursuit of libertinism.

While this may remind one of the work of Spener, we shall see that Kierkegaard was doing something very different from what Spener had offered in the seventeenth century. Unlike the German Pietist, who focused his efforts on emphasizing sin, the law, and the suffering of Christ in order to redirect the teaching of the German Lutheran church, the Danish Poet was proposing something much more radical. He was not interested in merely making adjustments to the present system, but in completely overhauling the entire structure. The whole edifice of Danish "Christianity" was a fraud, and the people needed to become aware that they were being misled and misdirected by their own religious leaders. "If Christianity is to be introduced here, then first and foremost the illusion must be removed. But since this illusion, this delusion, is that they are Christians, then it of course seems as if the introduction of Christianity would deprive people of Christianity. Yet this is the first thing that must be done; the illusion must go."[13] And again, "That the official Christianity, which we call Christianity, is not the Christianity of the New Testament, is not a striving toward it, has not the slightest resemblance to it—nothing is easier to see."[14] A break had to be made, he insisted, with what was posing for Christianity. Marie Mikulová Thulstrup is right in explaining that this extreme agenda points to a qualitative break with Pietism.[15] The answer for Kierkegaard did not lie in a

---

[12] *Postscript,* 374.

[13] *The Moment,* 107.

[14] Ibid., 169.

[15] Marie Mikulová Thulstrup, "Pietism," in *Bibliotheca Kierkegaardiana,* vol.6 (Copenhagen: C.A. Reitzels Boghandel, 1981), 173–222.

greater emphasis on conversion and sanctification. A radical solution was called for that challenged the very definition of the Christian faith that had established itself in the Lutheran church.

In order to understand how Kierkegaard hoped to accomplish this imposing task, this chapter will follow the three fundamental steps in the *ordo salutis* that he identified: "1) Imitation, in the direction of a decisive action by which the situation of becoming a Christian is created. 2) Christ as a gift. 3) Imitation as the fruit of faith."[16] Please note that these are not the same as the three stages (aesthetic, ethical, and religious) identified elsewhere in his writings. Moreover, as with the three stages, the division of these three steps in the order of salvation is not intended to suggest three temporally successive and independent periods, for all are present simultaneously. Nevertheless, this sequence does provide us with a rough framework of Kierkegaard's understanding of the Christian life and affords us the opportunity to consider, somewhat systematically, his understanding of these elements of the Christian life and their faithfulness to our guiding standard of *sola fide*.

Imitation and Despair

Kierkegaard's theological endeavor begins by considering the individual without the proper knowledge of her sin.[17] This is the case, he insisted, with most of Danish Christendom, despite its access to God's revelation. The scriptures have become commonplace, taken for granted, their moral principles reduced to clichés. The fact that Christendom possesses God's law has little meaning when all believe that they are Christian and are thereby no longer under the condemnation of the law.[18] The Danish church had allowed sin to be reduced to a concept, a doctrine; it no longer held the power to drive the individual to despair. Kierkegaard lamented, "But sin, that you and I are sinners (the single individual), has been abolished, or it has been illicitly reduced both in life (the domestic, the civic, the ecclesiastical) and in scholarship, which has invented the *doctrine* of sin in general."[19] His first task, then, in the revival of the Christianity of the New Testament was to reintroduce the law, not as doctrine, but as a means to bring individuals to despair; "since all truly Christian preaching is first and foremost the

---

[16] As quoted in Prenter, 153f.

[17] See further Henning Schröer's discussion of Per Lønning's Kierkegaard research in "Kierkegaard und Luther," *Kerygma und Dogma* 30 (1984): 227–248.

[18] See further Emanuel Hirsch, *Kierkegaard-Studien* (Gütersloh: Verlag C. Bertelsmann, 1933), 909ff.

[19] *Practice in Christianity,* 68.

preaching of repentance."[20] Theologically speaking, a person must be brought to the point of despair before there can be any hope of a reprieve; those who are ill must first be made aware of their ailment, not of the concept of illness in general. To assist the single individual in this existential journey, Kierkegaard provides copious works where he is preaching the law, not just preaching about the law. Nearly his entire *Works of Love* conveys to his readers the inadequacy of their own efforts at love. By holding up the standard of selfless love and shedding light on humanity's poor approximations, he wants to help his reader to despair of his own virtue and thereby come to rely on God in Christ for forgiveness. Likewise in his *Upbuilding Discourses*, Kierkegaard demonstrates his masterful ability to humble those who are comfortable or proud with their own piety. For example, to those who may pat themselves on the back for giving to the poor, he reminds them, "You were willing to give and assist someone in need who had nothing to give in return, and yet you demanded something from him: his respect, his admiration, his subservience—his soul."[21] All too often, he tells us, our good deeds are tainted with self-love.

Kierkegaard was quite adept at allowing the law to work in his readers in order to bring them to the realization that they are truly in need of God's mercy, that "God in heaven is capable of all things, and man of nothing at all."[22] Only when they reach this point of despair can they begin to seek for the cure to their condition. The Danish church, however, had failed to communicate God's law with its condemning effect. The result was complicity in the prevailing false assurance that salvation could be counted on by those who had been baptized. Kierkegaard responded by questioning this basis for his reader's confidence. "[Y]ou who are still on good terms with God, are you indeed on good terms with him; is your will, is it, and unconditionally, his will; are your wishes, every wish of yours, his command, your thoughts, the first and last, his thoughts—if not, how terrible that God is changeless, eternally, eternally changeless!"[23] He was determined not to let any rest comfortably in the belief that they were "on good terms with God" without first appropriating the fact that they were helplessly lost in their own sin. In so doing, Kierkegaard demonstrated himself to be superior to Luther, Melanchthon, and Spener—not in his understanding of sin and the law but in his ability to communicate them to others.

---

[20] *The Moment,* 18.
[21] *Eighteen Upbuilding Discourses,* trans. Howard V. Hong and Edna H. Hong (Princeton: Princeton University Press, 1990), 146.
[22] Ibid., 310.
[23] *The Moment,* 272f.

Christ: Pattern and Redeemer

Thus far, Kierkegaard had not suggested anything new or different from what many other Christian teachers had offered. He was not the first to insist that the law be fervently preached in order to afflict the comfortable, nor would he have claimed so. In this he saw himself in line with confessional Lutheranism: "The Augsburg Confession consistently teaches that it must be revealed to a man how great a sinner he is."[24] What he did bring to the discussion was an emphasis on the idea of "imitation." For too long, Kierkegaard felt, Christ had been viewed almost entirely as the redeemer alone; Christ must also be understood to be the example that his followers are to imitate. In fact, he insisted, one must first view Christ as the example to imitate before he can be understood as the redeemer. Proclaiming Christ as the example (i.e., the law) must necessarily precede the announcement of Christ as the savior, i.e. the gospel. In fact, teaching Christ as redeemer alone was a very strange idea to Kierkegaard. That his alleged followers would claim to surrender their lives to him and then not seek to follow the example he set for them is simply nonsensical.

> Instead of looking at him with respect to imitation, they dwelt on his good works and wished to be in the place of those to whom they were shown, which is just as upside down as to hear someone described as a prototype of generosity and then refuse to look at him with the intention of imitating his generosity but with the idea of wishing to be in the place of those to whom he showed generosity. So the prototype dropped out.[25]

More often than not, Kierkegaard preferred the language of *imitation* to that of the *law*. While there are significant ethical and exegetical implications that may be drawn from this change in language, what is important for this discussion is that he uses imitation as a synecdoche for the entire law. The new moral command of Jesus, that his disciples love one another as he had loved them, came to summarize and encompass all of God's law for Kierkegaard. While he recognized that debate on the specifics of ethics would continue unabated, he was confident that all could agree that the followers of Christ have an obligation to imitate the moral example of their Lord.

In focusing on Christ as the example to be imitated, Kierkegaard has led some to suggest that he has vitiated Luther's law/gospel distinction. Regin Prenter raises the question, "Has Kierkegaard rightly interpreted Luther's view of the relation between law and gospel in comparing it or even identifying it with his own distinction between Christ as example and Christ as

---

[24] As in Lowrie, *Kierkegaard,* 398.
[25] *The Moment,* 182.

redeemer (reconciliator)?...This is certainly not the case."[26] Prenter is particularly troubled with the notion that Christ as example represents the law. He insists, "According to Luther Christ as example does not belong to the realm of the law at all, but solely to that of the gospel."[27] He goes on to argue that Christ is the example in "the sense of the good shepherd" who leads his sheep, clearing their way so that they may follow him more easily. Prenter is convinced that Luther's teaching on the subject of law and gospel, and subsequently the principle of *sola fide*, have been violated by Kierkegaard, whom he insists, "transforms the gospel, the message of Christ the Redeemer, into a new law, still more severe than the law which requires perfect love for God and the neighbor."[28]

Prenter's concerns for the differences between Kierkegaard and Luther are appreciated, but in this case are clearly off base. To begin with, Luther most certainly did speak of Christ as the example functioning as law: "Now, the difference between faith and works is as great as the difference between a gift and an example."[29] Christ as gift, as was discussed in the first chapter, corresponds to faith, while Christ as example is related to our works; so Christ as example does not afford the forgiveness of sins (i.e. the gospel) any more than our works do. For Luther, Christ as the example to be imitated clearly falls under the category of the law.

Secondly, when Prenter describes the good shepherd who leads his sheep in paths of righteousness, doing so by being the absolute moral example, he is describing the third use of the *law*. For Luther, moreover, the primary function of the law—in this case with Jesus as example—must always be the second use, i.e. the mirror that shows sinners their own sin.[30] As with Kierkegaard, Luther believed that looking at Christ as a moral example has the power, first and foremost, to drive a person to repentance. Christ as example may serve in directing the redeemed in how they should live, but first and foremost this absolute moral pattern is in place to show humanity its own sin and weakness.

The attempt of the individual to imitate Christ is destined to end in failure. As discussed above, the purpose of this impossible standard is to compel the individual to seek help in God alone, rather than in his own strength. When that point has been reached, then Christ may become the redeemer—the savior who offers forgiveness. Christ is thus both pattern and

---

[26] Prenter, "Luther," 142f.
[27] Ibid., 143.
[28] Ibid., 145.
[29] *WA* 10[1], 1, 12.
[30] *LW* 26, 337.

redeemer. Kierkegaard explains, "so that when the striver sinks under the pattern, then the redeemer raises him up again, but at the same instant Thou art the pattern, to keep him continually striving."[31] While Kierkegaard is clear that the followers of Christ do not imitate him insofar as he is the savior of humanity,[32] there remains for all followers of Christ, at every point in their lives, the necessity of imitation. Kierkegaard's insistence on Christ as example, while not a primary theme in Luther, is most certainly consistent with the reformer's christology. At the same time, we should not assume that there are no differences between the two on this point. Kierkegaard insisted that Luther had failed to attend sufficiently to this aspect of Christ's work. Admittedly, Luther was responding to the deficiency in the Middle Ages that focused almost entirely on Christ's work as a moral model. Nonetheless, he failed to account adequately for his own corrective tendencies, especially insofar as they would be received by future generations. Kierkegaard's chosen task was to attempt to balance Christ's command that his disciples follow his example with Paul's primary insistence that grace and forgiveness come through Jesus Christ; he sought to do this while at the same time offering a corrective to the contemporary church's emphasis on the latter.

> [I]t is of great importance, to Protestantism in particular, to correct the enormous confusion Luther caused by inverting the relation and actually criticizing Christ by means of Paul, the Master by means of the follower. I, on the contrary, have not criticized the apostle, as if I myself were something, I who am not even a Christian; what I have done is to hold Christ's proclamation alongside the apostle's.... It is one thing to be able intellectually to make a dialectically true comment; it is something else to want to disparage, to weaken the apostle, something I am as far from doing as anyone.[33]

The Dialectical in Theology

When the law, or imitation, is excluded from Christian doctrine, Christianity ceases to exist. Where there is no struggle against the sinful flesh, there can be no faith. Luther had neglected the effective balancing of the law with the gospel at times. For Kierkegaard, if one is to "take away from the forgiveness of sins the battle of the anguished conscience (to which, according to Luther's excellent explanation, this whole doctrine is to lead)...then close the churches, the sooner the better."[34] As we have suggested, Luther failed to

---

[31] As quoted in Ernest B. Koenker, "Søren Kierkegaard on Luther," in *Interpreters of Luther*, ed. Jaroslav Pelikan (Philadelphia: Fortress Press, 1968), 246.

[32] *Pap.* X^1 A 132; as in *SKJP* 1:324. "For Christ's death is not a task for imitation but is the atonement."

[33] *The Moment*, 341n.

[34] *Works of Love*, trans. Howard V. Hong and Edna H. Hong (Princeton: Princeton University Press, 1995), 201.

communicate the requisite "anguished conscience" sufficiently in his writings, and Kierkegaard blamed him for the church's failure to make known the Christian requirement of imitation—a requirement necessary for both conversion and growing in one's faith. Luther seemed unaware at times that others do not share his personal struggle with sin. For most, Kierkegaard believed, the greatest temptation is not to doubt God's forgiveness, but to take advantage of it. Eduard Geismar has rightly pointed out, "Kierkegaard's enemy was another than the enemy of Luther. Luther's enemy was works righteousness, Kierkegaard's was worldliness."[35] Luther's corrective was not the same corrective that nineteenth century Denmark was in need of. Without the strict insistence on imitation, self-assured Christianity quickly travels down the road to moral apathy and the subsequent antinomianism.

The fundamental error that Luther made, according to Kierkegaard, was that he forgot to be dialectical in his theology; he forgot to take account of the legitimacy and necessity of the complement to his emphasis on grace. In terms of the analogy of the drunken peasant, he seemed unaware at times that he needed the assistance of the one on the other side of the horse...and that he should not push too hard on his own side. In fact, on the page following this earlier reference to Luther's analogy in *The Book on Adler*, Kierkegaard went on to explain that Luther, "admittedly with noble and lofty enthusiasm, knew how to defend Christian freedom against the pope but was not sufficiently dialectically attentive to defending it and himself against obtuse copycats and adherents."[36] The result was a Lutheranism that was as overly focused on grace and the gift of God in Christ as Roman Catholicism had been on works and the role of Christ as model.

Please note: the problem with Luther, as far as Kierkegaard was concerned, was not that he had simply emphasized one aspect more than another—that he had attempted to correct the church's misdirection by stressing the gospel more than the law—but rather that he had undertaken his project in a non-dialectical way. Kierkegaard considered himself a corrective to his own time as well. The difference, he believed, was that he would not forget to think dialectically, nor would he forget that he was a corrective. Ernest B. Koenker points out that Kierkegaard modeled himself in this regard after Socrates, the "true reformer," who never forgot that he was nothing more than "a corrective, a solitary witness, a midwife serving at the birth of truth."[37] Luther, on the other hand, allowed himself to get caught up in his reforming work to the point that he believed his own corrective should

---

[35] See Schröer's discussion of Eduard Geismar, "Kierkegaard und Luther," 232.
[36] *Adler*, 158n.
[37] Koenker, "Søren Kierkegaard on Luther," 240.

be the basis for the new evangelical theology. By insisting with such passion and enthusiasm that faith is given freely, *sola fide*, Luther shone such a bright light on the gospel that the demands of the law were often left in the shadows. Without making an allowance for the proper place of these demands in the theology of the church after the corrective had made its point, Luther had, in Kierkegaard's mind, left a Christianity that was as one-sided as the Roman church had been. Luther had become the father of a system rather than a voice crying in the wilderness.

> Luther has done incalculable harm through the fact that he did not become a martyr. And it may be that he during some years of his life is salt, then his later life is not without insipidity, of which Tischreden (Table Talk) are an instance! a man of God, who in all friendliness is throning surrounded by admiring devotees who believe that if he only farts then it is a revelation or the result of an inspiration.... Luther has, through his later habits of life accredited mediocrity. One is not on one's guard against the fact that in a certain sense a hero is needed when mediocrity for the first time is to be credited. This hero Luther was.[38]

The times needed a hero who would *accredit* mediocrity; but they did not need him to *establish* mediocrity as the norm. The contribution of Luther was necessary and correct, albeit non-dialectical. The essence of the problem was with the appropriation of Luther after his death. The early Kierkegaard placed the responsibility for this error on the followers of Luther—including himself at times—who were less tempted to doubt God's forgiveness and more tempted by worldliness and the tendency to gloss over the antinomian question. "The Lutheran attitude is excellent, it is the truth. I have concerning this excellent Lutheran attitude only one doubt. Not as regards the Lutheran attitude, no, it only concerns myself: that I have made sure that I am not an honest soul, but a sly fellow."[39] Later in life, as we have seen, the blame shifted to Luther himself.

Whether or not we should place the blame on Luther with Kierkegaard, or with later Lutheranism, like Spener, is to miss the point. Kierkegaard was responding to the worldly Christianity of his day by insisting that appeals to Luther's emphasis on grace need to take account of the fact that he was a corrective to a particular problem at a particular time. No theologian, especially a reformer, should ever have his or her theology enshrined as the norm for Christianity; yet this was what Lutherans had done with Luther. In order to respond to Lutheranism's comfortable and contented reliance on grace, which leads to worldliness, Kierkegaard began by introducing a counter-corrective to the institutionalized position of Luther: There must be

---

[38] Pap. XI¹ A 61; as in Prenter 162f.
[39] As in Prenter, 133.

imitation. At the same time, he was willing to admit that the time would come when his corrective would become unnecessary, and the voice of mediocrity would again need to be heard. It was his hope, however, that when that time arrived, his own contribution would not have been normalized and stand in the way of the latest corrective.

Law and Love

In placing such emphasis on the law, some have suggested that he failed to understand Luther's emphasis on faith and mercy. The Swedish Lutheran scholar Torsten Bohlin argued that, in a certain sense, Kierkegaard always lived under the law.[40] However, as we have seen, Kierkegaard's literary emphasis on the law should be understood as part of a theological corrective to make up for what he believed was lacking in Luther's theology. It should thereby be expected to contain an inflated emphasis on imitation. At the same time, it is hard to miss in Kierkegaard an underlying foundation for his work based on God's mercy, grace, and love. Walter Lowrie reminds us, "Love and forgiveness are the themes [he] was most inclined to dwell upon—even when he was meditating his attack upon the Church."[41] In Kierkegaard's own words, "I learned from [my father] what fatherly love is, and through this I gained a conception of divine fatherly love, the one single unshakable thing in life, the true Archimedean point."[42] Kierkegaard did certainly emphasize the law in a way that Luther never did. He used language, the language of imitation, in a way that is rarely found in Luther. Nonetheless, his reason for doing so—to drive the sinner to the point of despairing of her own strength and, hopefully, into the arms of the redeemer—is indeed most faithful to Luther. His hope was not to replace the gospel with the law, but to present the New Testament's radical moral demands strictly in order "that you admit that this is the requirement, and then have recourse to grace."[43]

The Leap

The precondition for asking the antinomian question, as we have said, is that one actually be justified. In order to be justified, Luther and Kierkegaard agreed, one must despair of ever meriting God's graciousness. The means to accomplish this is the law. After repentance, of course, one must come to the point of having faith. As Kierkegaard reminds us, however, "the first

---

[40] See Schröer's discussion of Bohlin on this point in "Kierkegaard und Luther," 229.
[41] Lowrie, *Kierkegaard*, 459.
[42] As quoted in *The Moment*, intro. xii.
[43] Ibid., 292.

condition, nevertheless, for my arriving at faith is that I become aware of whether I have it or not."[44] Faith cannot be something that one is born into, that I can inherit from my parents. None may assume that they have faith simply because they were born, baptized, and confirmed in a "Christian" nation. Rather, faith is a profound, immensely difficult, life-changing, and rare event. In fact, if one takes one's faith for granted, that is a good indicator that what one has is not genuine faith. "If anyone thinks he has faith and yet is indifferent toward this possession, is neither cold nor hot, he can be certain that he does not have faith. If anyone thinks he is a Christian and yet is indifferent toward being that, then he really is not one at all. Indeed, what would we think of a person who gave assurances that he was in love and also that it was a matter of indifference to him?"[45] Moreover, as should be apparent, knowledge of the teachings of the Lutheran church is no indicator that one has faith either. Kierkegaard introduces Johannes de Silentio, the pseudonymous author of *Fear and Trembling,* who gives a remarkably adroit exposition on what Christianity is, but confesses his inability to believe. "I cannot make the movement of faith," he tells us, "this courage I lack." For de Silentio, faith is such a remarkable and uncommon occurrence, that he confesses, "I wonder if anyone in my generation is able to make the movement of faith."[46] Kierkegaard wants to communicate, particularly in *Fear and Trembling,* that the leap of faith is a phenomenal event in an individual's life. By discussing faith in this way, Kierkegaard puts the breaks on the antinomian question. "[We may say]... 'if you have faith unto salvation, then you will be saved.' How lenient, how merciful! But is it also certain, then, that I have faith?"[47] Before someone makes the move to libertinism based on his justification, Kierkegaard wants that person to consider whether or not he indeed has the faith he is counting on to excuse him from judgment.

To begin with, the belief that all in Denmark are Christians, and are therefore people of faith because they were born into a Christian country, baptized, and even confirmed, is one that Kierkegaard could not accept. He both mocked and lamented the accepted principle that all baptized Danes could automatically enjoy the benefits that come with faith without its obligations, as we saw above in his remarks about the brothel owner. His comments about baptism, however, are cryptic. At times they appear to reject completely Luther's understanding of the sacramental value of the washing

---

[44] *Discourses,* 27.
[45] *Works of Love,* 26f.
[46] *Fear and Trembling,* 34.
[47] *Works of Love,* 378.

of rebirth in baptism.[48] At others, however, he hints at an understanding of baptism that parallels Spener's; baptism may save, but we still must appropriate the claims and faith of baptism later in life.[49] At the very least, we may say that Kierkegaard, like Spener, wanted to insist that his readers understand that faith is more than a seal-of-approval bestowed at baptism that eternally marks one as a person of faith.

For those who may have difficulty swallowing Kierkegaard's ambiguous views on infant baptism, his remarks about children will definitely get stuck in their throats. In *The Moment* he informs his shocked readers, "The truth is: one cannot become a Christian as a child; it is just as impossible as it is impossible for a child to beget children.... To become a Christian presupposes (according to the New Testament) a personal consciousness of sin and of oneself as a sinner."[50] This he believed children were unable to do, and therefore could not be included among those considered Christians. Does this mean that children cannot be "saved" or that they are excluded from justifying grace during their youth? Not necessarily, as we will see later in this chapter. Rather, Kierkegaard is reacting (some might say overreacting) to the diluted conception of faith that welcomed all people into its embrace because of the nation of their birth. Faith is much more than that.

For a person to come to faith, to take what Kierkegaard became famous for calling the "leap" of faith, necessarily involves a great deal of existential commitment from an individual. First, there is the requisite "sickness unto death"—the succumbing to despair discussed above. However, even more difficult than this radical repentance is the movement of faith itself. He sets the ideal before his readers in order that they might understand that faith is not the recitation of the creed or assent to the Formula of Concord; faith is seen in the examples of Abraham ("God himself will provide the lamb for the burnt offering, my son"[51]), of Job ("The Lord gave and the Lord has taken away; may the name of the Lord be praised"[52]), and of Paul ("I ask you, therefore, not to be discouraged because of my sufferings for you, which are your glory"[53]), to mention but a few. The commitment of most who claim to have faith pales in the face of these examples; they are forced

[48] See for example, *Postscript,* 363ff.
[49] Consider what Kierkegaard suggests a few pages after the above-mentioned quote. "Let it be ten times true that Baptism is a divine passport for eternity, but if light-mindedness and worldliness want to use it as a permit, is it then still a passport?" *Postscript,* 368. See also *Works of Love,* 379.
[50] *The Moment,* 238.
[51] See *Fear and Trembling.*
[52] See *Discourses,* 109ff.
[53] See *Discourses,* 80ff.

to reconsider whether what they thought they possessed is actually genuine faith. This is exactly what Kierkegaard wants them to do.

Faith and Ethics

In addition to holding these ideals before his readers, Kierkegaard also goes to great pains to distinguish genuine Christian faith from what often poses as Christianity. In his exhaustive consideration of the temptation of Abraham, a clear line is drawn between the spheres of ethics and faith. Abraham is praised and considered to be the father of faith, not because of a commitment to some universal standard of ethics, but because of his willingness to transcend the ethical realm. In agreeing to sacrifice his son, Abraham was turning his back on an ethical principle that Jews and Christians believe binds all people. Clearly he would have preferred to abide by the ethical standard that forbids such conduct. Nevertheless, he was willing to put aside his own desires, the future of his family, his wife's honor, and the indubitable moral proscription against such behavior for the sake of obedience to God. Clearly the movements of faith are found elsewhere than in abiding by society's accepted moral norms. However, what made Abraham a *"Knight of Faith"* was his willingness to believe also in the absurd promise that he would receive his son back. This is the model of faith for Kierkegaard. Ethics is a mere stepping-stone on the way to this ideal. Even the pseudonymous author of this work, de Silentio, who understands faith better than the vast majority of Christians, testifies to how difficult and rare this faith is. He tells us, "I cannot make the movement of faith, I cannot shut my eyes and plunge confidently into the absurd."[54]

Unfortunately, in recent years there has been a tendency to take what Kierkegaard made more difficult and once again make it easy enough for everyone to have. This principle, that faith stands above and beyond ethics, was intended not only as a rebuttal to the ethics of Kant and Hegel,[55] but as a call to recognize that faith is an exceptional spiritual movement that no one can take for granted or assume they possess because they have been baptized. Among some recent scholars, however, this latter theme seems to have been ignored. C. Stephen Evans, in discussing Kierkegaard's distinction between ethics and faith, makes the argument that the "situation of being 'outside the universal,' of finding something in life incommensurable with the life-view of a rational, social ethic is one that everyone who is truly honest will find

---

[54] *Fear and Trembling*, 34.
[55] See further Ronald M. Green, " 'Developing' *Fear and Trembling*," in *The Cambridge Companion to Kierkegaard*, eds. Alastair Hannay & Gordon D. Marino (Cambridge: Cambridge University Press, 1998) 257–281.

herself in. "[56] For Evans, all of humanity experiences being "outside the universal," that is, above and beyond the ethical realm. Kierkegaard only wants us to see that "it is at least possible for God to encounter a person directly, not simply through social ideas, and that such an encounter can provide a new self, a new identity, and a new understanding of the purpose of human existence."[57] While this notion of transcending one's culture and society does indeed fit well with the ideas of later existentialists, and can find some basis in Kierkegaard, this is certainly not his point in *Fear and Trembling.* In reading Evans' enthusiastic description of this move outside the universal, there is the sense that he is describing what will surely be a liberating experience. Completely missing is the horror that Abraham experienced, precisely by being outside the universal. When the move beyond the universal becomes an event that all of us make, almost as a matter of course, the road to faith becomes a lot smoother than what Kierkegaard took pains to describe.

John Caputo also makes use of this transcendence of the universal in his ethical theory. In *Against Ethics* he explains that the move beyond the universal means a move beyond law. There are no specific ethical rules on which one may rely to determine one's behavior. However, as in the case of Abraham, this makes things not easier but indeed more difficult. "Far from granting us unlimited licentiousness, lifting the universal makes things more difficult, more paralyzing. Divested of the guardrails of the universal, the single individual—Abraham—enters a fearsome sphere of singularity, silence, and incommunicability, where there is no law to fall back upon."[58] What remains is a guiding principle of love; the specific rules of ethics are removed. Rather than society's constraining dictates of the good, Caputo directs us to "one of the most beautiful maxims of the medieval masters: *dilige, et vis quod fac*: Love, and do what you will. Love—that is, answer the call wherever you are needed—and do what you will."[59] While this approach to ethics appeals to many in our postmodern world, it is problematical to base it on Kierkegaard, as Caputo seeks to do. To begin with, it should be obvious that removing the guardrails of particular notions of the good and relying on the principle of love would not have led Abraham to the point of agreeing to offer his son. Indeed, it was his own love for his son that made

[56] C. Stephen Evans, "Faith as the *Telos* of Morality: A Reading of *Fear and Trembling,*" in *International Kierkegaard Commentary: Fear and Trembling and Repetition,* ed. Robert L. Perkins (Macon, GA: Mercer University Press, 1993), 21.
[57] Ibid., 23.
[58] John D. Caputo, *Against Ethics* (Bloomington: Indiana University Press, 1993), 107.
[59] Ibid., 41.

the sacrifice so difficult. While Caputo describes the requisite judging after the suspension of the law as elastic, agile, flexible, and "a slippery affair,"[60] Kierkegaard's account of Abraham's move beyond the ethical is based not on his own reason, but on God's command. For Kierkegaard, the one who hears about the suspension of the ethical and announces, "That's for me!" has not understood what is entailed in such a move. There is a great deal that is appealing in Caputo; much could even fit within Luther's theology. However, his attempt to establish an ethic without guardrails based on Abraham's move beyond the universal is problematic. Abraham's move leads the individual outside ethics, not to a new ethical system. More importantly, this essential element in faith is based on a new connection to the divine, not simply the severing of ties with society.

Religiousness A and B

Beyond distinguishing the realm of faith from that of ethics, Kierkegaard wanted to make it clear to his readers that one may differentiate between religious experience and Christian faith; what he referred to in the *Postscript* as Religiousness A and Religiousness B. Kierkegaard's understanding of the nature of Christian faith is far more nuanced than an experience of the numinous. An existential pursuit of God, even the Christian God, was not sufficient to constitute faith for him. This type of religiousness is what the pseudonymous Johannes Climacus defined as Religiousness A. This type of religiousness does exhibit passion on the part of the believer; it is more than historical knowledge. Genuine and heartfelt concern, inward deepening, and existential interest in God are part of this religious expression. Moreover, it may very well be dialectical in its appreciation of the difference between God and humanity, and Kierkegaard never dared to disparage this type of religious experience. At the same time, however, he understood there to be a sharp distinction between Religiousness A and Religiousness B, the latter being the expression of genuine Christian faith.

Climacus offers the following definition: "Religiousness B...or paradoxical religiousness...makes conditions in such a way that the conditions are not the dialectical concentrations of inward deepening but a definite some-thing that qualifies the eternal happiness more specifically (whereas in A the more specific qualification of inward deepening is the only more specific qualification)."[61] This statement requires a little unpacking before we pro-ceed further. The essence of what Climacus is expressing is that in Religiousness A the qualification for relating oneself to the divine is inward

---

[60] Ibid., 108.
[61] *Postscript*, 556.

deepening, i.e. appropriation of the religious teachings by the individual. Religiousness B requires an additional condition: the acceptance of a specific principle that qualifies one for an eternal happiness. That specific principle is the belief in the paradox of the god in time, i.e. the incarnation.

The qualitative difference between Religiousness A and B is that in the latter, the believer has made the essential movement of faith: acceptance of the paradox. Adherents of Religiousness A seek to relate themselves to the divine directly through inward deepening, that is, through their own efforts to touch God directly, which Kierkegaard saw as impossible, and indeed a mark of Paganism. "All paganism consists in this, that God is related directly to a human being, as the remarkably striking to the amazed."[62] Those who partake of Religiousness B, on the other hand, couple the *pathos* of subjective religious interest with an embracing of the paradox, thereby creating a new *pathos*. The paradox of the god-man is essential to genuine Christian faith, for Kierkegaard, in that it offers the link from humanity to God. Embracing the paradox of the Eternal in time allows one to connect with God, not by one's own efforts to enter Eternity, nor by debasing the divine by bringing it into our finitude, like one finds with the Pagan gods, but by virtue of the "absurd" belief that God existed historically as a man. This existential commitment, then, is required of an individual before she can make the move required in Religiousness B.

The difference, then, between these two types of religious experience has to do with the embracing of the paradox as the condition that qualifies the believer for eternal happiness. However, Kierkegaard does not want his readers to see the acceptance of the paradox as merely one particular religious doctrine alongside other doctrines such as election, the sacraments, or ecclesiology. The paradox is far more than a doctrine. It is the life-changing condition that makes authentic living as a human being possible. Moreover, personally embracing a paradox as the moral and religious foundation for one's life is far from a simple task. The person who claims to have done this without the prerequisite existential *Angst* involved in grounding one's existence in an absurd belief has not made the movement of genuine Christian faith. Kierkegaard spilled a great deal of ink on this issue, not to make a contribution to Christian theology, dogmatics, or systematic theology, but to force his reader to ask whether he himself indeed has Christian faith. If not, the individual can no longer defend an indolent moral life on the basis of his status as a justified believer.

---

[62] *Postscript*, 245.

Subjectivity

Perhaps the most often misunderstood aspect of Kierkegaard's thought is found in his discussions of objectivity and subjectivity. His insistence that Christian faith must be subjective should not be understood as suggesting that the truth claims of the gospel are relative. Twentieth century notions of subjective truth cannot intrude upon his discussions of faith and knowledge without seriously compromising his thought. The meaning of the word "subjectivity" in this context is rather to be found among the Pietists of the previous two centuries. It is the same idea that Luther stressed in the sixteenth century. Subjectivity in this sense has to do with the personal appropriation of truth claims. As mentioned above, Kierkegaard's early encounter with Luther after the publication of *Either/Or* led him to recognize that he had found a kindred spirit in his insistence on the necessity of subjectivity in Christian faith.

The despair that follows from human attempts at imitation, the offense that is taken at the paradox of the god in time, and the leap of faith that leaves one without any firm epistemological grounding, none of these can be grasped through doctrine. Only when they are personally experienced do they become truth, "for only the truth that builds up is truth for you."[63] Kierkegaard's point here is not a metaphysical one; he is not presenting a new epistemology. His point is rather simple, and the Pietists had made it repeatedly in previous centuries. For example, I cannot say that I believe in hell and then not care about my own or anyone else's eternal destiny. I cannot say I love my father and then treat him with disregard. I cannot say that I believe the law and the gospel and then not manifest them in my life. With this approach to the subjectivity of knowledge, Kierkegaard is repeating what Luther and Spener had previously said. The claims of Christianity must be individually appropriated in order for them to be meaningful, effective, life changing, and, in Kierkegaard's words, true. Christianity does not consist of its truth claims, but in the individual's existential reception of the message of Christ: "Christianity is spirit; spirit is inwardness; inwardness is subjectivity; subjectivity is essentially passion, and at its maximum an infinite, personally interested passion for one's eternal happiness."[64]

It was the passionless Christianity of the nineteenth century Danish Church—a Christianity that generally assented to Lutheran doctrine and the cerebral system of Hegel, and sought explanation over experience—that was

---

[63] *Either/Or*, trans. Howard V. Hong and Edna H. Hong (Princeton: Princeton University Press, 1987), 2:354.
[64] *Postscript*, 33.

responsible for the sad state of affairs in Danish Christendom. These types of objective knowledge do not grasp the essentially Christian at all. "In relation to Christianity, however, objectivity is an extremely unfortunate category, and the one who has objective Christianity and nothing else is *eo ipso* [by that very fact] a pagan, because Christianity is precisely a matter of spirit and of subjectivity and of inwardness."[65]

In respect to subjectivity in Christianity, the problem Kierkegaard had with established Christendom was not so much the doctrines themselves, but the failure of the Danish clergy to assist their parishioners in appropriating these claims. He could repeat again and again, "I have no proposal to make concerning the established order."[66] "The *doctrine* is all right."[67] In this respect, Marie Thulstrup correctly compares Kierkegaard to his pietist forebears who had no intention of changing doctrine, but only its application. "[T]hey demanded an existential attitude and the implementation of doctrine in life."[68]

It is true that Kierkegaard's use of the category of subjectivity carried him further theologically than Luther and the Pietists had gone. His rejection of any objective basis for making the leap of faith took subjectivity to an entirely new level. Nonetheless, we may find at the base of his radical insistence on subjectivity the fundamental concern that Christianity must not be confused with a passionless religion which fails to change one's life and conveys a false assurance as to one's standing before God. By combating this misconception, Kierkegaard believed that he could counter the unspoken claims of so many in Denmark who believed that the life of sanctification need not be a primary concern for those who have been justified.

Freedom

Within the discussion of the leap of faith, Kierkegaard appealed greatly to individual freedom and, subsequently, individual responsibility with regard to the Christian life. Lowrie tells us, "He repudiated the doctrine of predestination and contended passionately for the freedom of the will."[69] In a way reminiscent of Melanchthon, Kierkegaard appears convinced that a greater emphasis on human freedom may manifest itself in less apathy or fatalism within Christendom. Each individual has the freedom and responsibility to decide whether or not to make the leap of faith. At the same time, as with

---

[65] Ibid., 43.
[66] *Pap.* X^3 A 187; as in *SKJP* 1:67.
[67] As quoted in *Attack upon "Christendom,"* trans. Walter Lowrie (Princeton: Princeton University Press, 1944), xxi.
[68] Thulstrup, "Pietism," 212.
[69] Lowrie, *Kierkegaard,* 8.

Melanchthon, some of his more forthright positions on freedom appear to be quite at odds with Luther.[70] Luther clearly rejected the notion that faith, or belief, comes from our own willing; it is the gift of God alone. We can hardly be surprised that Kierkegaard has been understood to be opposed to Luther's notion of the bondage of the will or anything that smacks of determinism.[71]

Did Kierkegaard, then, transgress against Luther's understanding of God as the architect and origin of Christian faith? Did he, like Melanchthon in the Synergistic Controversy, credit too much to humanity in order to avoid the libertinism that may flow from fatalism? I believe this is unlikely, although I would have to say that the legacy Kierkegaard has left us is unclear. To begin with, as one will recall from chapter two, the Synergistic Controversy dealt only with the initial point of conversion; the orthodox opponents of Melanchthon granted that after that point there is cooperation in the life of faith. Kierkegaard, however, wrote little about the moment of conversion. His concern was largely with the practical affair of having or maintaining faith *today*; abstract discussions regarding a specific point of time in the past held little interest for him. When Kierkegaard insists that faith necessarily exists in freedom, he is addressing his readers as they are today, not in their past (or future) religious conversion.

Secondly, Kierkegaard does have a great deal to say about the necessary preconditions for faith. Both the awareness of sin and the condition for faith come from God alone through Christ, the god in time. "[I]f a human being is to come truly to know something about the unknown (the god), he must first come to know that it is different from him, absolutely different from him. The understanding cannot come to know this by itself...if it is going to come to know this, it must come to know this from the god."[72] Likewise he tells us, "The condition [for faith] is a gift of God and a perfection that makes it possible to receive the good and perfect gift."[73]

Keeping in mind the intent of Kierkegaard's work as well as what he has written about the condition for faith coming from God alone, it would be premature to label Kierkegaard a synergist. As he was not particularly interested in discussing abstract theological questions, like whether or not humans are passive or cooperate in the singular moment of their conversion,

---

[70] Consider, for example, the "Interlude" in *Philosophical Fragments,* trans. Howard V. Hong and Edna H. Hong (Princeton: Princeton University Press, 1985): "belief is not a knowledge but an act of freedom, an expression of will." p. 83
[71] See Schröer, "Kierkegaard und Luther," 231.
[72] *Fragments,* 46. See further Paul Sponheim, "Is Forgiveness Enough? A Kierkegaardian Response," *Word and World* 16, no.3 (1996): 320–327.
[73] *Works of Love,* 137. See further *Fragments,* 63f.

we cannot pigeonhole him on this point. His preference for practical issues precludes us from answering definitively whether or not he was a synergist. While his comments about freedom certainly suggest disparity with Luther, we should remember that most of the comments are in the context of his response to Hegel's philosophy, maintaining that nothing in history, past or future, represents a logical process that is determined. He was certainly not suggesting that humans have the freedom to escape their own sin, or what is called "untruth" in the *Fragments*. The freedom that he was speaking of had little if anything to do with the freedom that Luther denied in *The Bondage of the Will*.

The Requirement

The final aspect of the Christian life that Kierkegaard wanted to problematize is the daily manifestation of the Christian faith, or what he called the "requirement." Being a Christian is not a free ride; there are obligations that are required of the children of God. Grace, of course, is clearly necessary for salvation. The question many of his readers have posed, as we shall see, is whether it is sufficient. Kierkegaard's discussions of the "requirement" that accompany faith tend to make orthodox Lutherans a bit nervous, and may partially explain the reluctance to make more use of him within orthodox circles. This requirement, or responsibility, was most clearly expressed later in his life,[74] and perhaps most directly in the tenth and final installment of *The Moment*, published after his death. Here he writes:

> A man dies and in his will designates someone as the heir to his entire fortune—but there is a condition, something that is required of the heir, and this does not please the heir. What does he do then? He takes possession of the fortune left to him—because, as he says, he is indeed the heir—and says good-bye to the responsibility.... It is the same with "Christendom." Christianity is a gift, if you will, stipulated for humanity according to the testament of the Savior of the world. But there is responsibility.... Christendom's skullduggery is to accept the gift and say good-bye to the responsibility.[75]

On the following page he reminds us that the responsibility is none other than the imitation of Jesus Christ. And so imitation reenters the picture. Now, however, it is not present as the mirror of the law to drive the sinner to despair, but as the requirement and responsibility for the Christian life. Please note that this latter use is not simply the third use of the law. Kierkegaard is making a bolder claim here than Melanchthon did in 1534. Imitation is not present simply to demonstrate how we *should* live, but as a

---

[74] See further Hirsch, *Kierkegaard-Studien*, 330ff.
[75] *The Moment*, 336.

demonstration of how we are *required* to live. Christians are required to live their lives in imitation of Christ. His language is striking. In the quote above, he is willing to grant that Christianity is a gift; it is the *"but"* that comes afterwards that troubles so many with Lutheran sensibilities.

If the notion of a requirement of imitation in Christianity appears somewhat demanding of human effort, the descriptions of this life of imitation double the responsibility. His accounts of what is entailed in imitation, especially in his later years, are remarkable. In an earlier installment of *The Moment*, Kierkegaard informs his readers, "In the New Testament, according to Christ's own teaching, to be a Christian is, to speak merely humanly, sheer agony, an agony compared with which all other human sufferings are almost only childish pranks."[76] And again, "the more you involve yourself with God and the more he loves you, the more you will become, humanly speaking, unhappy for this life, the more you will come to suffer in this life."[77]

Kierkegaard himself believed he had traveled this road of self-denial, although imperfectly, for the sake of his faith. In his journals he quotes Christian Scriver[78]: *"Aliis inserviendo consumor:* that fits my life, I am being sacrificed for others."[79] Clearly missing in his works are the descriptions of joy in life that one finds in Luther. At the same time, we should not forget that his reception of the gospel message brought him great joy as well. Nonetheless, he wanted to remind his readers that the Christian life is one of suffering…a requirement of suffering. Whether this was a corrective to Luther or a frank perception on his part is difficult to judge.

A great number of eminent Kierkegaard scholars have understood remarks like the ones above to suggest that he rejected Luther's position of *sola fide* as the basis for salvation. Walter Lowrie, the most influential Kierkegaard scholar from the United States, could not be more clear of his conviction that Kierkegaard rejected Luther's understanding of salvation: "With respect to the doctrine of 'works' [Kierkegaard] was clearly not in sympathy with the position characteristic of the Reformers…. [T]he reader has had abundant opportunity to observe other fundamental traits of his thinking which must have compelled him to discard Luther's characteristic assertion that salvation is 'by faith alone'."[80] He continues, "[I]t must have

---

[76] Ibid., 189.
[77] Ibid., 212.
[78] A man, interestingly enough, who had fallen under the influence of Spener. See further Thulstrup, "Pietism," 192f.
[79] As quoted in Thulstrup, "Pietism," 193.
[80] Lowrie, *Kierkegaard*, 375.

seemed to him that 'faith *alone'* was not only monstrous but impossible, equivalent to 'faith without works'."[81]

In a sense, Lowrie is correct. Kierkegaard did insist that works must accompany faith, and if a person claims to have faith and does not have works, that person cannot be considered a Christian and does not possess saving grace. In this sense, yes, Kierkegaard believed that faith cannot exist alone and it must be accompanied by works. The only problem for Lowrie, however, is that Luther maintained this as well. In the first chapter of this dissertation we saw that Luther had explained, "For God has made a coven-ant with those who are in Christ, so that there is no condemnation *if they fight* against themselves and their sin."[82] Likewise, the reverse also holds true. "Whoever has had faith at some time but now has no love, no longer has that faith."[83] Luther held that a Christian's faith must be accompanied by the "fight" against sin and the sinful nature; it must be accompanied by love. Kierkegaard used the word "imitation," but he was essentially saying the same thing. Lowrie is correct in saying that for Kierkegaard "faith alone" is not sufficient for a Christian. He is not correct, however, in his conclusion that this differentiates him from Luther.

The answer to this misunderstanding has already been elucidated in previous chapters. For Luther, it is faith alone that creates and sustains a saving relationship with the Creator. The good works, love, battle against sin, and imitation that follow are evidence of faith and assist the individual believer in continuing the life of faith; they do not contribute to one's salvation. In order for us to conclude whether or not Kierkegaard rejected Luther's understanding of *sola fide* as the sufficient source of salvation, we need to ask whether Kierkegaard saw the requirement of imitation in the same way that Luther understood the fight against sin.

The difficulty with finding allusions to the sufficiency of faith for salvation in Kierkegaard's writings is that he is writing as a corrective against those who would abuse it. As a result, he spends a great deal of time stressing the requirement that accompanies faith and spends considerably less on his belief that grace is freely given by God apart from any worthiness or cooperation on the part of the individual. And yet, this latter theme can be found. In his journals, one may find the following confession of a very Luther-an understanding of grace.

> The relation of Christ as redeemer to the believer is, I think, somewhat like that of an adult to children when the adult says: Now I will take care of everything; just be

---

[81] Ibid. See also his introduction to *Kierkegaard's Attack upon "Christendom,"* xvii.

[82] *LW* 32, 239, emphasis mine.

[83] *WA* 34[1], 168.

very calm and trust me—and then he becomes angry when the children, instead of being happy and letting him take care of things, want to do it themselves. I believe that Christ as redeemer is angered in the same way when the believer in any manner occupies himself with making restitution for his sin. No! The atonement is the decisive thing.[84]

While human beings want to contribute to the gift of salvation, Kierkegaard tells us, they not only are unable, they sin by even trying. The requirement of imitation that follows upon faith, then, plays no role in the saving act, of which God alone is the author. Koenker correctly explains that, for Kierkegaard, even the efforts born of gratitude, which lead to the fulfillment of the responsibilities of faith, are themselves grace.[85] These responsibilities should never be minimized or ignored, but neither should they be seen as providing any merit or support for one's status as a child of God. Koenker points to an entry in Kierkegaard's journals that is of considerable help in understanding the latter's understanding of grace and human works: "Christianity requires everything of you, but when you have accomplished everything it requires, all the same, that you realize you have been saved by grace alone and nothing else."[86] The Christian faith requires sinners to seek the life of imitation in order to discover their own moral depravity and need for God's grace. Moreover, this does not end with an individual's conversion. Christianity demands that one pursue this requirement throughout one's whole life, so that one's need for grace is never forgotten. Prenter correctly explains Kierkegaard's position: "But if the demand of imitation, the requirement of *existing* as a Christian, is not maintained without compromise, there will be no humiliation and consequently no forgiving grace.... And in this view he believed himself to be in profound harmony with Luther's doctrine about law and gospel."[87] The fundamental difference is that Kierkegaard emphasized what Luther feared to express. One must continually strive to be like Christ—to obey the law—in order to work out one's salvation; not because the works merit God's continued grace, but so that one is continually brought in fear and trembling to the throne of grace. Here again, there is no essential difference in *theology* between Luther and Kierkegaard, but only a difference in its *expression*.

One may object that Kierkegaard's language often *suggests* that works are necessary to earn salvation. This observation may have some merit, but

---

[84] *Pap* X² A 208; as in *SKJP* 1:428.
[85] Koenker, "Kierkegaard on Luther," 243. However, while Koenker points to this very Lutheran theme in Kierkegaard, he seems unaware that it comes from Luther himself.
[86] Koenker, 242; *Pap* X³ a 353. See also *Works of Love*, 379: "[God requires that] the human being itself not dare to think that he has some meritoriousness."
[87] Prenter, "Luther," 149.

no more merit than the observation that many of Luther's comments *suggest* libertinism or fatalism. It is difficult to find any essential works righteousness in the man who, when asked on his deathbed whether he relied upon grace, responded, "Naturally. What else?"[88]

To Be a Christian

As we have seen, one can always count on Kierkegaard to be difficult. On the one hand, we may read his deathbed confession of reliance upon grace. On the other, shortly before his death, in his last installment of *The Moment,* he explains to his readers, "I do not call myself a Christian; I do not speak of myself as a Christian."[89] Comments such as these have led to considerable confusion as to whether Kierkegaard truly experienced Christian faith. Questions regarding whether Kierkegaard was a Christian, or believed himself to be a Christian, often betray a failure to understand what he wanted to convey in remarks such as the one just quoted. To understand what he was trying to say, and why, the reader must overcome the habit of equating the word "Christian" with a recipient of God's saving grace. For Kierkegaard, they are not necessarily the same.

A "Christian," for Kierkegaard, is not simply a person who believes, but an individual whose life is a true witness to the truth; not in some partial way, but as one finds in the example of the apostles. The name "Christian" should be reserved, then, for those who live in a manner consistent with the teachings of the New Testament. Insofar as there are exceedingly few who fulfill this calling, he could say that Christians are extremely rare. He explained in a letter to the editor of *The Fatherland,* "I have no doubt at all that every individual in the nation will be honest enough to God and to himself to say in a private conversation, 'If I am to be honest, I do not deny it, I am not a Christian in the New Testament sense; if I am to be honest, I do not deny it, my life cannot be called a striving toward what the New Testament calls Christianity, toward denying myself, renouncing the world, dying to the world, etc.'"[90] This is certainly not to say that he did not believe there was one person in the whole nation of Denmark who possessed saving faith, who was justified in the eyes of God. He certainly believed that God had forgiven and forgotten his own sins.[91] Rather, he made a distinction between those who are justified and those who are living the Christian life as they have been called to do. For Kierkegaard, being a Christian and having faith are not

---

[88] Quoted in *Attack upon "Christendom,"* xvii.
[89] *The Moment,* 340.
[90] Ibid., 36.
[91] See Lowrie, *Kierkegaard,* 387.

synonymous. This is in clear contradistinction from the language of most of Christendom and of Luther as well. Prenter points out, "Here again is an essential difference between Luther and Kierkegaard. According to Luther taking refuge in God's forgiving grace is to be a *Christian* in the way in which it is required of everybody.... [W]e *are Christians in the strictest sense.*"[92]

The reason for this odd change in definitions is part and parcel of Kierkegaard's ongoing attempt to make the Christian life more difficult. Luther, he believed, had painted the picture of a Christian as such a mediocre fellow that there was no ideal left to strive for. Christianity was easy and required no real effort. The result was an indolent Christendom that took its alleged Christian faith for granted. This could be counteracted, he believed, by holding up the example of the true Christian, the Knight of Faith, the witness to the truth. This paragon, he believed, would compel the hypocrites to recognize their lack of faith and would provide those living with faith a model to remind them of their requirement and their continual need for forgiveness and grace. At the same time, he had no intention of allowing himself, as the author of this model, to be confused with the ideal; hence his odd comments about not considering himself a Christian. He explains, "Certainly it is of the utmost importance that in every generation the ideal picture of the Christian should be held up prominently, and illuminated precisely with a view to the errors of the time being; but he who draws this picture must above all things guard against mistaking himself for it."[93] Thus, we may understand his conviction that he should not be called a Christian, even in the last year of his life: "I do not call myself a Christian (keeping the ideal free),"[94] and "just because I do not call myself a Christian, it is impossible to get rid of me."[95] His own shortcomings could thereby never diminish what the life of a Christian should be, nor would he allow his own weaknesses to be viewed as permissible by those who followed him.

Kierkegaard's intent in redefining the word "Christian" in such a way as to compel others to continue striving was clearly an attempt to respond to the libertinism that followed from Luther's permissive attitude toward moral mediocrity. However, his cryptic and personalized definitions may do more harm than good insofar as few readers are able to discern what he was trying

---

[92] Prenter, "Luther," 149f.

[93] See Lowrie, 446. See also Kierkegaard's description of the poor soldier who must always be motivated by the aspiration of one day becoming a general, even if one know that the chances of this happening are exceedingly slim. *The Moment*, 314.

[94] *The Moment*, 341.

[95] Ibid., 342.

to convey by declaring that he was not to be called a Christian. Those who do not decode Kierkegaard's language may conclude that he is arguing that to be a Christian, i.e. to be "saved," requires that a person live an exceptional life. This may then lead either to attempts to earn one's salvation or a despair that fails to be comforted by the gospel. The others, who do come to understand Kierkegaard's new definition of "Christian," can simply comfort themselves with the knowledge that they can still receive saving grace without achieving this ideal standard. Kierkegaard's use of choice words and phrases to describe those who are truly paragons of Christian faith—as he does with "witness to the truth"—is a promising approach to responding to the contented and comfortable believer who is sure that all the necessary work of salvation was finished at the point of conversion. However, the games he plays with the word "Christian" only perpetuate misinterpretations of his understanding of grace and works. While this creative idea was well-intentioned and, strictly speaking, within the boundaries of *sola fide*, its considerable potential for confusion must be seen to outweigh its value as a response to the antinomian question.

Repetition

The last of Kierkegaard's contributions toward understanding the antinomian question that we shall treat here is found in his description of repetition. T. F. Morris has provided a wonderfully succinct definition of what Kierkegaard means by this word. He writes, "The task of repetition is to relate to something that has been found in the past to be meaningful, and to do so in the present."[96] What is in the future only resides with us in hope, while what has been in the past can only be recollected. Only what is carried in life in repetition can be truly present for an individual. Kierkegaard offered the following analogy in his 1843 work entitled *Repetition*: "Hope is a new garment, stiff and starched and lustrous, but it has never been tried on, and therefore one does not know how becoming it will be or how it will fit. Recollection is a discarded garment that does not fit, however beautiful it is, for one has outgrown it. Repetition is an indestructible garment that fits closely and tenderly, neither binds nor sags."[97] In the realm of Christianity, faith cannot be a movement of the past that is recollected or planned for in the future. As remarked on earlier, faith is not a previous action which one can look back on as evidence of one's justification; it must be enacted

---

[96] T. F. Morris, "Constanin Constantius's Search for an Acceptable Way of Life," in *International Kierkegaard Commentary: Fear and Trembling and Repetition*, ed. Robert L. Perkins (Macon, Georgia: Mercer University Press, 1993), 34.

[97] *Repetition*, trans. Howard V. Hong and Edna H. Hong (Princeton: Princeton University Press, 1983), 132.

repeatedly throughout one's life. In the *Postscript*, Kierkegaard submitted another image that suggests the necessity of repetition in the life of faith. "Sitting calmly on a ship in fair weather is not a metaphor for having faith; but when the ship has sprung a leak, then enthusiastically to keep the ship afloat by pumping and not to seek the harbor—that is the metaphor for having faith."[98]

The actions of faith must constantly be in motion if an individual is to possess the grace that is given through this faith. As we saw in Kierkegaard's cryptic remarks about baptism, even if this sacrament does confer the forgiveness of all sins, it can never be understood as a passport that forever grants admission to eternal happiness, for "a person is never saved except by 'working in fear and trembling.'"[99] As with Luther, Kierkegaard believed that faith is not guaranteed to persevere. Faith can be rejected; it can be lost. It may indeed be a free gift of God, but the human recipient must cooperate in the life of faith, fighting against sin and the sinful nature, acknowledging the responsibility and requirement of imitation. These works do not help earn one's eternal happiness, nor do they hold it fast; they rather strengthen and nourish faith so that it is not enervated to the point where it may be cast aside as useless. The failure to carry out one's faith in repetition—to continually repent, believe, and imitate Christ—is a sign of an emaciated or rejected faith. "If making a resolution is understood in this way to be the constant renewal of a crucial decision...then it remains fixed that resolution is a saving means."[100] Thus, for one to refuse the repetition of imitation is to neglect one's faith and undermine the basis for one's security. Faith, Kierkegaard would remind us, is more fragile than we realize.

While Luther shared this belief that saving faith must be enacted daily— that justification is not a talisman one wears around one's neck—there are differences between the two as to how they would communicate this belief. While Luther did maintain that faith can be lost, he spent little time discussing it. One reason was his fear that by focusing on the necessity of the believer's cooperation in holding on to faith, he might convey the message that one's works do indeed contribute to one's salvation. For this reason, his comments about individual responsibility in the ongoing struggle to work out one's faith in fear and trembling are few and far between. Others, like Spener, would emphasize this aspect of Luther's thought more during times which they believed were in need of hearing this message loud and clear.

---

[98] *Postscript*, 225n.
[99] *Discourses*, 183.
[100] Ibid., 352.

However, above and beyond this matter of a difference in emphasis, Kierkegaard's discussion of repetition carries with it another implication that Luther would have wanted to avoid. Part of Luther's insistence on faith alone as the sufficient condition for salvation was based on his concern that one may perceive oneself to be constantly losing and regaining one's faith. Fearing that this perception might undermine the joy, peace, and gratitude that spring from knowledge of one's salvation, and desiring that Christians trust in God's mercy rather than their own efforts for their eternal inheritance, Luther was wary of any theology or language that suggested that one's faith comes and goes on the basis of one's daily behavior.

While Kierkegaard never specifically suggested that faith is lost and reestablished on a regular basis among the faithful, his insistence on a constant renewal of the resolution to believe could be argued to suggest that one's standing before God is based on how one happens to act from day to day, or hour to hour. The potential fear that arises from constantly having to examine one's movements of faith, to see if they stand up to the admittedly difficult standards which Kierkegaard described, does hold the potential to undermine one's confidence in the mercy of God, placing the onus of salvation on one's own obedience to God. Again, as in the case of Kierkegaard's redefining of the word "Christian," there may be no fundamental point of disagreement between the theology of Luther and Kierkegaard—the doctrine of *sola fide* may be preserved in theory—but possible readings of Kierkegaard's descriptions of repetition do hold the potential for a serious undermining of trust in God as the sole author of one's salvation.

Conclusion

Walter Lowrie, in his authoritative biography, made the following remark about Kierkegaard's legacy. He wrote, "The effect of [Kierkegaard's] writings at that time, as it has been ever since, was to persuade some that they did not properly belong in the Church, to stimulate others to be better Protestants, and induce still others to take refuge in the Roman Church."[101] While the latter charge may have surprised him, he certainly had the first two in mind throughout nearly all of his writings. By raising the bar, some would be compelled to make an increased effort while others would decide to abandon the event in favor of easier labors. At the very least, Kierkegaard hoped, they would all recognize that the Christian faith is not a casual undertaking.

---

[101] Lowrie, *Kierkegaard,* 570.

His efforts to persuade Christendom of the difficulties of Christianity were clearly born of his concerns regarding the indolent approach to piety and faith within the Danish church. Luther's accreditation of mediocrity had become normative and the confidence in one's justification the basis for moral apathy. Moreover, this penchant for libertinism was not the result of cynical interpretations of the pastors' sermons, but the logical implication that followed from the preachers' diluted description of Christianity. The rigors of Christianity had to be restored.

For the most part, Kierkegaard's strong medicine—his lofty descriptions of the ethical life, the leap of faith, and the requirements for the Christian life—were a powerful corrective to the comfortable and easygoing patterns of life that the Church had made acceptable. In the world of spirit there can be no cheating, and the rules of the game, he insisted, are stricter than what was being communicated by the clergy. For those who desire to pursue the life of faith, the ideal must be elevated, for the watered-down requirements of Christendom have robbed the people of spiritual maturity and are making a mockery of the work of Christ.

The vast majority of Kierkegaard's theology fits within the parameters of Luther's thought. It has actually been misperceptions regarding the reformer's understanding of law and gospel that have led to various suggestions of their incompatibility. This is not to say that Luther would have approved of all that Kierkegaard said and did in his effort to restore Christianity, but his theology is indeed consistent with the principles of *sola fide* that Luther had described. The problem with Kierkegaard's contributions is not in their essential relation to the thought of Luther, but in their effects. His highly charged corrective to Lutheranism's antinomian tendencies often rings of Pelagianism, even if essentially it is not. The confusion following from the games he plays with the word "Christian" are a key example of the misunderstandings that easily arise from his passionate pursuit of the Christian ideal. Likewise, his focus on the daily requirements of repetition, while consistent with Luther in theory, is played out in such a way that one may easily conclude that one's faith comes and goes, day to day, on the basis of one's moral and religious conduct.

Kierkegaard offers a great deal in his own contributions toward a meaningful response to the antinomian question, and it is unfortunate that more of Lutheranism has not engaged his thought. His passion for religious seriousness and piety offer a much-needed corrective to tendencies in Protestant thought since the time of Luther's own corrective. At the same time, one needs to be careful when elevating the ideal in Christianity that one does not overshadow grace in the process. Kierkegaard may have been sufficiently dialectical in his own mind, but his writings do not always convey it so effectively.

○ℛ CHAPTER FIVE

Dietrich Bonhoeffer

"Cheap grace is the deadly enemy of our Church. We are fighting today for costly grace."[1] So begins the first chapter of Dietrich Bonhoeffer's influential, beloved, and most popular work, *The Cost of Discipleship*. His crusade against "cheap grace" has been an inspiration and clarion call for undertaking the rigors of the Christian life for every generation since his untimely death in 1945. With clarity and conviction, this first chapter points to the historical causes and unfortunate contemporary manifestations of Christian libertinism within the Protestant Church. With what would become the new slogan for those opposing antinomianism, he explained "cheap grace is the preaching of forgiveness without requiring repentance, baptism without church discipline, Communion without confession, absolution without personal confession."[2] The Church had been jumping the gun, proclaiming the benefits of faith without their necessary prerequisites and thereby operating as a peddler of cheap grace.

In Bonhoeffer's mind the fault does not lie, as it did for Kierkegaard, in the life and work of Luther. It was Luther, in fact, who had been called by God to restore the gospel of costly grace.[3] Luther had lived his life as a follower of Christ, demonstrating time and time again that he understood the precious gift of faith that he had been granted. The problem, Bonhoeffer tells us, is that while later generations repeated word for word Luther's doctrine, they neglected its requisite corollary, "the obligation of discipleship."[4] Again, in contrast to Kierkegaard, Bonhoeffer maintained that Luther did not need constantly to articulate this corollary, for it was manifest in his life. The fault lay with those who followed him, who took up the doctrine without understanding Luther's life of faith. "Judged by the standard of Luther's doctrine, that of his followers was unassailable, and yet their orthodoxy spelt

---

[1]*CD*, 45.
[2]Ibid., 47.
[3]Ibid., 50.
[4]Ibid., 53.

the end and destruction of the Reformation as the revelation on earth of the costly grace of God. "[5]

The result, as we have heard articulated in each of the three preceding chapters, was that society took advantage of the offer of free salvation. "The sacraments, the forgiveness of sins, and the consolation of religion are thrown away at cut prices."[6] The problem, Bonhoeffer explained, was that God's grace has been used to justify sin but not the sinner. The power of God is understood only to change the judgment against sin and not change the sinner herself. Add to this Lutheranism's radical insistence that sinners contribute nothing to their justification, and one has a recipe for libertinism based on cheap grace.

With such an immediate and outright attack on his culture's misappropriation of God's grace, in a book entitled *The Cost of Discipleship*, one would expect herein a systematic response to the flawed thinking behind this espousal of cheap grace. He certainly presented the central difficulty quite clearly in the first pages: "I can go and sin as much as I like, and rely on this grace to forgive me, for after all the world is justified in principle by grace."[7] One would think, then, that this text is the place to find some concrete answers to the antinomian question. Considering Bonhoeffer's reputation as a champion of costly grace, the reader who takes up this book for the first time, anticipating such a rebuttal, may be surprised to find that there are indeed no such answers provided. Page after page of insightful and inspiring material confronts the reader, but one is likely to reach the final page without ever having highlighted or underlined Bonhoeffer's "answer" to the antinomian question. And yet, to conclude on that basis that Bonhoeffer has not been responding to the question throughout would be to underestimate the contribution to Christian theology, and to the antinomian question, he made in this important work.

Bonhoeffer surprises us. To be certain, there is very little in this book that one might call a logical refutation of those indulging in libertine abuses of Christian freedom. One encounters a great deal more personal confession and mutual encouragement in this work than reasoned diatribe;[8] and it is this

---

[5]Ibid. See also his *Ethics*, where he argues, "the gospel became merely the call to conversion and the consolation in sin of drunkards, adulterers, and vicious men of every kind, and the gospel lost its power over good people." (62)

[6]Ibid., 45.

[7]Ibid., 54.

[8]For more on the autobiographical and existential underpinnings in Bonhoeffer's writing, especially in *Discipleship*, see Clifford J. Green, "Soteriologie und Socialethik bei Bonhoeffer und Luther," in *Bonhoeffer und Luther*, ed. Christian Gremmels (München: Chr. Kaiser Verlag, 1983), 107.

that functions as his strongest response to the antinomian question. Likewise, in his *Ethics*, there is less concern with sustaining an unassailable intellectual position and more concern for inspiring his readers' behavior. Eberhard Bethge explains, "The goal of the chapters [in *Ethics*] he was writing at the time was not simply to argue logically but to free people for action."[9] Bonhoeffer's reputation as a theologian and ethicist may have suffered because of this approach, but his legacy suggests that his grander goal of inspiring his audiences was by no means curtailed.

Bonhoeffer's writings not only fail to provide a logical answer to the antinomian question, they lack the other elements we might expect to find in a crusade against antinomianism as well. There is no harsh preaching of the law designed to leave the reader repenting in dust and ashes. One does not find emotional appeals to one's sense of honor or duty; he does not shame his audience by reminding them how much Christ suffered on the cross. There are no scare-tactics that force one seriously to question the reality or potential longevity of one's faith. In fact, one might finish *Discipleship*, or any of his other books, and be rather confused where indeed he earned this reputation as a leading opponent of cheap grace.

Yet we know that he has been an inspiration to countless people in their daily struggles with the life of faith, encouraging them to ever-increasing levels of work and commitment to discipleship. Moreover, as John W. de Gruchy has pointed out, the majority of those who have been so deeply affected by Bonhoeffer are not even aware of the finer points of his theology. He suggests, "Most of those who have been influenced by Bonhoeffer's legacy [through congregations, seminars, and workshops] have not been acquainted with the scholarly debates and issues which we have discussed. But they have found in Bonhoeffer's life and work a witness which has challenged then to greater Christian commitment and faithfulness."[10] Providing a bit more understanding into what captures people's hearts and minds in Bonhoeffer's legacy, de Gruchy goes on to quote from a "letter" which Korean feminist theologian Chung Hyun Kyung wrote in 1996: "You were the major theological mentor of our movement, not because we understood the details and nuances of your theology but because we were inspired by your life story."[11]

---

[9] *DB*, 721.
[10] John W. de Gruchy, "The Reception of Bonhoeffer's Theology," in *The Cambridge Companion to Dietrich Bonhoeffer*, ed. John W. de Gruchy (Cambridge: Cambridge University Press, 1999), 103.
[11] "Dear Dietrich Bonhoeffer: A Letter," in de Gruchy, ibid., 104.

If we are to understand *Discipleship*, then, we must recognize that there is more going on than his identification of the problem in the first chapter, even if we do not find the logical response or psychological arm-twisting that we might expect. What we find are three different approaches to the antinomian question in this text—complemented by his other theological works, sermons, and biography—that serve to respond to and minimize the destructive cheap grace which he believed was destroying the Church. First, Bonhoeffer left us a partial *"answer"* to the antinomian question in the form of a logical refutation of cheap grace. Far from being a systematic response to the problem he so deftly identified in the first chapter, his sporadic comments on the nature and necessity of *obedience* provide us with considerable insight into how he believed the problem of Christian libertinism is best addressed. Second, Bonhoeffer offers, quite consciously and forthrightly, an *example* of what Christian living looks like—in his sermons, his letters, and his life. Third, the *christology* he articulated, defined, and preached was specifically intended to encourage his audiences to become more active in the world; and he believed he could do this by correcting for the incomplete christology which Lutheranism had established for itself.

This fifth and final chapter will consider these three contributions that Bonhoeffer made to our understanding of how one may respond to the antinomian question, considering in turn the place of obedience, example, and christology in addressing abuses of Christian freedom. Once again, with the norm of *sola fide* as our guide, we will consider his faithfulness to Luther's understanding of grace as he used these three themes in his attempt to shatter the myth that Christ offers nothing more than cheap grace: "Grace without price; grace without cost! "[12]

Obedience

As with the three previous figures, Bonhoeffer was adamant that the Christian life involves a great deal more than the forgiveness of sins received freely through the sacrifice of Jesus on the cross. Contrary to what could often be conveyed by orthodox Lutherans, directly or indirectly, the life of faith entails more than simply trust in one's justification. In 1934 he expressed this to Erwin Sutz, reflecting, "Discipleship to Christ—I'd like to know what that is—it is not exhausted in our concept of faith."[13] He found that what needed to be stressed through Christian preaching and teaching was the place of obedience, or discipleship. His book *Discipleship* is full of state-

---

[12] *CD*, 45.
[13] *DBW* 13, 129. See also *DB*, 570.

ments that express the necessity of the active Christian life. He tells us, "The only man who has the right to say that he is justified by grace alone is the man who has left all to follow Christ."[14]

Obedience Before Faith

A considerable amount of the discussion of the Christian life in *Discipleship* focuses on the requirement of obedience prior to one receiving faith. Turning the tables on traditional discussions of obedience as the fruit of faith, Bonhoeffer insists, "In exactly the same way in which obedience is called the consequence of faith, it must also be called the presupposition of faith."[15] The individual must be obedient to God *before* he may enter into a justifying relationship with his Creator through faith in Christ. Obedience cannot wait until one has received saving grace but must take place even before one becomes a believer. Recalling Melanchthon's involvement in the Synergistic Controversy, and the relatively innocuous statements that put him in hot water with the orthodox party, these statements by Bonhoeffer would appear, at first glance, far to exceed what had been said four centuries before. Bonhoeffer, however, insisted that his position is consistent with the Lutheran Confessions[16] as he proceeded to explain his intention in these striking words: "Everything," he tells us, "depends on the first step. It has a unique quality of its own. The first step of obedience makes Peter leave his nets, and later get out of the ship; it calls upon the young man to leave his riches. Only this new existence, created through obedience, can make faith possible."[17] There must be some amount of obedience before one can come to the point of faith. The gift of faith remains the work of God alone, but one must obey God to the point of being in a position to receive the free offer of grace. "Although Peter cannot achieve his own conversion, he can leave his nets."[18] Likewise, we who live two thousand years after Christ are similarly called on to obey him, even before we may come to the point of faith. "Come to church! You can do that of your own free will. You can leave your home on a Sunday morning and come to hear the sermon. If you will not,

---

[14] *CD*, 55.
[15] Ibid., 70. See also *CD* 251.
[16] See further where he explains that the Confessions "find it both possible and necessary to leave room for the first external act which is the essential preliminary to faith." (*CD*, 70). At the same time, he admits that this matter is glossed over in these same confessions, "as though they were almost ashamed of it." (71)
[17] Ibid., 70.
[18] Ibid.

you are of your own free will excluding yourself from the place where faith is a possibility. "[19]

Bonhoeffer was responding to those who would deduce a fatalistic understanding of human obedience in the divine plan of salvation from the fact that human works contribute nothing to one's justification. He wanted to argue that this type of fatalism or moral apathy actually disqualifies one from potentially receiving the gift of justifying grace from God. Where this differs from Melanchthon is that Bonhoeffer was not speaking of cooperating with grace, as if one's obedience in this regard added to or complemented God's offer of salvation, but of allowing oneself to be in a position where grace may be received. The works of obedience that sit Peter at the feet of Jesus or put us in the pews on a Sunday morning have no merit in themselves, not even as cooperating behavior. Nonetheless, this initial act of obedience is required. "Once we are sure of this point, we must add at once that this step is, and can never be more than, a purely external act and a dead work of the law, which can never of itself bring a man to Christ. "[20]

This initial act of obedience also serves the purpose of allowing the sinner to see how much in need of God's free unconditional grace she is. "The end of all preparation of the way for Christ must lie precisely in perceiving that we ourselves can never prepare the way."[21] Bonhoeffer seems to be suggesting something akin to Kierkegaard's ethical stage, where one must come to despair of one's own efforts through an attempt at obedience. However, Bonhoeffer is never explicit in stating this. Perhaps believing that an explanation of why one needs to be obedient in this way would negate the effect, Bonhoeffer chose not to speak of this directly. This would serve to avoid the situation where his readers simply make the intellectual step without the requisite experience of attempting obedience. It would be too easy for them to say, "I understand that my attempts at obedience will bring about despair, for Bonhoeffer has explained this to me and I accept it. Therefore I can move to the next step of believing that my sins are forgiven in Christ." The full extent of what Bonhoeffer had in mind when he stressed the importance of obedience even before faith is difficult to gauge. He does not leave us a record of any strategy behind his words. Nonetheless, it does appear clear that this insistence on obedience prior to justification did have the expressed goal of both neutralizing moral fatalism and intensifying one's reliance on God alone for one's salvation.

---

[19] Ibid., 70f.
[20] Ibid., 71.
[21] *Ethics*, ed. Eberhard Bethge (New York: Macmillan Publishing Co., 1955), 140.

At the same time, while I have argued that Bonhoeffer insisted on obedience before faith in order to demonstrate the sinner's impotence, he was emphatic that this should not serve the purpose of making people identify with the most unworthy of God's servants. The Church should stop the practice of making its parishioners into the worst of sinners before presenting the gospel and describing the sanctified life.

> It is senseless and wrong, therefore, if one preaches to a Christian congregation today, as one can quite often hear done, that each and every man must first become like Mary Magdalene, like the beggar Lazarus, like the thief on the cross, like all these dim 'peripheral figures,' before he can become capable of hearing the final word of God. By speaking in this way one endeavors to emphasize the finality of God's word, but in reality one undermines it.[22]

Bonhoeffer appears concerned here that one's identification with the helpless would lead one again to fatalism. Unlike Kierkegaard, who did what he could to move people in the direction of a *"sickness unto death,"* Bonhoeffer believed the threat of moral apathy, based on despair, was the greater danger. This does not suggest, by any means, that he was opposed to the second use of the law or the idea that one needs to become aware of one's absolute dependence on God, but that during his time, moral paralysis based on identification with the helpless was a larger concern. Luther's day and age were different and necessitated such a corrective. *"It was very necessary to protest against that bourgeois self-satisfaction which, by a convenient reversal of the gospel, considered being good simply as a preliminary to be Christian and which supposed that the ascent from being good to being Christian could be accomplished more or less without a break."*[23]

As with Melanchthon, Bonhoeffer agreed that Luther had been right in his insistence that one needs to recognize oneself as a sinner before receiving forgiveness. Both Melanchthon and Bonhoeffer also believed, however, that subsequent generations had taken advantage of this knowledge of one's helplessness, using it as an excuse for inactivity. For this reason, Melanchthon insisted on synergism and Bonhoeffer on the necessity of obedience before faith. Melanchthon invited condemnation from the orthodox party by doing so; and not a few have cast a suspicious eye on Bonhoeffer's writings because of this as well.

---

[22] Ibid., 123f. See also Bonhoeffer's letter to Eberhard Bethge, dated June 30, 1944: "You see, that is the attitude that I am contending against. When Jesus blessed sinners, they were really sinners, but Jesus did not make everyone a sinner first. He called them away from their sin, not into their sin." *Letters and Papers From Prison*, 341.

[23] Ibid., 62.

The implications for the antinomian question are indirect but fairly apparent. Bonhoeffer has been speaking about obedience before faith, while the antinomian question is asked by those who believe themselves already to have faith. Nevertheless, the principle that holds for the initial acquisition of the gift of faith applies when one desires to keep hold of that faith as well. Like Luther, Bonhoeffer believed that faith can be forfeited.[24] By insisting that obedience precedes faith, he was not only arguing that obedience is required of those without faith but that this same obedience is required among believers for faith to continue. Obedience is not only the fruit of faith; it also allows the believer to remain in faith. "Christ alone creates faith. Yet there are situations in which faith is easier or more difficult."[25] Admittedly, he is toeing a thin line here between the initial obedience Luther spoke of and the synergism of Melanchthon. It was a line, however, that Bonhoeffer believed he had not crossed. As we continue we will have the chance to consider the question of whether or not he went too far in emphasizing the role of obedience and good works.

"Only He Who Believes Is Obedient, And Only He Who Is Obedient Believes."[26]

In this, one of Bonhoeffer's better-known formulations, he challenged the traditional understanding of the relationship between faith and works by moving beyond the idea that only those with faith obey God and adding the claim that only those who obey can be believers. Of course Bonhoeffer was far from suggesting that one earns one's faith by obeying. He helps us unpack this loaded phrase when he explains, "Discipleship is bound to Christ as the Mediator, and where it is properly understood, it necessarily implies faith in the Son of God as the Mediator."[27] Thus discipleship needs to be *understood* properly for one to have saving faith in Christ; and discipleship can be understood only through obedience. It brings one to the place where the Word of God may be heard, it allows one to see humanity's inability to save itself, and it is a sign of genuine saving faith.

While the language initially may sound quite disparate from that of Luther, the idea behind it is in keeping with the theology of the Reformer. By calling into question the idea that faith precedes works, as it has been portrayed for much of the history of Lutheranism, Bonhoeffer was aligning himself much more closely with Luther than might initially be apparent.

---

[24] "If we refuse to take up our cross and submit to suffering and rejection at the hands of men, we forfeit our fellowship with Christ and have ceased to follow him. *CD*, 101.

[25] *Ethics*, 36.

[26] *CD*, 69.

[27] Ibid., 64.

> Does not obedience follow faith as good fruit grows on a good tree? First, faith, then obedience. If by that we mean that it is faith which justifies, and not the act of obedience, all well and good, for that is the essential and unexceptionable pre-supposition of all that follows. If, however, we make a chronological distinction between faith and obedience, and make obedience subsequent to faith, we are divorcing the one from the other.[28]

Faith and works cannot be separate from one another; in theory, yes, one can differentiate between them for the purpose of explaining the work of God in the lives of human beings, but they are not distinct phenomena. It is when faith is conceived to be separate from works that one begins to find oneself in the quagmire of antinomianism. The individual begins to point to faith in order to excuse herself from a lack of works, as if to say they are distinct things. She may have one and not have the other. Bonhoeffer tells us, "From the point of view of justification it is necessary thus to separate them, but we must never lose sight of their essential unity. For faith is only real when there is obedience, never without it, and faith only becomes faith in the act of obedience."[29] Bonhoeffer's purpose behind the remarkable phrase, "Only he who believes is obedient, and only he who is obedient believes," was to draw the two essentials of the Christian life back together where they belong.

Lutheranism, in its never-ending effort to defend the doctrine of *sola fide*, had separated faith and obedience so often for the sake of articulating its view of justification that it failed to remind people that they are an essential unity. According to Bonhoeffer, Lutherans have emphasized the first half of the equation but have forgotten that faith and works necessarily exist together. They have neglected the principle that obedience is required for belief. "Our sinner has drugged himself with cheap and easy grace by accepting the proposition that only those who believe can obey."[30] Luther had emphasized their distinction in order to articulate, against the theological trend of the time, that humanity contributes nothing to its justification. What was needed in his own time, Bonhoeffer believed, was a reminder that faith and obedience belong together. He wrote his parents in 1943, "As long as a hundred years ago Kierkegaard said that today Luther would say the opposite of what he said then. I think he was right—with some reservations."[31]

While it is possible to reconcile Bonhoeffer's theological project with the thought of Luther, the fact remains that there are a number of statements

[28] Ibid., 69.
[29] Ibid.
[30] Ibid., 77.
[31] *Letters and Papers From Prison*, ed. Eberhard Bethge (New York: Macmillan Publishing Co., 1971), 123.

regarding obedience, particularly in *Discipleship*, that appear radically opposed to Luther's essential commitment to the principle of *sola fide*. Consider for example the following: "If you dismiss the word of God's command, you will not receive his word of grace. How can you hope to enter into communion with him when at some point in your life you are running away from him? *The man who disobeys cannot believe*, for only he who obeys can believe."[32] Bonhoeffer offers something of a qualifier on the next page, explaining, "This situation is therefore not the consequence of our obedience, but the gift of him who commands obedience."[33] Or again, "The step into the situation where faith is possible is not an offer which we can make to Jesus, but always his gracious offer to us."[34]

Bonhoeffer wants to find room for his radical statements within the parameters of Luther's thought, but, despite his qualifying statements, it is hard to avoid the sense that he exceeds them at times. There are statements that appear to rob one of confidence in one's justification. Bonhoeffer tells us, "Every day Christ's followers must acknowledge and bewail their guilt. Living as they do in fellowship with him, they ought to be sinless, but in practice their life is marred daily with all manner of unbelief.... No wonder that they must pray daily for God's forgiveness. *But God will only forgive them if they forgive one another with readiness and brotherly affection.*"[35] If only those who forgive one another with readiness and brotherly affection qualify for salvation, heaven will be a lonely place. And yet this is the same Bonhoeffer who explains that a believer who commits suicide can still receive forgiveness. He argues that one does not have to have time to repent after each sin in order to remain among the redeemed.[36]

These two apparently different attitudes toward the attainment of salvation are, despite their appearance, certainly compatible with one another. As we have seen with all four previous figures in this work, faith is understood to bring about a change in one's behavior. Where that change is not present, faith does not exist. At the same time, it has been consistently acknowledged that Christian believers also commit sins that do not necessarily disqualify them from salvation. Moreover, even when there is no opportunity to repent of a specific sin before death, one's status as a child of

---

[32] *CD*, 73, emphasis added. Consider also Bonhoeffer's remark, "But the Christ whom the Scriptures proclaim is in every word he utters one who grants faith to those only who obey him." Ibid., 93.

[33] Ibid., 74.

[34] Ibid., 94.

[35] Ibid., 186, emphasis added.

[36] *Ethics*, 166ff. Admittedly this argument is found in a later work, but the theological changes that Bonhoeffer underwent during these years do not include any radical shift in soteriology.

God is what assures one of justification, not the act of penance. The problem is that Bonhoeffer has set such a high standard at times for what behavior is consistent with genuine Christian faith that he excludes a great many who might be considered weak in their faith. "If the Christian would be saved, he must do good works, for those who are caught doing evil works will not see the kingdom of God."[37] As we have seen with others in this project, the enthusiasm to explain that works are necessary in the plan of salvation can lead to blanket statements that exclude weak believers and offend those with tender consciences. Bonhoeffer, like Spener, had a difficult time balancing his confidence that Christians will reflect their faith in their behavior with a belief in *simul iustus et peccator.*

For all intents and purposes, Bonhoeffer desired to remain true to Luther's theological Archimedean point of *sola fide.* Repeatedly he would insist that believers contribute nothing to their salvation. "We can then receive justification because we willingly renounce every attempt to establish our own righteousness and allow God alone to be righteous."[38] "But we are not to imagine that [strict exterior discipline] alone will crush the flesh, or that there is any way of mortifying our old man other than by faith in Jesus."[39] "We cling in faith to Christ and his works alone."[40] If there could be any doubt remaining as to where his allegiance lies, he states, "The origin and essence of all Christian life are comprised in the one process or event which the Reformation called justification of the sinner by grace alone."[41]

Bonhoeffer's excessive zeal in speaking of the necessity of obedience in *Discipleship*, while sympathetic as a response to antinomianism, led him to make claims that were problematic; at best they are misleading. Interestingly enough, Bonhoeffer himself, later in his life, acknowledged this overemphasis on the life of obedience. In a letter to Eberhard Bethge in July of 1944, he wrote, "I thought I could acquire faith by trying to live a holy life, or something like it. I suppose I wrote *The Cost of Discipleship* as the end of that path. Today I can see the dangers of that book, though I still stand by what I wrote."[42]

He appears to have come around to his friend Franz Hildebrandt's earlier concern that his work, in its focus on obedience, was becoming one-sided.[43] In a letter written in 1938, Bonhoeffer had responded to Hildebrandt in a

---

[37] *CD*, 333.
[38] Ibid., 309.
[39] Ibid., 189.
[40] Ibid., 334.
[41] *Ethics*, 120.
[42] *Letters*, 369.
[43] *DB*, 452.

jovial manner, "Watch, you antinomian, that you don't end up establishing a law of humanitarianism!"[44] Six years later he may have realized that his friend was right, and that *Discipleship* was a bit one-sided. Aside from Hildebrandt, however, the majority of scholars have concluded that Bonhoeffer's position was firmly in keeping with that of Luther as to the sufficiency of grace alone. Bethge explains, "Yet with his key formula, 'only the believer is obedient, and only those who are obedient believe,' he did not mean to question the validity of Luther's *sola fide* and *sola gratia*, but to reassert their validity by restoring to them their concreteness here on earth."[45] André Dumas, the influential French Bonhoeffer scholar, agrees. "Both Kierkegaard and Bonhoeffer are fully committed Lutherans. In relation to Luther's rediscoveries, they challenge neither salvation by faith alone nor the 'monastic' life within the world."[46] H. Gaylon Barker, who cites approvingly Gerhard Ebeling's comment, "In my heart, I believe Bonhoeffer and Luther are one," goes on to say that Luther was Bonhoeffer's defense against the Reformed influence of Barth, who sought to upset the Reformer's ordering of law and gospel.[47]

As we have seen, however, while Bonhoeffer may have wanted to be a faithful student of Luther, some of his writings certainly strayed from what his mentor would have approved of. James Burtness gives a more frank and realistic appraisal of his work, explaining that at times Bonhoeffer looked like a legalist, as in *Discipleship*, while at others he may have even resembled an antinomian, as in *Ethics*. The key to understanding him, Burtness tells us, is to view him through the lens of his christocentric focus, which we shall do below.[48] Similarly, Christian Gremmels has taken issue with Arvid Runestam's judgment that *Discipleship* is a stepchild of the evangelical ethic by insisting that Bonhoeffer's work be analyzed with an eye to the time and place of its authorship.[49]

---

[44] *DBW* 15, 23.

[45] *DB*, 454.

[46] André Dumas, *Dietrich Bonhoeffer: Theologian of Reality*, trans. Robert McAfee Brown (New York: The Macmillan Company, 1971), 118f. He goes on to say, "By insisting on this 'alien righteousness' that comes to us from beyond ourselves, Bonhoeffer finds himself in full accord with the preaching of the Reformation on justification by faith alone through grace." 132.

[47] H. Gaylon Barker, "Bonhoeffer, Luther, and *Theologia Crucis*," *Dialog* 34, no.1 (1995): 10-17.

[48] James Burtness, *Shaping the Future: The Ethics of Dietrich Bonhoeffer* (Philadelphia: Fortress Press, 1985), 95f.

[49] Christian Gremmels, "Rechfertigung und Nachfolge: Martin Luther in Dietrich Bonhoeffers Buch '*Nachfolge*,'" in *Dietrich Bonhoeffer Heute*, ed. Rainer Mayer und Peter Zimmerling (Giessen: Brunnen Verlag, 1992).

I believe that Dumas is correct in stating that Bonhoeffer was a fully committed Lutheran, just as Bethge is right in claiming that he did not question the validity of Luther's position. However, the question here is not what Bonhoeffer wanted to be, but what he was. The German pastor and theologian was obviously quite concerned with the effects of cheap grace, especially at a time when a call to moral virtue was so very much in need. His emphasis on obedience as a response to the antinomian question allowed him to make the very clear statement, "[G]enuine adherence to Christ also means adherence to the law of God."[50] The question is, however, whether he went too far in this emphasis, thereby compromising the gospel for the sake of the law.

There may have been a time, prior to 1938, during which Bonhoeffer was an accidental semi-Pelagian, as his letter to Bethge suggests. It is difficult to say exactly what he thought about the role of works at the time he was writing *Discipleship*; his various statements convey competing messages of *sola fide*, and *sola fide as long as you struggle constantly to be obedient*. While I cannot accept Gerhard Ebeling's claim that Bonhoeffer and Luther are one, the consensus among many scholars that Bonhoeffer wanted to be one with Luther seems to be on target. When Bonhoeffer, later in his life, realized that he might have strayed from that path a bit in *Discipleship* through some misleading comments, he was, much to his credit, perfectly willing to admit it. Gremmels is, I believe, quite on target when he reminds us that Bonhoeffer's work needs to be considered with some leniency that takes his context into account.

Freedom

Whenever the subject of a Christian's call to obedience is brought up, the antinomian cynic is liable to respond with a reference to a believer's freedom in Christ to offer protection from the demands of the law. This is not a topic that Bonhoeffer shies away from. However, Bonhoeffer's discussions of freedom, in the spirit of Luther, do not function as a way out of one's moral obligations but are a call to deeper levels of commitment. Jesus is the model of freedom from the law. "For the sake of God and of men Jesus became a breaker of the law. He broke the law of the Sabbath in order to keep it holy in love for God and for men."[51] One is forced to recognize, subsequently, that the life of Christian freedom does not exempt one from difficulty, persecution, and suffering. As in the case of Bonhoeffer taking part in the

---

[50] *CD*, 139.
[51] *Ethics*, 244.

conspiracy against the Nazis, freedom from the law means alienation and suffering, not opting out of one's ethical obligations.

Christian freedom does not make the life of discipleship easier, but more difficult. Admittedly, this freedom allows one liberation from the worries of whether or not one has behaved perfectly according to a particular legal code.[52] Christian liberty is designed, however, to free one to act more on behalf of one's neighbor, not less. "Permission and liberty do not mean that God now after all allows man a domain in which he can act according to his own choice, free from the commandment of God, but this permission and this liberty arise solely from the commandment of God itself."[53] Freedom conceived as an excuse for moral license is not the freedom that one attains through faith in Christ. "Obedience without freedom is slavery; freedom without obedience is arbitrary self-will."[54]

The Example

Bonhoeffer's attack on cheap grace and its subsequent antinomianism is more specific than a general call for obedience. Unlike many of Christianity's vigorous opponents of moral laxity, however, one will not find Bonhoeffer assaulting his audiences with strident condemnations of particular behaviors. He clearly preferred to model what is right and expected of the people of God; he would much rather have articulated and demonstrated what is expected of obedient people than point out the shortcomings of those around him.

Preaching the Law

Bonhoeffer's distaste for finger-pointing and moral witch-hunts was more than personal preference or style. It was part of a conscious approach to his ministry, with the expressed goal of helping others come to appreciate and accept the gospel message of the forgiveness of sins. While others have believed that pointing out another's sins is the best way to help them realize their need of a savior, Bonhoeffer thoroughly disagreed. "The secrets known to a man's valet—that is, to put it crudely, the range of his intimate life, from prayer to his sexual life—have become the hunting-ground of modern pastoral workers. In that way they resemble (though with quite different intentions) the dirtiest gutter journalists."[55]

---

[52] Ibid., 283
[53] Ibid., 281.
[54] Ibid., 252.
[55] *Letters*, 344.

To begin with, by pointing out one's particular sins, one runs the risk of conveying the message that the eradication of moral vice is the essence of Christianity, and that all one needs to do is eliminate those particular sins listed by the preacher. "If I condemn his evil actions I thereby confirm him in his apparently good actions which are yet never the good commended by Christ. Thus we remove him from the judgment of Christ and subject him to human judgment."[56] Lists of concrete sins may imply that the power and obligation to eradicate these problems lie within the individual. The preacher may stir up his conscience but will be unable to bring him to the point of shame. As Bonhoeffer explains in his *Ethics*, conscience only applies to certain actions, while shame embraces the whole of life.[57] Only by realizing that one's whole life exists in alienation from God can one come to see the need for a savior. Identifying particular moral shortcomings is not the way to bring one to despair. In fact, it is not so difficult to see how this could easily lead to pharisaism. We can understand, then, why Bonhoeffer would go on to say, "The moral preacher can only produce hypocrites."[58]

A second difficulty with this approach, related to the first, is that such identification of particular sins rarely gets to the heart of who an individual is. These lists tend to describe behaviors that are peripheral to a person's essential character. "Regarded theologically, the error is twofold. First, it is thought that a man can be addressed as a sinner only after his weakness and meanness have been spied out. Secondly, it is thought that a man's essential nature consists of his inmost and most intimate background; that is defined as his 'inner life', and it is precisely in those secret human places that God is to have his domain!" He continues to explain, "On the first point it is to be said that man is certainly a sinner, but is far from being mean or common on that account. To put it rather tritely, were Goethe and Napoleon sinners because they weren't always faithful husbands? It's not the sins of weakness, but the sins of strength, which matter here."[59] It is essential for the preacher to reach the "essential nature" of a human being, and this is not achieved by addressing moral foibles and shortcomings.

Moreover, these same preachers need to be very careful about addressing the sins of others. Very easily they fall into the trap of elevating themselves above their communities, holding them in contempt for those sins that they themselves most despise, or that affect them as the spiritual leaders of a community. "If when we judged others, our real motive was to destroy evil,

---

[56] *CD*, 205.
[57] *Ethics*, 24.
[58] Ibid., 313.
[59] *Letters*, 345.

we should look for evil where it is certain to be found, and that is in our own hearts. But if we are on the look-out for evil in others, our real motive is obviously to justify ourselves, for we are seeking to escape punishment for our own sins by passing judgment on others."[60] In fact, Bonhoeffer tells us, when pastors lose faith in their Christian communities, the problem should first be sought in their own hearts and in their inappropriate image of what that community should look like. Regarding such pastors, he tells us, "Let them accuse themselves of their unbelief, let them ask for an understanding of their own failure and their particular sin, and pray that they may not wrong other Christians."[61]

Rather than pointing out what is wrong in others' behavior, Bonhoeffer preferred the approach of describing what conduct is right. This may be a thin line, but it is an important one. The distinction between being told what is wrong with one's actions and what actions are to be undertaken is essential. In conveying what God expects of human beings, the individual is compelled to examine her own behavior in light of God's expectations; another person does not judge her. It is the positive command of God's will—the call to discipleship—that is presented to the believer. The example of Christ in his suffering and death becomes the model that confronts people in their innermost being in a way in which condemnations of particular behaviors could never do.

Sinners need to be called to obedience, both before conversion and after, as we have seen. It is through their own struggle with obedience, then, that they are confronted with their own impotence and thrust into the world, which is where faith is born and finds its life, as we shall see further below.

Bonhoeffer was talking, moreover, about more than abstract principles of discipleship. Dumas explains how in Bonhoeffer's theology, "To be called or summoned is to be confronted by a concrete commandment that cannot be divided into knowing versus doing, dogmatics versus ethics, or eternal principles versus worldly compromises."[62]

In light of this emphasis on obedience rather than repentance, we should not be surprised to find that Bonhoeffer understood the Sermon on the Mount, not simply as a law that shows us our sin, but as instructions to follow. "Humanly speaking, we could understand and interpret the Sermon on the Mount in a thousand different ways. Jesus knows only one possibility: simple surrender and obedience, not interpreting it or applying it, but doing

---

[60] *CD*, 206.

[61] *DBWE*, 5, 37f.

[62] Dumas, *Dietrich Bonhoeffer*, 123.

and obeying it. "[63] Moving away from the focus on the law as a mirror that brings us to despair, as we find in Luther and Kierkegaard, Bonhoeffer wanted the law to be considered with an eye to how it should be obeyed. It is true that one does not choose one or the other, for both are essential in Lutheran theology. Rather it is a question of emphasis, and Bonhoeffer's emphasis is clear. "It is evident that the only appropriate conduct of men before God is the doing of His will. The Sermon on the Mount is there for the purpose of being done (Matt. 7.24ff.). Only in doing can there be submission to the will of God. "[64]

None of this is to say that Bonhoeffer found no room for condemnation of illicit behavior. There is indeed a time and place for church discipline. "When another Christian falls into obvious sin, an admonition is imperative, because God's Word demands it. "[65] To ignore another's captivity to sin, or simply hope that it will change through good preaching, is a serious mistake. "Nothing can be more cruel than leniency which abandons others to their sin. Nothing can be more compassionate than that severe reprimand which calls another Christian in one's community back from the path of sin. "[66] However, this should not be the norm in the preaching of the law. Here Bonhoeffer always emphasized the call to obedience over the identification of specific sins.

In placing such emphasis on the importance of obedience, as in the Sermon on the Mount, Bonhoeffer has cast light on the essential difference between himself and Luther. For Luther, the primary purpose of the law is its second use, to show the sinner his sin. A third use for the law is present but difficult to find. In Bonhoeffer, on the other hand, it is the third use of the law that is primary, with the second use only hinted at between the lines. While the Sermon on the Mount is probably the best-known case of this difference, one finds Bonhoeffer's emphasis on following the law throughout his life and work. In 1932 and in 1938 he rephrased the official confirmation vow so that it would no longer contain any promises that would be impossible to fulfill. Contrary to what Luther argues in *The Bondage of the Will*, the law exists primarily to be followed, not just to point out our weakness.

---

[63] *CD*, 218f.

[64] *Ethics*, 43.

[65] *DBWE*, 5, 105.

[66] Ibid. See also *CD*, 324: "Nor is it enough [for the Church] simply to deplore in general terms that the sinfulness of man infects even his good works. It is necessary to point out concrete sins, and to punish and condemn them. "

Clifford Green suggests that Bonhoeffer may not even have been aware of this significant disparity, as he finds Bonhoeffer's descriptions of Luther to be thinly veiled self-portraits, focusing on his own ambitious attempts to storm the gates of heaven rather than the despairing Luther who struggles with guilt for hating God because of the impossibility of his commands.[67] Luther found rest for his wearied soul in Christ, who had finished the works of the law for him. His temptation was to doubt the sufficiency of Christ's sacrifice. Bonhoeffer, on the other hand, struggled with the temptation of a cerebral faith that was devoid of works, and found his faith when he became active in the world. As was indicated in the first chapter, Luther's experience may be the exception in human history, or at least since his time. As such, Bonhoeffer's emphasis on obedience may be just the remedy needed to counteract the cheap grace that he believed to be the legacy of the Reformation. While all of this points to a genuine difference between the theology of Luther and that of Bonhoeffer, it does not imply a disparate view of the principle of *sola fide*. Bonhoeffer's different understanding of the uses of the law is to be understood not as a betrayal of Luther's central theological tenet but as his response within the Church at a time very different from that of the Reformer.

At the same time, it must be admitted that much of this discussion of the second and third uses of the law is artificial. As was discussed in the case of Luther, the preaching of the law does not fall neatly into three distinct categories. Moreover, what is the second use of the law to one member of the congregation may be the third to another. Bonhoeffer certainly preached and taught in such a way that the call to obedience was explicitly foremost in his mind. At the same time, he understood that this call simultaneously functions as a mirror, reflecting the sins of his audiences back to them. He tells us, "There can be no Christian preaching of works without the preaching of the acknowledgment of sin and of the fulfillment of the law. And the law cannot be preached without the gospel."[68] We should be careful not to over-emphasize their differences here, as if to suggest a significant disagreement.

Another function of Bonhoeffer's preaching of obedience that differentiates him from the stereotype of a law-oriented preacher was his insistence that there is no place for emotional displays in a sermon. In general, Bonhoeffer was rather distrustful of those elevated experiences that create a different mood or affection on which the call to discipleship is based. Perhaps owing to the influence of his father's psychiatric profession, Bonhoeffer realized that such states are unreliable as a basis for one's life

---

[67] Green, "Soteriologie," 108ff.
[68] *Ethics*, 313.

and faith. "By sheer grace God will not permit us to live in a dream world even for a few weeks and to abandon ourselves to those blissful experiences and exalted moods that sweep over us like a wave of rapture. For God is not a God of emotionalism, but the God of truth."[69]

In Bonhoeffer's lectures on preaching, he warned his students against anything that would distract from the fundamental message of the Word of God. Preachers are to preach God's Word, not impress or awe their congregations with their oratory skills. "I must refuse to indulge in tricks and techniques, both the emotional ones and the rhetorical ones. I must not become pedantic and schoolmasterish, nor begging, entreating, urging. I do not try to make the sermon into a work of art."[70] Likewise, taking a page from Spener, he urged his students to avoid storytelling, illustrations, and quotations;[71] nor should the process of delivering a sermon leave the preacher drained or exhausted.[72] However, despite these sober guidelines, he differed significantly from Spener in that people loved to hear Bonhoeffer preach. He eschewed jargon and idiomatic theological language,[73] preached the Word of God without flair or ostentation, and received the admiration of his inspired students and congregations.

With unadorned, straightforward language, Bonhoeffer believed that the best way to embolden people to lives of discipleship was by simply telling them what was expected of them. It is enough to describe the Christian life, as in the Sermon on the Mount, for believers to know what behavior they need to change and what to repent of. What is not needed are pastors who search out their own pet peeves in the members of their congregations. "If the preacher wants to be certain about the truth of his preaching he should devote himself exclusively to the word of the text."[74]

Moreover, this preaching of the word of God must not become the communication of doctrine but must speak to people and be relevant to their lives. What has been leading to cheap grace, Bonhoeffer tells us, is this intellectualization of the faith. "An intellectual assent to that idea [of grace] is held to be of itself sufficient to secure remission of sins."[75] As was presented earlier in this chapter, Bonhoeffer's approach to discipleship and ethics was not based on presenting new theological paradigms or providing commentaries on doctrine. His approach was much more geared toward

[69] *DBWE*, 5, 35.
[70] Clyde E. Fant, *Bonhoeffer: Worldly Preaching* (Nashville: Thomas Nelson Inc., 1975), 138.
[71] Ibid., 158.
[72] Ibid., 139.
[73] See Dumas, *Dietrich Bonhoeffer*, 247.
[74] From Bonhoeffer's lectures on preaching in Fant, *Bonhoeffer*, 164.
[75] *CD*, 45.

reaching people on a personal level in the world, an approach in keeping
with his interest in religionless Christianity—a topic that regrettably cannot
be treated further here. With this tack, Bonhoeffer has inspired countless
readers with his direct communication of God's expectations for a life of
discipleship. "The dogmatically correct delivery of the Christian proclamation is not enough; nor are general ethical principles; what is needed is
concrete instruction in the concrete situation."[76] Otto W. Heick sees this
approach as reminiscent of Luther's rejection of the "god of the philo-
sophers" who contribute more to answering intellectual dilemmas about the
cosmos than transforming people's lives. Similarly, Bonhoeffer's rejection of
metaphysical speculation is comparable, in Heick's opinion, to Luther's rejection of the "theologians of glory."[77]

The Word of God is to be preached, Bonhoeffer tells us, without tugging
at heartstrings or dramatic calls for conversion. It is the Word of God itself
that has the power to transform lives. This living and active communication
is what changes a person, not reflection on its message. Bonhoeffer explains,
"The meaning of the proclaimed word, however, does not lie outside of
itself; it is the thing itself. It does not transmit anything else, it does not
express anything else, it has no external objectives—rather, it communicates
that it is itself: the historical Jesus Christ."[78] It is in the message that Jesus
Christ is actually present. For this reason Bonhoeffer insisted that emotional
appeals and psychological wrangling have no place in the sermon. One is to
preach the Word and allow the Spirit of God to work in people's hearts. He
advised his students, "The young preacher who thinks that he must produce
conversions is mistaken. He should leave the converting to God."[79]

Thus, to those who have analyzed Christian doctrine and found the moral
loophole of evangelical liberty, Bonhoeffer does not respond with a
theological argument that is also grounded in doctrine; rather, he confronts
them with the Word of God. He does not tell them why they should obey; he
presents them with Scripture's command that they shall obey. It is the Word
of God that will do the work in the life of his interlocutor, not his best efforts
at theological debate. And if the individual rejects the testimony and work of
the Spirit through the Word, Bonhoeffer's best efforts to win a theological

---

[76] *Ethics*, 354.
[77] Otto W. Heick, "Reflections on Bonhoeffer's Theology," *Concordia Theological Monthly*
40, no.4 (1969): 203–217.
[78] Fant, *Bonhoeffer*, 128.
[79] Ibid., 164. See also *CD*, 206: "Every attempt to impose the gospel by force, to run after
people and proselytize them, to use our own resources to arrange the salvation of other people,
is both futile and dangerous. It is futile, because the swine do not recognize the pearls that are
cast before them, and dangerous, because it profanes the word of forgiveness."

argument could hardly have been expected to change the other's heart. With this reliance on the Spirit in the Word, Bonhoeffer's response to the anti-nomian question takes the form of directing his audiences to the source. We have already seen this approach in his homiletics. Not surprisingly, he encouraged others to spend time each day in meditation on the Bible as well.[80]

Modeling Behavior

It is likely that Bonhoeffer's call to discipleship would have faded into obscurity over the past decades if it had not been so radically complemented by the witness of his life. Even before his death, his descriptions of what the Christian life should look like were underscored by his behavior. While teaching at the seminary he preferred not to point fingers at students for inappropriate behavior but modeled what was appropriate. Bethge tells the story of the second day at the seminary in Zingst when the kitchen staff requested help cleaning up after the meal. After a delay, during which no one volunteered, Professor Bonhoeffer quietly stood up and headed into the kitchen. When his students tried to follow his good example, trailing behind him, he would not let any of them in. He later joined his students on the beach and never said a word about the incident. Similarly, at the seminary in Finkenwalde, Bethge relates how students returning to their rooms would often discover with shame that their beds had been made by some anonymous benefactor.[81] It did not need to be pointed out what behaviors were wrong; the right behaviors were modeled quite clearly for them, and with much greater effect.

Later, while in prison, Bonhoeffer noticed, almost with embarrassment, that others in the prison were inspired by his conduct under such difficult circumstances. He remarked to Bethge in 1943, "Perhaps it will please you to hear that the prisoners and the guards here keep saying how they are 'amazed' (?!) at my tranquility and cheerfulness. I myself am always amazed about remarks of this kind. But isn't it rather nice?"[82] And there is of course the famous remark by the camp doctor at Flossenbürg, where Bonhoeffer was killed, who remarked, "In the almost fifty years I worked as a doctor, I have hardly ever seen a man die so entirely submissive to the will of God."[83]

---

[80] Cf. *CD*, 189, as well as Haddon Wilmer, "Costly Discipleship," in *The Cambridge Companion to Dietrich Bonhoeffer*, ed. John W. de Gruchy (Cambridge: Cambridge University Press, 1999), 183f.
[81] *DB*, 429.
[82] *Letters*, 134.
[83] *DB*, 928.

Similarly, when talking about the importance of recognizing and confessing one's sins, Bonhoeffer not only described what a believer should do but modeled it as well. In *Life Together* he would write, "There can be no genuine knowledge of sin that does not lead me down to this depth. If my sin appears to me to be in any way smaller or less reprehensible in comparison with the sins of others, then I am not yet recognizing my sin at all."[84] More powerful than this injunction, again, was that he modeled it in his life. When he preached, he was fully conscious that he was equally guilty of the sins he discussed from the pulpit. In a sermon from 1937, we read, "Indeed we know of ourselves that there are times when our ears are deaf. Those are the times we harden our hearts against God's will in willful disobedience and heap sin upon sin until we are finally no longer able to hear. At that point Satan has taken possession of us."[85] Bonhoeffer was a *Wir*-preacher, rather than an *Ihr*-preacher[86]. Again, this was much more than a homiletical strategy; Bonhoeffer truly felt what he described. In his letters from prison we see him painfully aware of his own shortcomings. In his well-known poem "Who am I?" he laments that while others see him as a beacon of faith and hope, he sees himself quite differently. He describes himself as: "restless," "struggling," "yearning," "thirsting," "trembling," "weary and empty at praying," "faint," "and ready to say farewell to it all."[87] Additionally, while in prison, he not only prayed for justice but asked his God, "Forgive my lack of faith and any wrong that I have done today, and help me to forgive all who have wronged me."[88] Even at Finkenwalde, at the same time he encouraged his students to practice private confession, he took part as well as a penitent. Bonhoeffer's willingness to demonstrate his conviction that all are sinners and need to repent of their misdeeds was what inspired his students, and many still today, to follow suit.

The example of his involvement in the conspiracy, similarly, has been an inspiration to many to take up the life of discipleship. The influence of his *Ethics* cannot help but be magnified exponentially through the knowledge of his life story. While misperceptions of his role in the conspiracy abound,[89]

[84] *DBWE*, 5, 97.
[85] "Sermon on a Psalm of Vengeance," trans. Daniel Bloesch, *Theology Today* 38 (1982): 465-71. Taken from "Predigt über einen Rachepsalm," *Gesammelte Schriften*, Band IV, 413-422.
[86] The German words *wir* and *ihr* translate as "We" and "You."
[87] *CD*, 18ff.
[88] *Letters*, 141.
[89] He was jailed and interrogated largely on the basis of his role in assisting certain pastors avoid enlistment in the military. His role in "Operation 7" and the assassination attempt on

and he would not have approved of all the descriptions of him as a martyr,[90] his willingness to sacrifice everything for a cause he believed in has stirred countless numbers of people to abandon the comfortable life of evangelical freedom for the responsibility of freedom that he insisted on.

Christology

Central to Bonhoeffer's theological project was the theme of christology. More than a touchstone to the legacy of Chalcedon, his development of this aspect of doctrine was designed to contribute to his work on ecclesiology, eschatology, epistemology, and, certainly not least, the life of sanctification. Heick points out that, consistent with Luther, Bonhoeffer believed that true theology finds its only grounding in Christ's incarnation and death on the cross.[91] Likewise, for both Bonhoeffer and Luther, a complete christology must include the life of the risen Christ who is still present in the world today. In Bonhoeffer's discussions of the resurrected Christ, it is not difficult to see his allegiance to Luther's belief in the ubiquity of Jesus Christ in body and spirit. He began his short work *Christology* with the sentence: "Jesus is the Christ present as the Crucified and Risen One. That is the first statement of christology."[92] At the same time, he wanted to correct for potential misunderstandings of this statement. First and foremost, the presence of the risen Christ may be incorrectly perceived to be his "effective historical influence." If this approach is adopted, Bonhoeffer believed, the resurrection is effectively being denied; he had little patience for Schleiermacher's metaphorical understanding of the resurrection, which he believed destroyed the Church.[93] "Only the Risen One makes possible the presence of the living person and gives the presupposition for christology, no longer dissipated into historical energy or an intuited ideal of Christ."[94] The resurrected Christ is truly present still today.

In addition to his rejection of symbolic interpretations of Christ's resurrection, from early in his career he also rejected the christology of his teacher Karl Holl as well. While he appreciated Holl's revival of the doctrine of "by grace alone" against what Bethge labels the "vague cultural Protest-

---

Hitler were extremely minor, although he did admit that he would be willing to be directly involved with the latter. See *DB*, 751f.

[90] See *DB*, 834. He can be considered a martyr only if the term is used somewhat loosely, as Archbishop Bell did when he stated that "Dietrich himself was a martyr many times before he died." *CD*, 7.

[91] Heick, "Reflections," 205.

[92] *Christology*, trans. John Bowden (London: Collins, 1966), 43.

[93] Ibid., 43ff.

[94] Ibid., 45.

antism" of the time,[95] he found its foundation in Luther's christology to be sorely lacking. He expressed this at the University of Berlin in his inaugural address as a lecturer. "Holl defined Luther's religion as a religion of conscience. With this there went, as should first simply be noted here, a remarkably scant estimation of Luther's christology."[96] Christology was essential to Bonhoeffer for all other aspects of the Christian life and doctrine.

Even the orthodox Lutherans who embraced Chalcedon and Luther were guilty of only perceiving half the picture of who Christ was and why he came. The Mediator not only exists as the end of the law, who frees sinners from their guilt and proclaims freedom; he is also the goal of the law, the model, example, and pattern for imitation. Jonathan Sorum explains further, *"The Cost of Discipleship* is Bonhoeffer's insistence that Christ is both the end *and* the goal of the law: only the one who has faith obeys (Christ is the end of the law), and only the one who obeys has faith (Christ is the goal of the law). Each is true because of the other, and neither is true without the other."[97] It has been the unfortunate legacy of much of Lutheranism that Christ as the *end* of the law receives full attention while his function as the *goal* of the law gets short shrift.

Reminiscent of Spener's argument that Christ be fully appreciated as prophet, priest, and king, Bonhoeffer wanted to make sure that the Church's christology not neglect particular aspects of Christ's work on behalf of humanity. In addition to discussions of the Savior as the end and goal of the law, Bonhoeffer wanted to round out the Church's understanding of the Messiah in another way. Rather than the three functions that Spener pointed to, Bonhoeffer addressed the three works of the incarnation, crucifixion, and resurrection. "In the incarnation we learn of the love of God for His creation; in the crucifixion we learn of the judgment of God upon all flesh; and in the resurrection we learn of God's will for a new world. There could be no greater error than to tear these three elements apart."[98] Thus, Bonhoeffer understood the resurrection as evidence not only that God has honored the sacrifice of the Son, but also that there is a plan for renewal in which all human beings are to take part. A fuller and more developed christology reminds Christians that Jesus' work did not end with his atoning death on the cross. Easter is not just God's stamp of approval on the sacrifice of Jesus.

---

[95] *DB*, 69.
[96] Quoted in Barker, "Bonhoeffer, Luther, and *Theologia Crucis*, 11.
[97] Jonathan Sorum, "Barth's 'Gospel and Law' and Bonhoeffer's *The Cost of Discipleship.*" in *Essays in Honor of F. Burton Nelson,* ed. Geffrey B. Kelly and C. John Weborg (Chicago: Covenant Publications, 1999), 222.
[98] *Ethics*, 130f.

The Savior's resurrection is the power to live and work in the world through the power of the indwelling Spirit of Christ for the purpose of carrying out God's plan for a new earth. A more complete christology, then, serves the purpose of demonstrating what is expected of believers in this world; the mandate that comes with Christ's resurrection cannot be ignored as incidental to christology or the Christian life. "Christian life means being a man through the efficacy of the incarnation; it means being sentenced and pardoned through the efficacy of the cross; and it means living a new life through the efficacy of the resurrection. There cannot be one of these without the rest. "[99]

Christ Has Come Into the World

Christ's incarnation, his coming into the world as a human being, has placed a positive valuation on the world that, Bonhoeffer regrets, is often overshadowed by concerns for spiritual matters alone. As Barker explains, since God entered into the world in Christ, this world is not to be abandoned by his disciples; it is in the midst of this world that we meet God.[100] The incarnation tells us not only that God loves the creation, but that God's children are to do likewise. We are to remember that Jesus lived a life among people, not in isolation or religious seclusion, and he insisted that his followers do likewise. "Unlike the founders of the great religions, he had no desire to withdraw them from the vulgar crowd and initiate them into an esoteric system of religion and ethics. "[101] Christians today, therefore, are to engage the world actively as citizens of the world. There can be no withdrawal from the life or responsibilities of a member of the human community. "We should have so much love for this contemporary world of ours…that we should declare our solidarity with it in distress as well as in its hope. "[102]

The most apparent targets of such comments were those who would pursue the Christian life from a monastery. "So Christians, too, belong not in the seclusion of a cloistered life but in the midst of enemies. There they find their mission, their work. "[103] However, Bonhoeffer was never one to chastise

---

[99] Ibid., 133.

[100] Barker, "Bonhoeffer," 17.

[101] *CD*, 223. See also his letters to Bethge from 1944: E.g. "He must therefore really live in the godless world, without attempting to gloss over or explain its ungodliness in some religious way or other. He just lives a 'secular' life, and thereby shares in God's sufferings." *Letters*, 361. "The Christian is not a *homo religiosus*, but simply a man, as Jesus was a man— in contrast, shall we say, to John the Baptist." *Letters*, 369.

[102] *DBW* 10, 285.

[103] *DBWE* 5, 27.

members of another Christian community without direct relevance to his own situation. These comments were far from a critique of Roman Catholicism.[104] Protestants can be just as guilty of hiding from the challenges of the real world in their own religious isolation. He wrote to Theodore Litt, "Solely because God became a poor, suffering, unknown successless man, and because from now on God allows himself to be found only in poverty, in the cross, we cannot disengage ourselves from man and from the world."[105] It is not only Roman Catholic monks whom one may find retreating from the life of the world.

Bonhoeffer was very distrustful of self-appointed Christian groups that split themselves off from the Church, or at least found their own little corner of it in which to be alone. His work on behalf of international ecumenism is testimony that he believed strongly that ghetto communities of Christians, who stick to themselves in their limited lives of mediocre discipleship, are offending against the God who came to be a part of the world. While the expressed goals of many of these groups—to study the Bible and support one another in faith—may be laudatory, the dangers of Protestant monasticism are real. "In other words, a life together under the Word will stay healthy only when it does not form itself into a movement, an order, a society, a *collegium pietatis*, but instead understands itself as being part of the one, holy, universal Christian church, sharing through its deeds and suffering in the hardships and struggles and promise of the whole church."[106] Isolationism, which may spring from an inadequate christology, inhibits Christians from living the active life of discipleship they were meant to undertake. And more importantly, perhaps, for the antinomian question, this incomplete christology may manifest itself through preaching that fails to articulate the importance of following Christ's example to be living and active in the world.

The focus on this world that springs from Bonhoeffer's christology also serves to draw people away from the tendency to focus excessively on the afterlife. This undue emphasis on eternal life is often a product of preaching that speaks of Christianity as nothing more than the forgiveness of sins. Bonhoeffer believed that both of these errors are corrected for when one remembers to express that Christ's work in the world is our model and example. "It is not with the beyond that we are concerned, but with this world as created and preserved, subjected to laws, reconciled, and restored. What is

---

[104] We should remember that he himself spent time in the Roman Catholic Ettal Monastery in 1940 and 1941.

[105] *Gesammelte Schriften*, ed. Eberhard Bethge (München: Chr. Kaiser Verlag, 1960), 3:32.

[106] *DBWE* 5, 45.

above this world is, in the gospel, intended to exist *for* this world. "[107] This was not to suggest that eternal life is unimportant; but the Christian life takes place on this earth, not in starry-eyed expectation of what is to come. Bonhoeffer was concerned that excessive *"otherworldliness"* would alienate Christians from their life and responsibilities in this world. Indeed, Christians have been saved from sin, death, and the devil, "Yet it remains true that the whole purpose of our new creation in Christ is that in him we might attain unto good works. "[108]

This brings us to another crucial difference between Luther and Bonhoeffer. For Luther, the security and gratitude that comes from knowing that one is justified and will enter eternity with one's Creator is the starting point for the Christian life. Trust in the gift of one's eternal destiny with God is the basis for acts of love in this world. For Bonhoeffer, more modeling of the behavior required of believers is needed on the part of clergy. The faith that brings about works of love needs to be strengthened, not by focus on the hereafter, but by life in the world. While the early Bonhoeffer attempted to make faith stronger by obedience, he later found that it is the experience of living in the midst of God's world that makes one stronger in faith.

> I discovered later, and I'm still discovering right up to this moment, that [it is] only by living completely in this world that one learns to have faith. One must completely abandon any attempt to make something of oneself, whether it be a saint, or a converted sinner, or a churchman (a so-called priestly type!), a righteous man or an unrighteous one, a sick man or a healthy one. By this-worldliness I mean living unreservedly in life's duties, problems, successes and failures, experiences and perplexities. In so doing we throw ourselves completely into the arms of God, taking seriously, not our own sufferings, but those of God in the world—watching with Christ in Gethsemane. That, I think, is faith; that is *metanoia*; and that is how one becomes a man and a Christian.[109]

This difference does not suggest any substantive disparity between Luther and Bonhoeffer. As with the uses of the law, there is room for debate on the subject of emphases. Both men understood the life of discipleship to spring from faith. However, how that faith is best kindled to create the burning desire to live the Christian life is less than clear and is certainly different for different people. Bonhoeffer was firmly convinced that Lutheranism had neglected the incarnational implications of Jesus Christ's life. The rediscovery of this neglected aspect of doctrine, he believed, could

---

[107] *Letters*, 286.
[108] *CD*, 334.
[109] *Letters*, 369f.

make up for some of the otherworldly focus among believers that kept them sitting pretty in their justification while the world around them went to hell.

Christ as the Church

Bonhoeffer's insistence on the importance of christology, as we have seen, has important implications for the life of the Church. To gain further insight into what he wanted to communicate about this relationship, we must be clear about what he meant when he spoke of "the Church." The Church, for him, is not simply a collection of believers who remember Jesus Christ, believe him to have been the messiah, and seek to model their lives after his example. The Church is the actual presence of Christ in the world. It does not simply possess the Word of God; it *is* the Word of God. "The Community is therefore not only the receiver of the Word of revelation; it is itself revelation and Word of God. Only in so far as it is itself the Word of God can it understand the Word of God."[110] The resurrection of Jesus was not just his own victory over death, or evidence of his disciples' future glory, but it made possible his real presence in the world until the end of time. Christ in Word and Sacrament is truly present to the people of God. Working in human hearts and hands, the divine Logos exists in the world to proclaim the good news of salvation. "The Word is *in* the community in so far as the community is a recipient of revelation. But the Word is also itself community in so far as the community is itself revelation and the Word wills to have the form of a created body.... The community is the body of Christ. But here is not just a metaphor. The community *is* the body of Christ, it does not *represent* the body of Christ."[111]

While Bonhoeffer was raised outside a Church community—his family very rarely attended public worship—he developed a love and concern for the family of believers that would inspire not only those who were fortunate enough to live and work with him but the millions of readers of his books as well. He was generally distrustful of theology or religious practice that placed much emphasis on the existential spiritual journey of Christian faith.[112] The personal struggle of faith has its place but must come to the point of manifesting itself in the Christian community and getting its hands dirty in the world. The solitary pursuit of holiness that fails to recognize its essential part in the body of Christ is neglecting not only brothers and sisters in Christ, but also the real presence of the Word of God in this world.

---

[110] *Christology*, 60.
[111] Ibid.
[112] As for the Father of Existentialism, Bonhoeffer generally approved of Kierkegaard, but he did not find much use for the Dane in his own work, and held little more than a basic knowledge of his theological contribution.

If we regard sanctification as a purely personal matter which has nothing whatever to do with public life and the visible line of demarcation between the Church and the world, we shall land ourselves inevitably into a confusion between the pious wishes of the religious flesh and the sanctification of the Church which is accomplished in the death of Christ through the seal of God. This is the deceitful arrogance and the false spirituality of the old man, who seeks sanctification outside the visible community of the brethren. It is contempt of the Body of Christ as a visible fellowship of justified sinners.[113]

The importance of understanding that the Church exists as the presence of Christ in the world is far from being abstract theology. If individual Christians are part of this real presence of God in the world, they are responsible for carrying out the work of God here and now. The Christian life, like the life of Jesus, is not to consist in the preaching of the kingdom alone, which has been the mistake of many in Protestantism. The presence of God in the world as Jesus Christ is the model for how believers are to conduct themselves as the present manifestation of Christ: teaching, preaching, healing the sick, comforting the afflicted, welcoming children. "It is not only Christ who is both *donum* [gift] and *exemplum* [example] for us human beings, but in the same way also one human being is so for another."[114] Christians must be as much a part of the world, as active in this world, as Jesus Christ was during his earthly pilgrimage two thousand years ago. "The danger of the Reformation...lies in the fact that it devotes its whole attention to the mandate of the proclamation of the word and, consequently, almost entirely neglects the proper domain and function of the Church as an end in herself, and this consists precisely in her existence for the sake of the world."[115] When Christian leaders understand this implication of christology, they place themselves in a better position to convey to their communities the responsibilities of the Christian life. They are thereby able to hold up the pattern believers are to follow. Once again, Bonhoeffer is not providing a concrete answer to the antinomian question but allowing his readers to see the difference between what a Christian life is, and what it is not. With this clearer presentation of the model for Christian behavior, as we have seen, Bonhoeffer believed he could inspire others to pursue discipleship with more enthusiasm and conviction.

---

[113] *CD*, 315.
[114] *DB*, 213.
[115] *Ethics*, 301.

Conclusion

The previous century's most famous proponent of costly grace was a man who has inspired countless people to take up their crosses in renewed lives of discipleship. He championed the cause of eradicating cheap grace and its subsequent antinomianism without preaching fire and brimstone, making emotional pleas to one's sense of duty, or even providing a logical response to the antinomian question. His clarification of what the moral life should look like, the witness of his life in support of his convictions, and his willingness to let the Spirit of God change people's hearts, these were his responses to those who might be tempted to take advantage of the freedom that comes with faith. Certainly this response to the problem has been more productive than his best efforts to refute the cynical logic behind the antinomian question could have ever been.

In fact, we have seen that his attempts to respond logically to those threatening libertinism may have created more problems than it has solved. While it is certainly possible to judge his more radical comments on obedience in *Discipleship* to be consistent with the doctrine of *sola fide*, many of these early comments carry the potential for grave misunderstanding. As in the case of others we have considered in this project, Bonhoeffer's enthusiasm to explain that genuine faith can be recognized by its fruits led him to identify characteristics that hold the potential to exclude others on the basis of the relative value of their behavior rather than the trust they have in their Creator to grant them forgiveness. The effect can be that while the antinomian cynic is unimpressed, those with tender consciences are robbed of the joy and gratitude that come from the assurance of one's salvation from the hand of God. Over and above this concern for the weak in faith, Bonhoeffer's extreme statements in *Discipleship* also contribute to suspicions among those who guard the principle of *sola fide* most carefully. The result can be that those who might benefit most from his inspiring message and call to obedience push him aside on the basis of a suspicion that he has compromised the gospel.

Nonetheless, Bonhoeffer's legacy has been substantial. People and organizations of vastly different theological orientation, from atheists to liberation theologians to orthodox Lutherans, have embraced him.[116] He has become many things to many people. However, as much as one may become involved with understanding the finer points of his theological work, the impression one receives from the first line of the first chapter of *Discipleship* ought to be the guiding one in any attempt to fathom the life and work of

---

[116] See John W. de Gruchy, "The Reception of Bonhoeffer's Theology."

Dietrich Bonhoeffer. He needs to be viewed through the lens of his commitment to the life of serious Christian discipleship, and I suspect that Haddon Wilmer is right when he claims this is best done when one is actively involved with the life of discipleship oneself. "Attempting to make sense and use of Bonhoeffer, outside of a discipleship like and with his, will result in serious misreading."[117]

---

[117] Haddon Wilmer, "Costly Discipleship," 188.

☙ EPILOGUE

Throughout this project, I keep returning to the thought that a great many Lutheran theologians would have considered Luther himself to be an antinomian if not for the fact that he was the hero of the Reformation and their theological namesake. His almost fatalistic description of the bondage of the will prior to faith, his enthusiastic espousal of Christian freedom, his vehement attacks upon anything that suggested legalism, and his clear preference for teaching and preaching the gospel over the law, together would have qualified him as an antinomian in the minds of more than a few among his many audiences. This might have been the case if it were not for his recovery of the *"pure gospel"* at a time when the tyranny of the law was believed to have stolen the joy and comfort that Christ had intended to bring to his people. For his great personal sacrifices and courage in confronting the Papacy, Luther has been granted almost apostolic authority among many Lutherans, so that corrections, criticisms, or alterations to his theology must be made with considerable discretion and caution. The task of re-presenting Luther's doctrine in a way that curbs its potential for the abuse of Christian freedom was undertaken by the four theologians discussed above with considerable success. Not everyone, however, has been pleased with all of their suggestions.

Melanchthon was one of the first to experience the unwillingness of the orthodox party to accept theological disparity within the ranks. Motivated chiefly by his concerns for the antinomian implications that followed from some of Luther's more radical comments and positions, Melanchthon suggested a few corrections to ensure that Luther's theology would not be used as an excuse for moral laxity. The immediate response of the Gnesio-Lutherans demonstrated that this was going to be a problem. Admittedly, some of Melanchthon's suggestions did violate Luther's solifidianism. His synergism is the clearest example of this. His concern for the implications of fatalism led him, in this case, to propose a solution that could not be reconciled with the principle of *sola fide*. At other times his language suggested a message contrary to that of Luther, as in the case of the Majorist Controversy, although it is certainly possible to reconcile the two if one is willing to put the best construction on what Melanchthon was saying. These more controversial points aside, Melanchthon did leave the Church a significant theological arsenal for dealing with antinomianism. His third use of the law, discussion of temporal rewards and punishments, and elucidation of the sin against the Holy Spirit are three of his most significant intellectual approaches toward curbing the abuse of Christian freedom.

Melanchthon never ascended a pulpit to preach. He did not leave us a collection of inspiring sermons or devotional writings. Germany's great *praeceptor* was from first to last a theologian. While history may judge him to have strayed from the parameters of Luther's thought, his conviction that the developing evangelical theology must not become an occasion for libertinism helped indicate the direction in which the dawning movement would turn. He was, arguably, the first and most influential corrective in the history of Lutheran theology.

Spener, whose concern for antinomian abuses of Christian freedom was much more apparent, was quite outspoken and direct when attempting to respond to the antinomian question. At the same time, his was not a theological approach as much as a pastoral one. Spener was convinced that spiritual development was as important a component in eradicating libertinism as theology. His focus on Bible studies, small group meetings, catechesis, and meditations on the suffering of Christ were central to his project. He firmly believed that if he could motivate his parishioners to expose themselves to the scriptures and meditate on their meaning, the moral loophole of antinomianism would close itself. At the same time, he had a responsibility for those who did not attend his *collegia pietatis*. In order to make up for the contented moral apathy among many Lutheran laity, Spener's sermons focused much more heavily on the law than did those of Luther. While the gospel was always present, and Spener forthrightly rejected any compromise of the doctrine that salvation comes by grace alone through faith alone, he was adamant that the law be preached with force and conviction.

Unfortunately, Spener was not content to stop there. His attempt at theological innovation regarding sin led him to a position that was clearly in violation of Luther's fundamental premises. His delineation of sins of weakness and sins of malice led not only to a departure from Luther's *simul iustus et peccator*, it also contributed to his troubling statements about what behavior is indicative of those without faith. By differentiating between different kinds of sins in this way, he placed himself in the position of judging others' salvation from the relative value of particular behaviors. In so doing, he was contravening the principles he wanted so very much to hold on to.

It is apparent that Spener's legacy has had an enormous impact on the life of the Church. His insistence on small group Bible studies—with all of their potential complications—has completely changed the way countless congregations view their mission and purpose; the Church does more than convey doctrine on Sunday mornings. Likewise, Spener has demonstrated that the vigorous preaching of the law can exist among clergy committed to the principle of *sola fide*. At the same time, Spener's foray into constructive theology led him to a conclusion that carried implications he probably did not want to make. While he may not have realized the danger in some of his preaching and teaching, others have. As a result, he continues to be judged with some suspicion, or to be lumped together with other Pietists, and is thereby neglected in circles that might otherwise benefit from his insights.

In the case of Kierkegaard, we have seen that the Father of Existentialism did not have the same reluctance as others to criticize Luther. As he grew older, Kierkegaard's frustration with the work of the Reformer increased to the point where he held him largely responsible for the state of moral apathy in Danish Christendom. Luther had accredited mediocrity in the life of faith, and subsequent generations were paying the price. The answer, or corrective, that Kierkegaard provided was to make the Christian life more difficult. His lofty descriptions of the nature of repentance and faith cut the legs out from underneath those who would make a quick appeal to Christian faith to justify their vices. Not everyone born and baptized in Denmark could claim to have Christian faith, he insisted. In fact, most had not even seriously engaged the ethical life, a prerequisite of faith.

By elevating the precondition for faith, and faith itself, to a level that clearly did not include every Tom, Dick, and Harry, Kierkegaard could respond to the antinomian question by challenging its fundamental assumption: that the one posing it did indeed already have faith. At the same time, this elevation, with its cryptic use of language, could serve to confuse his readers more than help them mature in faith. His peculiar use of the word "Christian," which suggested that genuine Christians are exceedingly rare, potentially conveys the message that none of his readers can consider themselves to have saving faith. Likewise, his discussions of repetition, while essentially in keeping with Luther's understanding of the nature of faith, could lend themselves to the perception that faith is a phenomenon that comes and goes depending on one's religious and ethical diligence. Kierkegaard's self-described project of making Christianity more difficult was a remarkable and inspiring response to his times, and an ingenious way of dealing with the antinomian question. However, as with Spener, we may see that too much of a good thing can get one into trouble. Kierkegaard's portrayal of the person of faith became so lofty that his readers might easily despair, not of their own depravity, but of God's willingness to grant them the gift of salvation, a fear that stands in stark contrast to the liberating theology of *sola fide*.

Lastly, Bonhoeffer's approach in responding to the antinomian question, primarily through descriptions of what the Christian life should look like, finds its strength not in logical debate but in his unshakable belief that God is present in the Word and in the community of believers. It is not Christians who convert others, either to faith or to sanctified living, but the Spirit of Christ. His use of the scriptures to describe the life of obedience, and his willingness to underscore this with the witness of his own life and death, have served as perhaps the most influential and inspiring call to discipleship within the history of Lutheranism. While Kierkegaard regretted that Luther had not died a martyr's death, thereby perpetuating the Lutheran church's slouching toward mediocrity, Bonhoeffer's victimization at the hands of the Nazis made it crystal clear to Christendom that the Christian life is not about waiting around for one's turn to enter paradise. As he never tired of explaining, Christ's life and work in this world are to be the model of how Christians should behave during their earthly pilgrimage. His death placed the exclamation point at the end of this conviction in a way that a continuing academic career could never have accomplished.

At the same time, Bonhoeffer was more than an inspirational pastor. He was a theologian. While it is true that his legacy is not based on theological genius, his contributions in this area have been significant and do lend themselves toward addressing the problems of antinomianism. The development and articulation of his christology was largely based on his desire to emphasize that the Christian life needs to be active in the world. Christ's incarnation is a witness to the call for all Christians to get their hands dirty in and among humanity. His resurrection is the promise and testimony that he is still present in the life of the Church, giving it strength to continue his work on behalf of all people. Bonhoeffer's theological critique of the place of obedience in the Church, likewise, was a call to remember that sanctification is not distinct and separate from justification. Obedience is necessary at every stage in one's spiritual development, even before faith. To neglect obedience at any point is to remove oneself from the place where salvation is given.

Unfortunately, his hopes and expectations for what this obedience looks like led him, like Spener, to define what behaviors one will find among the redeemed to such an extent that he allowed himself to condemn others if their behavior did not meet what he expected to see. He fell into the trap that so many others have succumbed to: In his desire to clarify that a believer cannot and will not live a life of vice, he moved beyond recognizing a tree by its fruits and created his own litmus test based on the behavior he wanted to see in order to determine whether an individual has saving faith. The effect is unfortunate, for the antinomian cynic still brings up the claim of *sola fide*, and those who are weak in faith or struggle with their unworthiness come to doubt or despair of their redemption.

Orthodoxy and Orthopraxy

On the basis of this brief summary, it should be apparent that orthodoxy and orthopraxy are not two mutually exclusive theological concepts. While different religious movements may emphasize one over the other, it cannot be claimed that orthodoxy is accentuated only at the expense of orthopraxy, or vice versa. The vast majority of Melanchthon's efforts to combat moral inactivity were based on theological innovations. He firmly believed that a correctly formulated systematic theology would be able to help keep Christians on the straight and narrow. Likewise, the christological developments of both Spener and Bonhoeffer were intended to provide a more accurate and complete understanding of Jesus Christ with the express goal of thereby reminding believers of their moral responsibilities. Kierkegaard's insistence on a more precise definition of faith, in the same way, demonstrated his conviction that, when Christianity is more accurately communicated, believers are more likely to lead lives in imitation of Christ.

Bonhoeffer in particular, especially in his encounters with Americans, was convinced that the idea that orthopraxy is brought about in believers apart from rigorous theological investigation was absurd. In his *Ethics* he tells us, "We are sick and tired of Christian programmes and of the thoughtless and superficial slogan of what is called 'practical' Christianity as distinct from 'dogmatic' Christianity."[1] Good works cannot simply be emphasized. Correct behavior cannot be exacted from people by simply calling on them to be virtuous. The works of the law follow from faith and understanding of the life, death, and resurrection of Jesus Christ. "There can be no Christian preaching of works without the preaching of the acknowledgment of sin and of the fulfilment of the law.... The moral preacher can only produce hypocrites."[2]

---

[1]*Ethics*, 80.
[2]Ibid., 313.

In this way, the four figures we have discussed in the previous chapters were fundamentally in agreement with Luther in his essential understanding of the life of sanctification. Good works proceed from faith in Christ, and one must understand the work of Christ in order to have faith. While all four theologians were strong adherents of a third use of the law, and certainly emphasized the life of obedience more than Luther, they also understood that people require a reason to undertake the life of discipleship. This may be accomplished in a variety of ways, as we have seen throughout this project: the modeling of proper behavior, reminders of one's duty, threats of temporal punishments, and, yes, the articulation of the Church's theology. Orthodoxy was not an afterthought for these men when encouraging orthopraxy, but its prerequisite. Where orthodoxy is under-emphasized, the moral life of the Church will suffer. "False doctrine corrupts the life of the Church at its source, and that is why doctrinal sin is more serious than moral."[3]

Any confusion regarding orthodoxy and orthopraxy as opposite poles, or piety and orthodoxy as competing ideals, causes the central unity of correct faith and correct behavior to be overlooked. Just as Luther understood justification and sanctification to be the work of the same gift of grace, so the more insightful Lutherans through the past five centuries have realized that insistence on proper doctrine is not at odds with the demand for proper behavior. We have seen that the greatest opponents of cheap grace held passionately to their orthodox moorings to assist in their work. Similarly, one of the most celebrated orthodox opponents of Pietism, Valentin Löscher, was also quite concerned with the problem of antinomianism in the Church. In fact, he has left us one of the simplest and most direct responses to the antinomian question. In the midst of a stinging attack on those who would mix righteousness by faith with works, he explains, "Nevertheless, in order to guard against the base misuse of the evangelical basis and comfort, one can say that faith which is without good works is in very great danger of losing its righteousness and salvation."[4] The ones asking the antinomian question should carefully consider whether the faith they are counting on to save them is not in danger of being lost. We see, then, that while room exists for different emphases on orthodoxy or orthopraxy, depending on the needs of the time and the particular community, there is no place for the notion that they are competing principles.

---

[3]*CD*, 330n.
[4]Löscher, *Timotheus Verinus*, 125.

A Final Analysis

The central question throughout this entire project has not been the antinomian question but rather, "How can Lutherans respond to the antinomian question without compromising the principle of *sola fide?*" We could make a rather extensive list of the approaches our four Lutheran theologians have suggested. A more helpful procedure, however, would be to consider the specific angles of attack that these different figures took to the problem. To begin with, there are two fundamental approaches in responding to the antinomian question: (1) responses to the question itself, and (2) responses to the individual asking the question. On top of these two approaches, I believe we can identify two different frames of mind that differentiate our figures as well: (1) the passive theologian and (2) the active theologian. Together they make up four possible ways in which the antinomian question may be addressed, four ways that the four figures in this project represent.

Responding to the Question or Questioner

The first approach to dealing with this problem is to attack the question itself. By engaging the internal logic or presuppositions of the antinomian question, it is possible to frame an effective response to its suggestion of libertinism. To a certain degree we might consider this a theological approach to the problem. This is the approach to antinomianism that we find in Melanchthon and Kierkegaard.

Melanchthon's approach to our problem was certainly the most theological of the four we have considered. His concern for an increased emphasis on the role of works—demonstrated through his third use of the law, his belief in the necessity of good works for salvation, and his synergism—displayed itself in theological innovations that would remove barriers which stood in the way of a proper understanding of doctrine. He was convinced that if he could remove the false fatalism that some were deducing from Luther's various works, he would be making headway against the internal logic of the antinomian question. Likewise, he believed Luther's undue emphasis on the gospel over that of the law could be corrected by introducing a stronger third use. Melanchthon's development of the idea of the sin against the Holy Spirit, in the same way, was yet another way of demonstrating the weakness behind the logic of the antinomian question. Through the articulation of a clearer theology, Melanchthon believed he could refute those pressing forward with what was perceived to be the moral loophole within solifidianism.

Kierkegaard also engaged this theological approach in his response. By presenting his understanding of the ethical life and faith in such elevated language, he sought to undercut the presuppositions of the antinomian question. The logic behind the question begins with the assumption that the one asking already has faith. Kierkegaard attacks this premise simply by defining faith as an elevated and rare phenomenon. The result is that the initial argument falls apart. Not satisfied simply to call into question the faith of his interlocutor, he seeks to show that the necessary precursor for faith, i.e. the ethical life, may also be absent in the individual's religious journey. It is as if to say that the one who is trying to forgo moral responsibility by an appeal to grace has demonstrated that she does not take the ethical life seriously. The person who has not taken up the ethical life, however, is ineligible for faith. *Ergo* the one who considers the antinomian question with an eye to libertinism cannot have the requisite faith that allows the question even to be asked.

Kierkegaard, with his descriptions of faith and the stages of religious development, has done an impressive job of responding to the antinomian question directly by virtue of his theological acumen. At the same time, while we can acknowledge his more pastoral approach in *Works of Love* and *Upbuilding Discourses*, it was in works like *Fear and Trembling, Concluding Unscientific Postscript*, and *Sickness Unto Death*, where he makes the ethical and religious life more difficult, that his theological legacy was established. It was here that he undercut any foundation for moral vice based on an appeal to faith.

The second approach to antinomianism is not an assault on the logic behind the position but a confrontation of the person asking the question. Instead of demonstrating the weakness in the argument, those utilizing this approach tend to address the person in such a way that the question is withdrawn. We find this more pastoral approach to be at the heart of the work of both Spener and Bonhoeffer.

Spener placed a great deal of trust in the power of the law to curb antinomian influences. In his preaching and teaching, he wanted to expose his parishioners to the demands of the law in a way he believed had been neglected by other Lutherans. His catechesis and *collegia pietatis* were designed with the intent of helping others see that theology and the Christian life entail more than the message of justification. The Bible has a lot to say about sanctification, and Spener did too. His insistence that believers remember that Christ is prophet, priest, and king was likewise intended to remind others that Christian preaching does not end with the forgiveness of sins but must include Jesus' call to a new life and the responsibility to obey. Even his meditations on Christ's suffering are in large part a preaching of the law, intended to remind the believer what Christ underwent because of one's sins, and that his followers rarely honor his sacrifice in their actions.

The purpose of this considerable use of the law is not to make a rebuttal to the antinomian question. In fact, it contributes very little toward demonstrating any weakness in the argument itself. Rather, Spener believed that the preaching of the law would serve to drive one to repentance, and the one who is in the throes of sorrowful confession cannot at the next moment contemplate an abuse of the freedom that is being provided by Christ. Spener did not need to address the antinomian question itself, as did Melanchthon and Kierkegaard;[5] he simply responded with questions like, "Do you know that your behavior merits your condemnation? Do you know how much Christ suffered for you? And do you know that this same Christ has told you to stop such behavior?" He was convinced that genuine believers who daily consider these questions could no longer contemplate abusing the grace they had received freely at such a cost to their redeemer. Spener's response was oriented not toward the question but the questioner. While some might object that this does not represent a real answer to the problem, I suspect Spener would disagree. With such an approach, the hypocrite who still asks the antinomian question betrays his lack of faith with a lifestyle characterized by sin; the true believer would be ashamed of having even contemplated such libertinism.

In the same way, Bonhoeffer hoped to dissolve the antinomian question without having to address it directly. Aside from his brief comments about the necessity of obedience prior to faith, his approach to the problem was quite similar to that of Spener. He preached the law, exposed people to the scriptures, encouraged confession and mutual accountability, and reiterated the claim of Jesus, Paul, and James that a life characterized by vice cannot truly have been redeemed. There was, however, one fundamental difference between the two. While Spener used the law to point out the sins of his audience, Bonhoeffer used the law to point to what behavior should be followed; Spener wanted his hearers to realize what great *sinners* they were, while Bonhoeffer preferred to demonstrate what great *Christians* they should be.

Bonhoeffer's theological development of his christology was intended to support this approach in that it emphasized Christ's role as the example to be imitated. The life of Jesus Christ holds value not only in its redemptive work, providing justification, but also in its message that the people of God are to be living and active in the world. Quite apart from an intellectual response to

---

[5]In fact, when he tried to do this with his differentiation of sins of weakness and sins of malice, he clearly stepped outside the boundaries of Luther's theology.

the flawed reasoning behind the antinomian question, Bonhoeffer assailed the position of cheap grace by pointing to the appeals toward godly living in the Bible and providing his own life as a witness as well. By virtue of this rather indirect approach, he may have done more to salvage costly grace than any logical assault on antinomianism ever could.

Passive or Active Theology

By differentiating between passive and active theologians, I do not intend to suggest that one is lazy and the other industrious, or that one is more concerned with sanctification than the other. Rather, passive theologians believe that they are responsible for preaching the law and gospel clearly and effectively, but then the change in peoples' behavior is dependent on the work of the Spirit of God in their lives. The active theologians believe that they need to be more involved in shaping the responses and behavior that follow after the preaching of the Word. They do not suggest that God is inactive, but that human beings benefit from additional guidance, direction, and encouragement.

Luther certainly belonged to the former category. He had little interest in trying to shape people's behavior. God alone would do that through the work of the Spirit in faith. While Melanchthon could become rather frustrated with Luther's neglect of the law, he also falls into the category of a passive theologian. He believed that a proper presentation of the law and gospel was sufficient for the spiritual development of an individual. His introduction of a formal third use of the law was an attempt to present the Word of God more completely. His rejection of fatalism, likewise, was intended to clarify Christian doctrine, as were his warnings about the sin against the Holy Spirit and his development of forensic justification. Nevertheless, after the correct doctrine was presented in a clear and balanced way, the change that takes place in the life of the individual is in God's hands. Melanchthon had no special techniques for helping his audiences internalize God's Word. His self-chosen task was to present the doctrine as clearly as possible, and he believed that doing this effectively offered the best response to antinomianism.

Likewise, Bonhoeffer placed sole responsibility for changes in human behavior in God's hands. The preacher is to explain what behavior God commands, announce the forgiveness of sins, and let God do the rest. As he has told us, it is not preachers who convert people but God. Bonhoeffer found no room for emotional displays or appeals in the Church. As he explained in his christology, the resurrection event means that God is now active in the Church through his people; Christians are not dependent solely on historical accounts of what Jesus has done for them to motivate them to good works.

Christ is truly present for them in Word and Sacrament in order to lead them in sanctification. The preacher, on the other hand, is responsible only for providing an accurate and complete account of God's Word. It is God alone who will see to it that libertinism does not hold sway in the Church as long as the preachers are doing their job correctly.

We can consider Spener, on the other hand, to be an active theologian when it comes to responding to antinomianism in the Church. Not content just to present the doctrines of law and gospel to the people, Spener believed he could be of additional service by constantly driving home the message of the law. While certainly not a fire and brimstone preacher, Spener often used the law with an eye toward changing his parishioners' behavior. Rather than wait for the Spirit to move a person, and then provide them with direction as to how they should live, Spener wanted to improve the moral conduct of his audiences by providing additional motivations, like guilt and duty. The meditations on Christ's suffering, for example, not only strengthen faith, they make use of the principle of shame to curb sinful conduct. His direct preaching of the law, likewise, functions as a psychological tool to alter his congregations' behavior insofar as it makes use of guilt to eradicate moral vice. The Church simply cannot wait for the behavior of believers to change on the basis of love for God alone. As the fallout of the Thirty Years War illustrated, such an approach provides too little too late. Luther's attempt to wait for the Spirit to inspire a person to righteous living was obviously inadequate; the Lutheran countries were in complete moral disarray. The behavior of Christians needs to be kept in check for the sake of the individual and of the Church as a whole. Where the people's faith is not manifesting itself adequately in appropriate behavior, the law can be used to help keep them on the straight and narrow. While the Spirit is working in a person, bringing change from the inside, Spener believed the pastor has a responsibility to guide that person in morally virtuous behavior through other means as well.

Kierkegaard, similarly, was not content to provide a response to the antinomian question and let God do the rest. He was not satisfied simply to correct for faulty doctrine by providing more accurate definitions of faith and ethics and then leave his readers in the hands of God. He understood that faith cannot be brought about by the objective communication of doctrine. His message of the requirements of faith needed to be communicated indirectly. He needed to capture and inspire his readers and force them into a subjective engagement with the material. Whether through his account of Abraham's struggle to believe God or his parables of geese on their way to morning worship, Kierkegaard demonstrated his conviction that the Christian teacher must do more than provide information and wait for God to do the rest. Unlike Melanchthon, he could not address the antinomian question with definitions and doctrines; he had to inspire the readers himself. He needed to help them truly understand what is involved in faith. Faith is certainly the indwelling of God's Spirit who transforms people's lives. However, the doctrines that must be understood before one may come to faith require a messenger who can help others appreciate the message on an existential level. As with Melanchthon, the response to the antinomian question may take the form of information; nevertheless, the one providing the information should not passively communicate doctrines but inspire the other to subjectively engage the material.

On the basis of these final thoughts, I have no intention of suggesting that one approach is superior to another. There are too many confounding variables involved for us ever to claim one approach as the best response to the antinomian question. If Luther's colleague at Wittenberg had been a theologian like Bonhoeffer rather than Melanchthon, it is hard to believe that the young Evangelical movement would have succeeded as it did. Likewise, another systematic theologian of Melanchthon's quality in the early twentieth century would not likely have had the same impact on the Church as did Bonhoeffer. In the same way, as much as Spener would have been out of his league in Kierkegaard's intellectual world, Kierkegaard would likely have been ill equipped to handle the congregations Spener was called to.

This is not to say that the value of all four contributions is relative. The reader will likely find aspects of one approach more attractive than others. Disagreement may continue as to whether the law should be preached by example or condemnation. The antinomian question, however, as was discussed in the beginning, appears in a variety of forms. It is unlikely that one response or approach could be sufficient for all cases when it appears. The material presented here provides a foundation for addressing this perpetual theological conundrum and demonstrates that Lutherans can indeed respond *effectively* to the antinomian question without compromising the doctrine of *sola fide*. No "answer" to the antinomian question is possible within the parameters of Luther's theology; nonetheless, the contributions made by these four figures toward a fuller understanding of the relationship between justification and sanctification are essential, I believe, for the one who desires to know what it means to be a Christian.

◯Ω BIBLIOGRAPHY

Althaus, Paul. *The Theology of Martin Luther*. Robert C. Schultz, trans. Philadelphia: Fortress Press, 1966.

Arndt, Johann. *True Christianity*. Peter Erb, trans. New York: Paulist Press, 1979.

Barker, H. Gaylon. "Bonhoeffer, Luther, and *Theologia Crucis*." *Dialog* 34, no.1 (1995): 10–17.

Barth, Karl. *Evangelium und Gesetz* . Zürich: Evangelischer Verlag a.g., 1940.

Bente, F. *Historical Introductions to the Book of Concord*. St. Louis: Concordia Publishing House, 1965. First published in *Concordia Triglotta*, 1921.

Bethge, Eberhard. *Dietrich Bonhoeffer*. by Victoria J. Barnett, ed. Minneapolis: Fortress Press, 2000.

Beyreuther, Erich. *Geschichte des Pietismus*. Stuttgart: J.F. Steinkopf Verlag, 1978.

Blume, Helmut. "The Age of Confessionalism." *Protestant Church Music*. Helmut Blume, ed. New York: W.W. Norton & Co., 1974.

Bonhoeffer, Dietrich. *Christology*. John Bowden, trans. London: Collins, 1966.

———. *The Cost of Discipleship*. R. H. Fuller, trans. New York: Macmillan Publishing Company, 1959.

———. *Dietrich Bonhoeffer Werke*. Eberhard Bethge, ed. 17 vols. Gütersloh: Chr. Kaiser, 1986 – 1999.

———. *Dietrich Bonhoeffer Works*, English edition. Wayne Whitson Floyd, Jr., ed. 7 vols. to date, Minneapolis: Fortress Press, 1996–.

———. *Ethics*. Eberhard Bethge, ed. New York: Macmillan Publishing Co., 1955.

———. *Gesammelte Schriften*. 3 vols. Eberhard Bethge, ed. München: Chr. Kaiser Verlag, 1960.

———. *Letters and Papers From Prison*. Eberhard Bethge, ed. New York: Macmillan Publishing Co., 1971.

———. "Sermon on a Psalm of Vengeance." Daniel Bloesch. Trans. *Theology Today* 38 (1982): 465–71.

The Book of Concord. Theodore G. Tappert, ed. and trans. Philadelphia: Fortress Press, 1959.

Bornkamm,Heinrich. *Luther in Mid–Career*. E. Theodore Bachmann, trans. Philadelphia: Fortress Press, 1983.

Braaten, Carl E. and Jenson, Robert W., eds. *Union with Christ: The New Finnish Interpretation of Luther*. Grand Rapids: William B. Eerdmans, 1998.

Brecht, Martin. *Geschichte des Pietismus*. Göttingen: Vandenhoeck & Ruprecht, 1993.

Burtness, James. *Shaping the Future: The Ethics of Dietrich Bonhoeffer.* Philadelphia: Fortress Press, 1985.

Caemmerer Sr., Richard R. "The Melanchthonian Blight," *Concordia Theological Monthly* 18, no.5 (May 1947): 321–338.

Campbell, Ted A. *The Religion of the Heart: A Study of European Religious Life in theSeventeenth and Eighteenth Centuries.* Columbia: University of South Carolina Press, 1991.

Caputo, John D. *Against Ethics.* Bloomington: Indiana University Press, 1993.

Dumas, André. *Dietrich Bonhoeffer: Theologian of Reality.* Robert McAfee Brown, trans. New York: The Macmillan Company, 1971.

Ebeling, Gerhard. *Wort und Glaube.* Tübingen : J.C.B. Mohr (Paul Siebeck), 1960–1969.

Eck, Johann. *Enchiridion of Commonplaces.* Ford Lewis Battles, trans. Grand Rapids: Baker Book House, 1979.

Elert, Werner. "Eine theologische Fälschung zur Lehre vom Tertius usus legis," *Zeitschrift für Religions–und Geistesgeschichte* (1948), 168–70.

———. *The Christian Ethos.* Trans. Carl J. Schindler. Philadelphia: Muhlenberg Press, 1957.

———. *The Structure of Lutheranism.* Walter A. Hansen, trans. St. Louis: Concordia Publishing House, 1962.

———. *Law and Gospel.* Edward H. Schroeder, trans. Philadelphia: Fortress Press, 1967.

Erb, Peter C. "Pietist Spirituality: Some aspects of Present Research," *The Roots of theModern Christian Tradition.* Kalamazoo: Cistercian Publications, Inc., 1984.

Evans, C. Stephen. "Faith as the *Telos* of Morality: A Reading of *Fear and Trembling,*" in *International Kierkegaard Commentary*: Fear and Trembling *and* Repetition. Robert L. Perkins, ed. Macon, GA: Mercer University Press, 1993.

Fant, Clyde E. *Bonhoeffer: Worldly Preaching.* Nashville: Thomas Nelson Inc., 1975.

Forde, Gerhard O. "Forensic Justification and the Law in Lutheran Theology." *Justification by Faith.* Minneapolis: Augsburg Publishing House, 1985.

———. *The Law–Gospel Debate.* Minneapolis: Augsburg Publishing House, 1969.

Green, Clifford J. "Soteriologie und Socialethik bei Bonhoeffer und Luther." *Bonhoeffer und Luther.* Christian Gremmels, ed. München: Chr. Kaiser Verlag, 1983.

Green, Ronald M. " 'Developing' *Fear and Trembling,*" *The Cambridge Companion to Kierkegaard.* Alastair Hannay & Gordon D. Marino, eds. Cambridge: Cambridge University Press, 1998.

Gremmels, Christian. "Rechfertigung und Nachfolge: Martin Luther in Dietrich Bonhoeffers Buch 'Nachfolge.'" *Dietrich Bonhoeffer Heute.* Rainer Mayer und Peter Zimmer-ling, eds. Giessen: Brunnen Verlag, 1992.

de Gruchy, John W. "The Reception of Bonhoeffer's Theology." *The CambridgeCompanion to Dietrich Bonhoeffer.* John W. de Gruchy, ed. Cambridge: Cambridge University Press, 1999.

Grünberg, Paul. *Philipp Jakob Spener.* 3 vols. Göttingen: Vandenhoeck & Ruprecht, 1893–1906.

von Harnack, Adolph. *History of Dogma,* vol. 6. Neil Buchanan, trasns. New York: Russell and Russell, 1958.

Heick, Otto W. "Reflections on Bonhoeffer's Theology," *Concordia TheologicalMonthly.* 40, no.4 (1969): 203–217.

Hirsch, Emanuel. *Kierkegaard–Studien*. Gütersloh: Verlag C. Bertelsmann, 1933.

Hoffman, Bengt R. *"On the Relationship Between Mystical Faith and Moral Life in Luther's Thought."* *Encounters with Luther*. vol. 1. Gettysburg: Lutheran Theological Semin-ary, 1980.

Holl, Karl. "Die Rechtfertigungslehre in Luthers Vorlesung über den Römerbrief mit besonderer Rücksicht auf die Frage der Heilsgewißheit." *Gesammelte Aufsätze zurKirchengeschichte*, 3d ed., 3 vols. 1:126–29. Tübingen: J.C.B. Mohr/Paul Siebeck, 1923.

Janssen, Johannees. *History of the German People at the Close of the Middle Ages*, Vol. 4. A.M. Christie, trans. St. Louis: B. Herder, 1908.

Joest, Wilfred. *Gesetz und Freiheit*. 2nd ed. Göttingen: Vandenhoeck & Ruprecht, 1956.

Kierkegaard, Søren. *Attack upon "Christendom."* Walter Lowrie, trans. Princeton: Princeton University Press, 1944.

———. *The Book on Adler*. Howard V. Hong and Edna H. Hong, trans. Princeton: Princeton University Press, 1998.

———. *Concluding Unscientific Postscript to Philosophical Fragments*. Howard V. Hong and Edna H. Hong, trans. Princeton: Princeton University Press, 1992.

———. *Eighteen Upbuilding Discourses*. Howard V. Hong and Edna H. Hong, trans. Princeton: Princeton University Press, 1990.

———. *Either/Or*. Howard V. Hong and Edna H. Hong, trans. Princeton: Princeton University Press, 1987.

———. *Fear and Trembling*. Howard V. Hong and Edna H. Hong, trans. Princeton: Princeton University Press, 1983.

———. *The Moment and Late Writings*. Howard V. Hong and Edna H. Hong, trans. Princeton: Princeton University Press, 1998.

———. *Philosophical Fragments*. Howard V. Hong and Edna H. Hong, trans. Princeton: Princeton University Press, 1985.

———. *Practice in Christianity*. Howard V. Hong and Edna H. Hong, trans. Princeton: Princeton University Press, 1991.

———. *Repetition*. Howard V. Hong and Edna H. Hong, trans. Princeton: Princeton University Press, 1983.

———. *Søren Kierkegaard's Journals and Papers*. Howard V. Hong and Edna H. Hong, trans. Bloomington: Indiana University Press, 1967–78.

———. *Søren Kierkegaards Papirer*. 2. enlarged edition by Niels Thulstrup. Copenhagen 1968–78.

———. *Works of Love*. Howard V. Hong and Edna H. Hong, trans. Princeton: Princeton University Press, 1995.

Kiessling, Elmer Carl. *The Early Sermons of Luther and Their Relation to the Pre-Reformation Sermon*. Grand Rapids: Zondervan Publishing House, 1935.

Kinder, Ernst und Haendler, Klaus, ed. *Gesetz und Evangelium*. Darmstadt: Wissenschaft-liche Buchgesellschaft, 1968.

Koenker, Ernest B. *"Søren Kierkegaard on Luther."* *Interpreters of Luther*. Jaroslav Pelikan, ed. Philadelphia: Fortress Press, 1968.

Krodel, Gottfried G. "Luther—an Antinomian?" in *Lutherjahrbuch.* Göttingen: Vanden-hoeck & Ruprecht, 1996.

von Loewenich, Walther. *Martin Luther: The Man and His Work.* Lawrence W. Denef, trans. Minneapolis: Augsburg Publishing House, 1986.

Lohse, Bernhard. *Martin Luther: An Introduction to His Life and Work.* Robert S. Schultz, trans. Philadelphia: Fortress Press, 1986.

Löscher, Valentin Ernst. *The Complete Timotheus Verinus.* Milwaukee: Northwestern Publishing House, 1998.

Lowrie,Walter. *Kierkegaard.* New York: Harper and Brothers, 1962.

Luther, Martin. *Luther's Works.* 55 vols. Philadelphia and St. Louis: Fortress Press and Concordia Publishing House, 1958–1986.

———. *Dr Martin Luther Werke.* 65 vols. Weimar: H. Böhlau, 1883–1993.

———. *Sermons of Martin Luther: The House Postils.* Eugene F. A. Klug, trans. Grand Rapids: Baker Books, 1996.

Maurer,Wilhelm. *Der junge Melanchthon zwischen Humanismus und Reformation,* 2 vols. Göttingen: Vandenhoeck and Ruprecht, 1967,1969.

Maxcey, Carl E. *Bona Opera: A Study in the Development of the Doctrine of Philip Melanch-thon.* Chicago: Nieuwkoop B De Graaf, 1980.

McGrath, Alister E. *Iustitia Dei: A History of the Christian Doctrine of Justification.* 2nd ed. Cambridge: Cambridge University Press, 1998.

McIntosh, John. "Proposals for Godliness in the Church." *The Reformed Theological Review* 35, S–D (1976): 79–88.

Melanchthon, Philip. *A Melanchthon Reader.* Ralph Keen, trans. New York: Peter Lang Publishing, 1988.

———. *Corpus Reformatorum. Philippi Melanchthonis opera quae supersunt omnia.* Karl Bretschneider and Heinrich Bindseil, eds. 28 vols. Halle and Braunschweig: Schwetschke, 1834–1860.

———. *Loci Communes Theologici* (1521). Wilhelm Pauck, ed. Philadelphia: The West-minster Press, 1969.

———. *Loci Communes Theologici* (1555). Clyde L. Manschreck, trans. New York: Oxford University Press, 1965.

———. *Melanchthons Briefwechsel: Kritische und kommentierte Gesamtausgabe.* Heinz Scheible, ed. 10 vols. to date. Stuttgart–Bad Cannstatt: Frommann–Holzboog, 1977–.

Morris, T. F. "Constanin Constantius's Search for an Acceptable Way of Life." *International Kierkegaard Commentary:* Fear and Trembling *and* Repetition. Robert L. Perkins, ed. Macon, Georgia: Mercer University Press, 1993.

Mühlenberg, Ekkehard. "Humanistische Bildungsprogramm und reformatorische Lehre beim junge Melanchthon." *Zeitschrift für Theologie und Kirche* 65 (1968): 431–44.

Nevile, Donald. "Pietism and Liturgical Worship: An Evaluation." *Consensus* 16, no.2 (1990):91–106.

Pauck,Wilhelm. "Luther and Melanchthon." *Luther and Melanchthon in the History and Theology of the Reformation.* Philadelphia: Muhlenberg Press, 1960.

Pelikan, Jaroslav. *From Luther to Kierkegaard.* St. Louis: Concordia Publishing House, 1950.

Pietists: Selected Writings. Peter C. Erb, ed. New York: Paulist Press, 1983.

Pinson, Koppel S. *Pietism as a Factor in the Rise of German Nationalism*. New York: Octagon Books, 1968.

Prenter, Regin. "Luther and Lutheranism." *Bibliotheca Kierkegaardiana*. Copenhagen: C.A. Reitzels Boghandel, 1981, 6:121–172.

Preus, Robert D. *The Theology of Post-Reformation Lutheranism: A Study of Theological Prolegomena*. St. Louis: Concordia Publishing House, 1970.

Pustejovsky, John. "Philipp Jakob Spener," *Dictionary of Literary Biography*. Detroit: Gale Research Inc., 1996, 164: 321–329.

Richter, Matthias. *Gesetz und Heil*. Göttingen: Vandenhoeck & Ruprecht, 1996.

Ritschl, Albrecht. "'Prolegomena' to the *History of Pietism*." *Three Essays*. Philip Hefner, trans. Philadelphia: Fortress, Press, 1972.

Schaff, Philip. *History of the Christian Church*, vol. 7. Grand Rapids: William B Eerdman's, 1910.

Scheible, Heinz. "Luther and Melanchthon." *Lutheran Quarterly* 4 (Autumn, 1990): 317–339.

Schmauck, Theodore E. and Benze, C. Theodore. *The Confessional Principle and the Confessions of the Lutheran Church*. Philadelphia: General Council Publication Board, 1911.

Schröer, Henning. "Kierkegaard und Luther." *Kerygma und Dogma* 30 (1984): 227–248.

Schurb,Ken. "Twentieth–Century Melanchthon Scholarship and the Missouri Synod." *Concordia Theological Quarterly*, 62, no. 4 (1998): 287–307.

Schwarzwaller, Klaus. "Verantwortung des Glaubens."*Freiheit als Liebe bei Martin Luther.* Dennis Bielfeldt and Klaus Schwarzwaller, eds. Frankfurt: Peter Lang, 1995.

Sorum, Jonathan. "Barth's 'Gospel and Law' and Bonhoeffer's *The Cost of Discipleship*." *Essays in Honor of F. Burton Nelson*. Geffrey B. Kelly and C. John Weborg, eds. Chicago: Covenant Publications, 1999.

Spener, Philip Jacob. *Pia Desideria*. Theodore G. Tappert, trans. Fortress Press, 1964.

———. *Philipp Jakob Spener Schriften*. Erich Beyreuther, ed. Hildesheim: Georg Olms Verlag, 1979–.

Sponheim, Paul. "Is Forgiveness Enough? A Kierkegaardian Response." *Word and World* 16, no.3 (1996): 320–327.

Stein, K. James. *Philipp Jakob Spener: Pietist Patriarch*. Chicago: Covenant Press, 1986.

Stoeffler, F. Ernest. *German Pietism During the Eighteenth Century*. Leiden, Netherlands: E.J. Brill, 1973.

———. *The Rise of Evangelical Pietism*. Leiden, Netherlands: E.J. Brill,1965.

Thulstrup, Marie Mikulová. "Pietism." *Bibliotheca Kierkegaardiana*. Copenhagen: C.A. Reitzels Boghandel, 1981, 6:173–222.

Tillich, Paul. *Systematic Theology*. vol. 3. Chicago: University of Chicago Press, 1963.

Wallmann, Johannes. *Philipp Jakob Spener und die Anfänge des Pietismus*. Tübingen: J.C.B. Mohr / Paul Siebeck, 1970.

———. "Postillenvorrede und *Pia Desideria* Philipp Jakob Speners." *Der Pietismus inGestalten und Wirkungen*. Bielefeld: Luther–Verlag, 1975.

Weiss, James Michael. "Erasmus at Luther's Funeral: Melanchthon's Commemorations of Luther in 1546." *Sixteenth Century Journal* 16.1 (1985): 91–114.

Wengert, Timothy J. *Human Freedom, Christian Righteousness: Philip Melanchthon's Exegetical Dispute with Erasmus of Rotterdam*. New York: Oxford University Press, 1998.

————. *Law and Gospel: Philip Melanchthon's Debate with John Agricola of Eisleben over Poenitentia*. Grand Rapids: Baker Books, 1997

Wiedenhofer, Siegfried. *Formalstrukturen humanistischer und reformatorischerTheologie bei Philip Melanchthon*. 2 vols. Frankfurt: Peter Lang, 1976.

Wilmer, Haddon. *"Costly Discipleship." The Cambridge Companion to Dietrich Bonhoeffer*. John W. de Gruchy, ed. Cambridge: Cambridge University Press, 1999.